Better Writing Through Editing

D0465936

Better Writing Through Editing

JAN PETERSON

Edmonds Community College

STACY A. HAGEN

Edmonds Community College

McGraw-Hill
College

Boston   Burr Ridge, IL   Dubuque, IA   Madison, WI   New York
San Francisco   St. Louis   Bangkok   Bogotá   Caracas   Lisbon   London   Madrid
Mexico City   Milan   New Delhi   Seoul   Singapore   Sydney   Taipei   Toronto

McGraw-Hill College

A Division of The McGraw·Hill Companies

BETTER WRITING THROUGH EDITING

Copyright © 1999 by The McGraw-Hill Companies, Inc. All rights reserved. Printed in the United States of America. Except as permitted under the United States Copyright Act of 1976, no part of this publication may be reproduced or distributed in any form or by any means, or stored in a data base or retrieval system, without the prior written permission of the publisher.

 This book is printed on recycled, acid-free paper containing 10% postconsumer waste.

890 BKM BKM 09876

ISBN 0–07–049885–7

Editorial director: *Thalia Dorwick*
Publisher: *Tim Stookesberry*
Developmental editors: *Marietta Urban/Pam Tiberia*
Marketing manager: *Pam Tiberia*
Project manager: *Renee C. Russian*
Production supervisor: *Enboge Chong*
Designer: *Gino Cieslik*
Interior designer: *Joel Davies/Z Graphics*
Senior photo research coordinator: *Carrie K. Burger*
Compositor: *David Corona Design*
Typeface: *10/12 Times Roman*

Chapter Openers 1, 2, 3, 5, 6, and 7: *PhotoDisc*
Chapter Opener 4 and Part 2, p. 45: *Weatherstock*

Library of Congress Cataloging-in-Publication Data

Peterson, Jan, 1955–
    Better writing through editing / Jan Peterson, Stacy A. Hagen. — 1st
ed.
        p.   cm.
    ISBN 0–07–049885–7
    1. English language—Textbooks for foreign speakers. 2. English
language—Rhetoric—Problems, exercises, etc. 3. English language—
Grammar—Problems, exercises, etc. 4. Report writing—Problems,
exercises, etc. 5. Editing—Problems, exercises, etc. I. Hagen,
Stacy A., 1956–   . II. Title.
PE1128.P43   1999
428.2'4—dc21   98–39803
                                                       CIP

CONTENTS

Better Writing Through Editing is a writing and editing book for intermediate students of ESL/EFL. The book works best when used as a systematic approach to writing, sentence structure, and editing skills. Recommendations for how to do this can be found in the comprehensive Teacher's Edition, which includes this student book, sample course outlines, sample lesson plans, quizzes, and suggestions for using this text in a variety of different classroom situations.*

---

* The Teacher's Edition listed here accompanies *Better Writing Through Editing*. Please contact your local McGraw-Hill representative for details concerning policies, prices, and availability as some restrictions may apply. For more information, call Customer Service at 1-800-338-3987.

Acknowledgments

We would like to acknowledge the following people for their roles in helping *Better Writing Through Editing* come to life.

Thank you to . . . first and foremost, our students, whose unending curiosity and dedication inspire us; our colleagues at Edmonds Community College, for their feedback and support; Garnet Templin-Imel, for field testing our project with her students at Bellevue Community College; our reviewers, Julie Cloninger, Maria Parker, Linda Prue, Janine Goerlitz, and Anne Ediger, for their valuable comments and opinions; Marietta Urban, for her careful editing skills and many helpful suggestions; Tim Stookesberry and Pam Tiberia, for their enthusiasm and belief in the project; and our close friends and families, for their encouragement and understanding.

Dedication

To Mark, Sarah, and Erik—my wonderful "ginks"
JP

In memory of my mother, Patricia Ann Hagen, who patiently taught me the craft of editing.
SH

Better Writing Through Editing is a book that will help you improve your writing. You will learn about your strengths and weaknesses as a writer. You will also learn how to *edit* your writing in order to find and correct common mistakes. Of course, the best way to improve your writing is to write a lot! This text will give you many opportunities to see sample sentences, paragraphs, and essays, and to write similar ones of your own.

The three sections of this book are the following:

Part 1   *Getting Started*

This section will teach you a system for finding and correcting the errors that you make in your writing. By completing the Beginning Editing Assessment, you will know which topics in the Editing Focus section (Part 3) you need to complete in order to become a better, clearer writer.

Part 2   *Writing Focus*

This section reviews different types of English sentences. You will see how you can make your writing more interesting by including more sentence variety. All of the topics for the writing assignments are found in this section of the book.

Part 3   *Editing Focus*

This section helps you recognize and correct common errors in written grammar and expression. By completing the exercises in these chapters, you will improve the editing skills that you use when you check your writing. As a result, your writing will be much clearer and easier to understand.

The Importance of Editing

Editing is extremely important for all writers—especially ESL/EFL students. Editing is the final step in the writing process when you check your writing assignments for correct grammar, sentence structure, word choice, punctuation, and spelling.

Many intermediate students have important ideas that they want to express. Unfortunately, their English vocabulary and skills sometimes aren't good enough to express their ideas clearly. Often these students are trying to translate their ideas directly from their language into English. They also haven't learned how to edit their writing carefully for grammar. As a result, their writing can be difficult to understand.

If this is true for you, we hope that you will learn to think in English as you write, to use more natural-sounding English expressions, and to check your writing for common grammar mistakes. Your writing may sound a little simple to you, and you may not be able to express all of your ideas, but the reader will understand what you mean.

Tips for Improving Your Writing

As you learn more about editing, you may want to use one or more of these techniques that many students find useful:

- If your assignment is to be completed outside of class, put your finished assignment away for a period of time. This could be 30 minutes or an entire day, depending on the assignment. Then go back to it later, and check the writing carefully. This fresh look can be helpful in finding any mistakes that you might have missed when you first wrote the assignment.

- Read your completed assignment aloud (outside of class) or quietly (in class), listening for how each sentence sounds. Some students can hear natural-sounding expressions or correct grammar better than they can see it in their writing.

- Look at each sentence in your assignment. Write S above each subject and V above each verb. Then check to see that the following are correct: Is the subject singular or plural? Does the verb agree with the subject? Does the sentence use the correct verb tense and verb form? Is the sentence a complete sentence? Checking for these areas can help you avoid many typical errors.

- Learn to check your assignment carefully for the types of errors that you usually make. You can keep a list of your previous errors and their corrections in the Student Notebook section in the back of the book. Look at your new writing to be sure you haven't repeated the same errors or types of errors. As you continue through the Editing Focus section of this book, you will learn a lot about how to avoid these errors.

Your writing will improve if you read in English, listen to English on the radio or TV, and speak to others in English as much as possible. Little by little, it will be easier for you to think in English as you write and to use more natural-sounding expressions and grammar.

This book has been written to help you learn about and work on your individual problems. You can use this book as a textbook for class or by yourself. Either way, you will need to think about your strengths and weaknesses in writing. You will need to become a better *editor* of your own writing. Finally, you will need to concentrate on improving your writing and recording your improvement. If you work hard, you will make a lot of progress.

Suggestions for Self-Study

This book will be very useful if you are working by yourself to improve your sentence structure and editing skills. You can do most of the exercises in this book on your own. Just check the Answer Key carefully.

Even if you don't have a teacher to help you practice editing your own writing assignments, you may be able to ask a friend who is good in English or a native speaker of English who can check your editing with you. That person may not be able to explain all of the reasons why a word or expression is better than another or may not know the grammar words we use in this book. Nevertheless, you can learn a lot from friends.

Use the appendices in the back of the book to find additional information about irregular verbs, count and noncount nouns, word forms, and so on. You may also want to have a more complete grammar book and an ESL/EFL dictionary to check for more information.

To use this book for self-study, the following steps are recommended:

1. Start with the Beginning Editing Assessment in Part 1. This exercise will help you discover your individual editing strengths and weaknesses.

2. Next, look at your results on the Beginning Editing Assessment. Choose the area that has the most errors (for example, "Verbs"). In Part 3, Editing Focus, find the chapter for that topic (for example, Chapter 5, Verbs). Study the examples and explanations and do each of the exercises. Check your answers carefully in the Answer Key.

3. Then, choose another Editing Focus chapter to do according to the Beginning Editing Assessment.

4. At the same time, you can begin working on the chapters in Part 2, Writing Focus. (If you have someone who can check your writing for you, you may want to do one of the longer writing assignments that you will find at the end of each chapter.) Do the Writing Focus chapters in order.

5. Continue to work on the Editing Focus chapters that seem useful to you until you feel you have a good understanding of basic English grammar and editing. Some students may want to do the entire book, while others will want to focus on their weaker areas only.

6. When you have finished all of the chapters in the Writing Focus section, and you have finished as much as you want to do in the Editing Focus section, take the Final Editing Assessment in Chapter 17. Compare your results with your Beginning Editing Assessment to see how your editing skills have improved.

We wish you all the best as you move toward better writing through editing!

Getting Started

CHAPTER 1

Beginning Editing Assessment

Before you begin working on the Editing Focus exercises in this book, it will be helpful for you to find out what you already know about English. That way you find out your strong points and can focus on the areas you want to improve.

This assessment will help you find out your feeling for correct and incorrect English. This is not a test for a grade. It is to help you (and your teacher) see what you know about English now. Don't worry if you are not sure about the answers. Just do your best. The suggested time for this assessment is 45 minutes.

Directions

The Beginning Editing Assessment is divided into sections or parts. Each part will focus on a special language point in English. For example, the sentences in the section on verbs will have correct or incorrect use of verb tense or verb form. You will decide if the sentence is correct or incorrect, and then you will write the answer on the answer sheet on the next page. If there is no error, choose **C** for *correct.* If there is an error, choose **I** for *incorrect.*

Examples:

Verbs

1. Tomas and Stephen usually take the bus to school.   1. Ⓒ I
2. Yesterday I goed to a movie.   2. C Ⓘ

For the verb section, just think about the verbs. Don't worry about spelling or any other type of mistake.

In each section there is a short description for the topic. If you don't understand, you can still take the assessment. Just do your best to decide if it seems like correct or incorrect English to you.

(*Note:* Some teachers may prefer to use a scantron answer card. If so, use **A** for correct and **B** for incorrect.)

Answer Sheet

Tear this answer sheet out of your book and use it to take the Beginning Editing Assessment on pages 7 to 9.
Circle C for *correct* if there is no error. Circle I for *incorrect* if there is an error.

1. C I	26. C I	51. C I
2. C I	27. C I	52. C I
3. C I	28. C I	53. C I
4. C I	29. C I	54. C I
5. C I	30. C I	55. C I
6. C I	31. C I	56. C I
7. C I	32. C I	57. C I
8. C I	33. C I	58. C I
9. C I	34. C I	59. C I
10. C I	35. C I	60. C I
11. C I	36. C I	61. C I
12. C I	37. C I	62. C I
13. C I	38. C I	63. C I
14. C I	39. C I	64. C I
15. C I	40. C I	65. C I
16. C I	41. C I	66. C I
17. C I	42. C I	67. C I
18. C I	43. C I	68. C I
19. C I	44. C I	69. C I
20. C I	45. C I	70. C I
21. C I	46. C I	
22. C I	47. C I	
23. C I	48. C I	
24. C I	49. C I	
25. C I	50. C I	

Fragment

(The sentence, or one of the sentences, is not a complete sentence.)

1. British Columbia is a Canadian province with beautiful cities. Such as Vancouver and Victoria.

2. Many tourists come to visit British Columbia from all over the world.

3. In Vancouver, visitors can walk around Stanley Park, go to several wonderful museums, or shop on Robson Street.

4. On a sunny day, the views around Vancouver are beautiful. Because you can see the mountains.

5. If you ever have the chance to go to Western Canada. You should try to visit British Columbia.

Run-on or Comma Splice

(Two sentences are written incorrectly as one sentence.)

6. At first, life was difficult for me in the United States, I didn't understand English.

7. I could speak only a few words of English, so it was very hard to communicate.

8. Luckily, I had some friends who spoke English they could help me a lot.

9. When I needed to fill out applications or go to the doctor, my friends translated for me.

10. Now I can do everything by myself because I speak and understand English quite well, and I am getting along fine.

Verbs

(The problem can be the verb tense or verb form.)

11. The new city library near my house built in 1990.

12. Every day I am going to the library to study in a quiet place.

13. Yesterday I studied in the library for three hours.

14. Residents are allow to check out books, CDs, and tapes from the library.

15. I had my own library card since last August.

Singular/Plural

(The noun form for *one* or *more than one* isn't correct.)

16. Students usually have homeworks every day.

17. I always have to read book and write summary.

18. I sometimes learn useful information in my reading assignments.

19. This week we are reading stories from several country.

20. I'm learning about tradition and custom in Chile.

Subject–Verb Agreement

(The subject and verb don't match.)

21. Both the book and the tapes for our listening class is available in the college bookstore.

22. One of my favorite hobbies are looking at books in a big bookstore.

23. The people who work in the bookstore are very helpful.

24. Every student need to know how to get to the bookstore.

25. The bookstore opens at 8:00 A.M. and closes at 8:00 P.M. on weekdays.

Noun–Pronoun Agreement

(Words such as *he, him, his, it* are not used correctly.)

26. My friend, she works at a CD store.

27. I bought a great new CD. I've listened to it many times.

28. If you need to get special CDs, you can order it at the store.

29. I hope to have own music store someday.

30. It's a dream I've had all of my life.

Word Choice

(One or more words are wrong. A different word or expression should be used.)

31. I really enjoy meeting other country's people.

32. Every Friday night I play bowling with my friends.

33. I was very tired last night, so I went to bed early.

34. When I am sick, I take some medicine.

35. I hope I will spend a good life.

Word Form

(The wrong form of a word is used.)

36. My friend loves playing basketball and to swim.

37. He and another friends often have a basketball game after class.

38. My friend thinks basketball is the most exciting sport in the world.

39. However, when I watch basketball games, I'm very boring.

40. I'm unusual because almost all young men seem to like basketball.

Word Order

(The words are correct, but they are in the wrong place in the sentence.)

41. My nieces and nephews I love a lot.

42. I especially enjoy playing fun games with them.

43. My nephew is in the second grade whom I babysit for often.

44. Babysitting is good practice to learn for me how to be a parent.

45. However, I like it when I can give the kids back to their parents at the end of the day.

Prepositions

(Words such as *on, in, at,* or *to* are used incorrectly.)

46. I feel very sorry for my friend.

47. He has been living in here for three years.

48. Now he has to go back his country because his father died.

49. He has to quit school and get ready to leave in Friday.

50. I'll go to the airport with him to say good-bye.

Articles

(The words *a, an,* or *the* are used incorrectly.)

51. My aunt lives in a small apartment in a big city.

52. She moved to New York, which is biggest city in the United States.

53. Unfortunately, the cost of living in New York City is very expensive.

54. My aunt is looking for better job that pays more money.

55. She may take computer classes at a local college to improve her skills.

Punctuation

(The marks , ; : ' ". . ." are used incorrectly.)

56. Paul Newman, who is a good actor is also an unusual businessman.

57. His company makes a variety of spaghetti sauces and salad dressings.

58. Unlike most companies, Newman's company gives all of its profits to help people who are poor, handicapped, or sick.

59. I really like to watch Newman's movies, and I feel good about buying his food products.

60. He's starred in some of my favorite films, such as; *Butch Cassidy and the Sundance Kid* and *Nobody's Fool.*

Capitalization

(A big or small letter is used incorrectly.)

61. Many international students attend colleges and universities in North America.

62. At my College, they often study Business classes.

63. I have several Vietnamese friends at school.

64. They speak english at school, but they use vietnamese at home.

65. Next semester a friend and I will take Introduction to Psychology.

Spelling

(A word is not spelled correctly.)

66. I'm waiting to recieve an important package in the mail.

67. I hope it will arrive tommorrow.

68. I ordered a new printer from a computer magazine.

69. Computers have become extremely important in modern society.

70. I'll be able to write essays for my writting class at home instead of using the computer lab.

Editing Assessment Results

If you are using this book in a class, your teacher may correct your answers on the Beginning Editing Assessment. If you are using this book for self study, you can check your own answers using the Answer Key on page 351 of this book.

When you get your corrected answer sheet, follow these steps to find your stronger and weaker areas:

1. Put a slash (/) through the number of each of your incorrect answers. For example, if you answered items 1, 4, and 5 incorrectly, draw a slash through those numbers below.

   ## Beginning Editing Assessment Results

Fragment	1	2	3	4	5
Run-on or Comma Splice	6	7	8	9	10
Verbs	11	12	13	14	15
Singular / Plural	16	17	18	19	20
Subject–Verb Agreement	21	22	23	24	25
Noun–Pronoun Agreement	26	27	28	29	30
Word Choice	31	32	33	34	35
Word Form	36	37	38	39	40
Word Order	41	42	43	44	45
Prepositions	46	47	48	49	50
Articles	51	52	53	54	55
Punctuation	56	57	58	59	60
Capitalization	61	62	63	64	65
Spelling	66	67	68	69	70

2. Count up your total score: number correct _____ (out of 70). This gives you a general idea of your overall score.

3. Draw a star in front of the areas that had no mistakes or only 1 mistake. These areas are your strong points, or your strengths.

4. Put an X in front of the areas that had the most mistakes. These areas may be your weak points. You will want to focus on these areas in the Editing Focus section.

CHAPTER 2

The Editing System

Study the following system used in this book to describe typical errors. These errors can be divided into bigger problems and smaller problems.

For each error, you will see the Editing Focus chapter number, the name of the problem, a description of the problem, the symbol commonly used for this problem, and at least one example of the incorrect and correct sentences.

Bigger Problems

These problems can get in the way of people understanding your writing.

Editing Focus Chapter	Problem	Symbol
1	**Unclear** Some part of your sentence is not clear or does not sound like English. It may be a translation.	**Uncl**

No: My other suggestion is too much homework.

Yes: My other suggestion is for teachers to give less homework.

No: It can be difficult to open minds each other friends.

Yes: It can be difficult to express your feelings with friends.

Yes: It can be difficult to share your ideas with friends.

Editing Focus Chapter	Problem	Symbol

2

Fragment   The sentence is not a complete sentence.   **Frag**

No: I felt cold yesterday. Because I forgot my jacket.

Yes: I felt cold yesterday because I forgot my jacket.

No: Tom doesn't like fast food. For example, hamburgers and tacos.

Yes: Tom doesn't like fast food, for example, hamburgers and tacos.

No: Suzanne a good friend of mine.

Yes: Suzanne is a good friend of mine.

3

Run-on Sentence   Two sentences are written incorrectly as one sentence.   **Run-on**

No: I have a cat her name is Kiki.

Yes: I have a cat. Her name is Kiki.

4

Comma Splice   A comma is not used to separate two sentences.   **CS**

No: It's really difficult to learn English, it takes a long time.

Yes: It's really difficult to learn English. It takes a long time.

Yes: It's really difficult to learn English because it takes a long time.

Yes: It's really difficult to learn English, for it takes a long time.

Yes: It's really difficult to learn English; it takes a long time.

5

Verbs / Verb Tense   The time of the verb is not clear or not correct.   **V**

No: Tomohiko was a student since 1988.

Yes: Tomohiko has been a student since 1988.

Verb Form   The form of the verb is not correct.   **V**

No: He can goes to the party.

Yes: He can go to the party.

Editing Focus Chapter	Problem	Symbol
6	**Singular / Plural** The noun form for *one* or *more than one* is not correct.	S/Pl

No: I had to buy three book.

Yes: I had to buy three books.

No: The book contained a lot of informations.

Yes: The book contained a lot of information.

7	**Subject–Verb Agreement** The subject and verb don't match.	SV

No: Ms. Watson work at a bank.

Yes: Ms. Watson works at a bank.

8	**Noun–Pronoun Agreement** Words such as *he, him, it* are not used correctly.	N-PN

No: My books were heavy, so I didn't want to carry it.

Yes: My books were heavy, so I didn't want to carry them.

Smaller Problems

These problems probably don't stop the reader from understanding you, but they are mistakes that make your writing sound non-native. Some of the problems, such as prepositions, articles, and word choice, take time to learn completely, but you can improve a lot with practice. Other problems, such as punctuation and capitalization, are much easier to study and correct.

Editing Focus Chapter	Problem	Symbol
9	**Word Choice** A different word or expression should be used.	WC

No: It improved my writing much better.

Yes: It made my writing much better.

Yes: It improved my writing.

Editing Focus Chapter	Problem	Symbol

10

Word Form   The wrong form of the word is used.   **WF**

No: Please tell me the true.

Yes: Please tell me the truth.

No: My writing is more better now.

Yes: My writing is better now.

No: They have to improve programs and continuing research.

Yes: They have to improve programs and continue research.

11

Word Order   The words are correct, but they are in the wrong place in the sentence.   **WO**

No: My friend lives in San Jose who is a computer programmer.

Yes: My friend who is a computer programmer lives in San Jose.

12

Preposition   Words such as *on, in,* or *at* are used incorrectly.   **Prep**

No: Vancouver is surrounded from mountains.

Yes: Vancouver is surrounded by mountains.

No: I need to go back my country.

Yes: I need to go back to my country.

13

Articles   The words *a, an,* or *the* are used incorrectly.   **Art**

No: I went to movie.

Yes: I went to a movie.

No: She'll take next bus.

Yes: She'll take the next bus.

14

Punctuation   The marks **, ; : ' ". . ."** are used incorrectly.   **Punc**

No: I'm studying grammar writing and reading.

Yes: I'm studying grammar, writing, and reading.

No: I came from my brothers house.

Yes: I came from my brother's house.

Editing Focus Chapter	Problem	Symbol
15	**Capitalization** A big or small letter is used incorrectly.	*Cap*
	No: Last Spring I went to michigan.	
	Yes: Last spring I went to Michigan.	
16	**Spelling** A word is not spelled correctly.	*Sp*
	No: My writting has improved.	
	Yes: My writing has improved.	

CHAPTER 3

Sample Writing

If you are using this book for a class, your teacher will probably mark the errors on your paper. Here is a sample of a student's writing and two ways a teacher may mark the errors: with symbols or with numbers according to the chapters used in the Editing Focus section. When the student repeated exactly the same error, the teacher used parentheses ( ).

Using Symbols

Why I Came to Canada

Prep
I came to Canada on March, 1997. I wanted to learn English.

V   WO   Sp
I study/in my country/only grammer and reading, so I wanted

WF   Art   SV
study speaking. I live with Canadian girl and she speak to me
                              ∧

Prep
often, so I can use English now. She told to me my English

V   Prep   WF   Prep
getting better. I also came to here for having fun and learning
                                                              ∧

WF   WF   (Prep)   S/Pl   S/Pl
other culture. I enjoy to learn other custom and lifestyle.

WC   V
Maybe I will study regular college classes if I will have time.

Art   Sp   WC/WO   Prep
Few monthes or one year later, I will go back my country and
                                                ∧

Art
find job.
∧

Why I Came to Canada

12   5
I came to Canada on March, 1997. I wanted to learn English. I study in

11   16   10
my country/only grammer and reading, so I wanted study speaking. I live

13   7
with ˄ Canadian girl and she speak to me often, so I can use English now.

12   5   12
She told to me my English getting better. I also came to here for

10   (10) 12 10   10 (12)   6
having fun and learning other culture. I enjoy to learn other custom
                        ˄   ˄

6   9   5
and lifestyle. Maybe I will study regular college classes if I will have

13   16   9/11   12
time. Few monthes or one year later, I will go back my country and
      ˄

13
find job.
      ˄

CHAPTER 4

Sample Charts

A good way to learn more about your strengths and weaknesses in writing is to keep a record of your errors. You will see which areas to work on and which areas are improving. After every writing, fill out an individual Error Chart.* Here is a sample of the chart for the previous student sample "Why I Came to Canada" from Chapter 3.

Error Chart

Name: **Sample**   Title: **Why I Came to Canada**   Writing # __1__

After your teacher has marked your writing, use this chart to record which types of errors occurred.
Put a check (✓) in the correct row for each error. Then add up the totals and write them on your Progress Chart.

Editing Focus Chapter	Error Type	Symbol		Totals
1	Unclear Meaning / Translation	(Uncl)		
2	Fragment	(Frag)		
3	Run-on Sentence	(Run-on)		
4	Comma Splice	(CS)		
5	Verb Tense / Verb Form	(V)	✓ ✓ ✓	3
6	Singular / Plural	(S/Pl)	✓ ✓	3
7	Subject–Verb Agreement	(SV)	✓	1
8	Noun–Pronoun Agreement	(N-Pn)		
9	Word Choice	(WC)	✓ ✓	2
10	Word Form	(WF)	✓ ✓ ✓ ✓	4
11	Word Order	(WO)	✓ ✓	2
12	Preposition	(Prep)	✓ ✓ ✓ ✓ ✓	5
13	Article	(Art)	✓ ✓ ✓	3
14	Punctuation	(Punc)		
15	Capitalization	(Cap)		
16	Spelling	(Sp)	✓ ✓	2

* *Note: This Error Chart can be found in the Student Notebook section at the back of this book.*

Next, transfer the totals to your Progress Chart.* Here is a sample of the "Why I Came to Canada" writing on a Progress Chart. You will see your progress as you add results from each writing. Your Progress Chart will also help you decide which chapters in Editing Focus to work on.

Progress Chart

Name: _____

This chart will help you see your progress. You'll see which areas are improving and which areas need more study. Record the totals from the Error Chart for each writing assignment.

Editing Focus Chapter		Writing:	1	2	3	4	5	6	7	8	9	10
1	Unclear Meaning / Translation	(Uncl)										
2	Fragment	(Frag)										
3	Run-on Sentence	(Run-on)										
4	Comma Splice	(CS)										
5	Verb Tense / Verb Form	(V)	3									
6	Singular / Plural	(S/Pl)	3									
7	Subject–Verb Agreement	(SV)	1									
8	Noun–Pronoun Agreement	(N-Pn)										
9	Word Choice	(WC)	2									
10	Word Form	(WF)	4									
11	Word Order	(WO)	2									
12	Preposition	(Prep)	5									
13	Article	(Art)	3									
14	Punctuation	(Punc)										
15	Capitalization	(Cap)										
16	Spelling	(Sp)	2									
	Total Number of Errors:											
	Grade:											

(Title / Why I Came to Canada)

* Note: This Progress Chart can be found on the inside front cover of this book and in the Student Notebook section at the back of this book.

CHAPTER 5

Sample Rewrite

The best way to improve your writing is to correct your errors in a rewrite. Your teacher may ask you to rewrite by yourself or to work with another student. Then return your original writing, your individual chart, and your rewrite to your teacher. He or she will help with any additional changes at that time.

Here is the rewrite of "Why I Came to Canada" and the teacher's suggestions.

Why I Came to Canada

I came to Canada in March, 1997. I wanted to learn English. In my country I studied only grammar and reading, so I wanted to study speaking. I live with a Canadian girl and she speaks to me often, so I can use English now. She told me my English is getter better. I also

(no 'in' with 'here')   about another (= 1 more)   about

came in here to have fun and learn other culture. I enjoy learning

take

other customs and lifestyles. Maybe I will go to regular college

a   A

classes if I have time. A few months or one year after, I will go back

to my country and find a job.

Good rewrite!
(Check carefully
so you make all of
the changes.)

Use the Beginning Editing Assessment and your Progress Chart to help you decide which Editing Focus chapters to study. As you work on those chapters and practice editing your own writing, you will see your writing improve.

Writing Focus

CHAPTER 1

ESL Students

Simple Sentences

Quick Facts   ESL Students

- Every day, English is spoken by more people as a second language than as a native language.

- Millions of people all over the world study English as a foreign language.

- International students at colleges and universities:
  Canada: 60,000 (1994)   U.S.: 450,000 (1995)

- Average number of immigrants and refugees who came to North America each year from 1990–1995:
  Canada: 215,000   U.S.: 900,000

- Percentage of people in the U.S. over five years old who reported speaking a language other than English at home:
  6.2 percent (1990)

- Percentage of people in Canada who reported speaking a language other than English or French at home:
  7 percent (1991)

Words to Know

ESL   (English as a Second Language) Studying English if English is not your native language. Sometimes this also means you are studying in a country that uses English.

EFL   (English as a Foreign Language) Studying English in a country that does not use English as a native or official language.

international student   A person who comes to another country to study and then returns to his or her country.

immigrant   A person who comes to another country to live permanently.

refugee   A person who comes to another country because of war or danger in his or her home country.

ESOL   (English for Speakers of Other Languages) This term is often used for both ESL and EFL situations.

And You?

- Are you studying ESL or EFL?

  If you are an ESL student, are you an international student, immigrant, or refugee?

  What are your reasons for studying English?

Form

A simple sentence has at least one subject and one full verb and tells a complete thought. It consists of one independent clause.

Simple sentences look like this:

```
                              S V
                    S and   S V
              S, S, and   S V
                              S V   or V
                              S V   and V
                              S V,  V, and V
                    S and   S V   and V
              S, S, and   S V   and V
```

Simple sentences can be very short.

```
              S    V
       Chan is an immigrant.
```

Simple sentences can also be long.

```
       S                                          V
The tall young man with dark hair and glasses speaks nearly fluent English.
```

Example Sentences

S = subject
V = verb
hv = helping verb

The following sentences are simple sentences about students in an ESL class. Note the subjects and verb in each sentence.

```
       S    V
```
1. Tariq is an ESL student.

```
       S    V
```
2. Kim came to Canada three years ago.

```
       S   V
```
3. Li wants to be an English teacher.
   Note: to be is the object in this sentence. It is not a verb.

```
          S    V
```
4. Teresa loves living in a foreign country.
   Note: living is the object in this sentence. It is not a verb.

```
          S      hv    V
```
5. ESL students should try to speak with native speakers.

```
       V
```
6. Study hard!
   Note: The subject you is understood in commands.

Simple sentences may have more than one subject and more than one verb, but the subjects are together and the verbs are together. They are connected with *and* or *or*.

        S   S   V

7. Canada and the U.S. have many immigrants.

       S   S   S   hv   V

8. Immigrants, refugees, and international students may study together in one class.

   Note: Three or more items in a list (subjects or verbs) need commas. The comma before *and* is preferred, but not necessary.

            S   hv   V   V

9. Next year, Stephan will study at a college or get a job.

   Note: You do not need to repeat the helping verb *will* with the second verb *get.*

            S   V   V

10. Every day after class, Young Sil practices her speaking and does her homework with a study group.

     S   V   V   V

11. Chang immigrated to Los Angeles, got a job, and now owns his own company.

    S   S   V   V

12. Irina and Sarah study English and run a day-care.

Watch Out For . . .

Be sure you write a complete sentence with a subject and a verb. Note the following incomplete sentences, called fragments.

See Fragments on page 93 for more information and practice.

A Make sure you have a verb in the sentence.

         S

No: English a very difficult subject.

         S   V

Yes: English is a very difficult subject.

         S

No: My school far away.

         S   V

Yes: My school is far away.

B In formal writing, words such as *because, if, although,* and *when* cannot begin a simple sentence. They are used in complex sentences.

See Adverb Clauses on page 53 for more information.

No: Although I'm homesick.

Yes: I'm homesick.

Yes: Although I'm homesick, I will stay here for two years.

C If you use *for example* and *such as,* make sure you have a subject and a verb in the sentence.

No: For example, San Francisco.

Yes: For example, San Francisco has many Chinese immigrants.

No: Such as Ukraine.

Yes: Many recent immigrants come from Eastern European countries, such as Ukraine.

Sentence Practice

Exercise 1

Write S above the subject(s) and V above the verb(s).

Studying English as a Second Language

1. Many ESL students come to the United States and Canada to start a new life.

2. Other ESL students come to North America to study English and other subjects.

3. Most ESL students enjoy getting to know students from around the world.

4. Yumiko, Abdullah, and Kwang Ho are ESL students at North City Community College.

5. They are studying English and taking other college classes.

6. Hwang and Christine take classes and work full-time.

Exercise 2

Write **S** above the subject(s) and **V** above the verb(s). Then write **SS** in the blank if the sentence is a simple sentence or **F** if the sentence is a fragment (incomplete sentence).

Studying English as a Foreign Language

1. _____ Thousands of students all over the world study English in their own countries.

2. _____ Because English has become an international language.

3. _____ When people study English in a non-English-speaking country.

4. _____ It is sometimes called English as a Foreign Language, or EFL.

5. _____ Elementary students, junior high students, and high school students often take English in school as a required subject.

6. _____ Some EFL students take special English classes to help them pass a test.

7. _____ Such as a college entrance exam or the TOEFL* test.

8. _____ English a very popular language nowadays.

---

* Test of English as a Foreign Language

Exercise 3

On another piece of paper, write a paragraph by combining each group of sentences into one simple sentence. Use *and* or *or*. Think carefully about commas. Your paragraph should have six sentences.

ESL Students

1. Thousands of ESL students live in North America.
   Thousands of ESL students study English at high schools, colleges, and universities.

2. International students study ESL to improve their lives.
   Immigrants study ESL to improve their lives.
   Refugees study ESL to improve their lives.

3. Many international students work on ESL first.

   Many international students take regular college classes later.

4. International students take classes for fun.

   International students study for college degrees.

   International students improve their English for their profession.

5. Immigrants study ESL to survive in an English-speaking country.

   Immigrants study ESL to take college classes.

   Immigrants study ESL to get good jobs.

   Refugees study ESL to survive in an English-speaking country.

   Refugees study ESL to take college classes.

   Refugees study ESL to get good jobs.

6. They often study ESL.

   They often have a job.

   They often take care of their families.

Writing Practice (Optional)

Ten Perfect Sentences

To practice writing simple sentences and to practice editing carefully for grammar problems, you will write ten perfect simple sentences. Your teacher may ask you to write about students in your class or about another topic that he or she chooses.

a. Your sentences must be the type of sentences you are practicing, for example, simple sentences. The punctuation must be correct. All additional grammar points must be correct.

b. Try a variety of types of simple sentences (SSV, SVV, etc.). Check the sentences very carefully for correct grammar, punctuation, spelling, and expression. It is important to write and check these sentences by yourself.

c. Your teacher will check your sentences and circle the number of the correct sentences. Congratulations!

d. If a sentence has any problems or is not a simple sentence, your teacher will make the corrections in the sentence.

e. Then your teacher (or you) can count the number of correct sentences. If you wrote ten perfect simple sentences, great! You are finished with this exercise. You can work on self-study. If you didn't write ten perfect sentences, you need to write new (different) sentences until you have a total of ten perfect sentences.

This is more difficult than you think! It may take you several tries. Keep working on your sentences until you are finished.

The student sample that follows will help you understand.

Here is an example of a student's Ten Perfect Sentences. This student wrote sentences about her family.

Ten Perfect Simple Sentences

1. My father work at computer factory.

2. My Mother/ she stay and work at home.

3. My sister is studying in high school.

4. My grandmother and my grandfather live with my aunt and help with her children.

5. I love and respec my parent.

6. If you will meet my family, you will like them.   **(Not a simple sentence)**

7. My brother/ He is only six year old.

8. Sometime I play with my brother and cousin.

9. My sister or I make dinner every Saturday.

10. I always help my mother in the kitchen.

(**6 more**)

(Note that the student wrote four perfect simple sentences. She needed to write six more sentences. They must be different sentences. First, she looked at her old sentences to see what mistakes she had. Then, on the same piece of paper, she wrote six new sentences.)

1. My family and I came to the United State three years ago.

2. My father plays piano and likes to read.

3. My sister likes (very much) her friends and her classmates.

4. I have many cousins.

5. Some of the my cousins live in the United State^s.

6. My brother and his friend are on a soccer team.

3 more

(She wrote three more.)

1. My sister and her friends like to go rollerblading.

2. I live together with my family in a little house.

3. My mother likes to read and sew.

OK

(She finished Ten Perfect Sentences.)

 Writing Topics

Your teacher may ask you to write a paragraph or essay on one of the following topics:

1. Interview another student in your class. Write about his or her life and/or future plans.

   (Narration)

2. Describe an English as a Second Language class or an English as a Foreign Language class you have had. Write about the teacher, students, and activities in class.

   (Description)

3. What are your reasons for studying English? How will knowing more English benefit you?

   (Reasons)

Exercise 1

                S   V
1. Many ESL students come to the United States and Canada to start a new life.

              S   V
2. Other ESL students come to North America to study English and other subjects.

              S   V
3. Most ESL students enjoy getting to know students from around the world.

        S   S   S   V
4. Yumiko, Abdullah, and Kwang Ho are ESL students at North City Community College.

        S   hv   V   V
5. They are studying English and taking other college classes.

        S   S   V   V
6. Hwang and Christine take classes and work full-time.

Exercise 2

                          S   V
1. __SS__ Thousands of students all over the world study English in their own countries.

                      S   hv   V
2. __F__ Because English has become an international language.

                     S   V
3. __F__ When people study English in a non-English-speaking country.

           S hv   V
4. __SS__ It is sometimes called English as a Foreign Language, or EFL.

                   S   S
5. __SS__ Elementary students, junior high students, and high school

                   S   V
          students often take English in school as a required subject.

                   S   V
6. __SS__ Some EFL students take special English classes to help them pass a test.

7. __F__ Such as a college entrance exam or the TOEFL test.

                   S
8. __F__ English a very popular language nowadays.

Exercise 3

Best answer:

Thousands of ESL students live in North America <u>and</u> study English at high schools, colleges, and universities. International students, immigrants, <u>and</u> refugees study ESL to improve their lives. Many international students work on ESL first <u>and</u> take regular college classes later. International students take classes for fun, study for college degrees, <u>or</u> to improve their English for their profession. Immigrants <u>and</u> refugees study ESL to survive in an English-speaking country, to take college classes, or* to get good jobs. They often study ESL, have a job, <u>and</u> take care of their families.

---

* *and* could be used here, but *or* is a better answer because most students takes classes for one of those reasons, not for all of them.

Note: The commas are optional before connecting words in lists of three or more.

CHAPTER 2

Siblings

Less Formal Compound Sentences

Quick Facts   Siblings

- Average family size: U.S.: 3.19   Canada: 2.9
- Average number of children per mother: U.S.: 2.06   Canada: 1.81
- The number of twins, triplets, and other multiple births has tripled since 1990 due to older women having babies and to fertility treatments. Twenty-five percent of the women who receive fertility treatments to help them become pregnant have more than one child (twins, triplets, quadruplets, quintuplets).
- The largest number of children born at one time to one mother: 10

- The birth order of some famous people:

  First-born: Rock singer Courtney Love, Presidents Bill Clinton and George Washington, Chinese Leader Mao Tse Tung

  Middle-born: Civil Rights Leader Martin Luther King, Jr., Cuban Leader Fidel Castro, actor Michael J. Fox, President Richard Nixon, journalist Barbara Walters

  Last-born: Indian Leader Mahatma Gandhi, actor Eddie Murphy, actress Goldie Hawn

  Only child: Artist Leonardo da Vinci, singer Elvis Presley, model Brooke Shields

Words to Know

sibling   Brother or sister.

twins   Two children born to the same mother at the same time.

triplets   Three children born to the same mother at the same time.

quadruplets   Four children born to the same mother at the same time.

quintuplets   Five children born to the same mother at the same time.

And You?

- How many siblings do you have?

  Are you a first-born, middle-born, youngest, or only child?

  Are there twins, triplets, or other multiple-birth children in your family?

Form

Compound sentences are two simple sentences (two "independent clauses") that are joined together because of their meaning. There can be more than one subject or more than one verb in the simple sentence. This chapter discusses less formal compound sentences with connecting words like *and, but, or,* and *so.*

Note: Connecting words are sometimes called *coordinating conjunctions.*

Less formal compound sentences look like this:

```
   S      V         , connecting word     S      V         .
 SENTENCE                                SENTENCE

                     , and

                     , but

                     , or

                     , so
```

The two sentences have equal importance.

_____

Note: Compound sentences need a comma after the first simple sentence unless the sentences are very short.

Example Sentences

The following sentences are informal compound sentences about two sisters. Note the subjects and verbs in each sentence and the meaning of the connecting words.

Very common connecting words: *and, but, or, so.*

S = subject
V = verb
hv = helping verb
cw = connecting word

```
   S    V        cw   S    V
```
1. Terri has twins, and Beth has triplets.
   Note: and shows a similarity.

```
    S       V              cw  S    V
```
2. They both love their children, but they have questions about raising them.
   Note: but shows a difference.

```
   S   hv   V                    S   hv   V
```
3. Beth will stay home with the children, or she will go back to work.
   Note: or shows a choice and is often in the future.

```
    S      V                          cw   S   V
```
4. They wanted to find others with twins or triplets, so they formed a parents' group.
   Note: so shows a result.

Less common connecting words: *for, yet, nor.**

<pre>
        S   V   cw S   V
</pre>
5. Terri's twins aren't identical, yet people still have trouble telling them apart.

   Note: yet shows a difference. It is like *but* only more formal.

<pre>
        S   hv   V   cw S   V
</pre>
6. Terri's twins don't dress alike, for they want to be different.

   Note: for shows a reason and means *because.*

<pre>
        S   hv   V   cw hv S   V
</pre>
7. Terri's twins don't look exactly alike, nor do they act alike.

   * *Note:* **nor** is a very unusual connecting word. It means "not this and not that." After *nor*, the word order is like a question.

Watch Out For . . .

A In very formal English, do not begin a sentence with a connecting word. In informal writing, it is usually OK to begin a sentence with a connecting word, but not too often.

No: And my mother is an only child.

Yes: My father is the youngest child in his family, and my mother is an only child.

No: But, my roommate comes from a large family.

Yes: I come from a small family, but my roommate comes from a large family.

No: So she used fertility drugs.

Yes: Pat couldn't have children, so she used fertility drugs.

No: Or, I may have triplets.

Yes: The doctors think I will have twins, or I may have triplets.

B In written English, you cannot begin a line with a comma. Put it at the end of the line instead.

No: Thomas is interested in sports

, but his twin brother prefers reading.

Yes: Thomas is interested in sports,

but his twin brother prefers reading.

C The words *also* and *then* are not connecting words. You need more than a comma (a period or a semicolon) to use them between sentences.

No: My brothers fought as children, then they were friends later.

Yes: My brothers fought as children. Then they were friends later.

No: My brothers share many interests, they also look alike.

Yes: My brothers share many interests; they also look alike.

Sentence Practice

Exercise 1

Write **S** over the subjects and **V** over the verbs in the following compound sentences.

Twins

1. Twins are two children born to the same mother at the same time, and there are two types of twins.

2. Identical twins are from one egg, but fraternal twins are from two eggs.

3. Identical twins have the same blood type, and they also have identical fingerprints.

4. Some identical twins look almost exactly alike, so it can be very difficult to tell them apart.

5. Identical twins are always the same sex, but fraternal twins can be the same or different sex.

6. Fraternal twins can be two girls or two boys, or they can be a girl and a boy.

7. Fraternal twins may not look very much alike, for they are actually the same as other sisters or brothers.

Exercise 2

Mark **S** over the subjects and **V** over the verbs in the following sentences. Then decide if they are simple or compound sentences. In the blanks, write **SS** for a simple sentence and **CS** for a compound sentence. Add commas to the compound sentences. The first sentence is done for you.

Birth Order

1. __CS__   Psychologists have studied children according to their birth order,

                  and they have discovered the following general results.

2. _____   First-born children often have strong personalities and like

                  to be leaders.

3. _____   They usually get high grades in school but they also get angry

                  more easily than other children.

4. _____   Middle children are usually satisfied with their place in the family

                  and they are quite flexible.

5. _____   Middle children generally follow the rules so they don't get into

                  trouble very much.

6. _____   The youngest children in the family like to get along with other

                  people and to try new things.

7. _____   Only children often need their parents but they are also

                  self-confident.

8. _____   These descriptions may fit your family well or they may not

                  describe the children in your family.

9. _____   Each family is different so no description of birth order is perfect.

On another piece of paper, combine each pair of sentences into one simple or compound sentence. Use *and, but, or, so,* or *for.* Be sure to use commas correctly.

Quadruplets

1. Christine and Lyle wanted to have another baby.

   Christine was not able to get pregnant.

2. She had an operation to help her get pregnant.

   It worked.

3. Seven months later, Christine gave birth to quadruplets.

   Aili, Daisey, Max, and Nathan joined the family.

4. At first, Christine panicked at the babies' crying.

   After a few months, she learned to help one and say "just a minute" to the others.

5. Having four babies is a lot of work.

   Christine has learned to ask for help from friends and neighbors.

6. Nine-year-old brother Benjamin is good at changing diapers.

   He likes making faces at the babies and watching them smile.

Writing Practice (Optional)

Write Ten Perfect Compound Sentences. Use each of the common connecting words, and be sure that they make sense for the meaning of the sentence. Check carefully for commas and other grammar and punctuation. You may want to write about your family or about another topic your teacher suggests. *(See pages 30–32 for instructions and an example.)*

Your teacher may ask you to write a paragraph or essay on one of the following topics:

1. If you have siblings, describe how they are similar or different from you or from each other (or describe two siblings you know well). If you have more than one child, discuss how they are similar or different.

   (Comparison / Contrast)

2. Are you a first-born, middle-born, youngest, or only child? Do you fit the descriptions given in Exercise 2? Why or why not?

   (Reasons)

3. Discuss the advantages and disadvantages of being an only child or coming from a large family. You can write from your own experience or the experience of others.

   (Advantages / Disadvantages)

Exercise 1

                   S   V

1. Twins are two children born to the same mother at the same time, and

       S   V

there are two types of twins.

           S   V   S   V

2. Identical twins are from one egg, but fraternal twins are from two eggs.

           S   V   S   V

3. Identical twins have the same blood type, and they also have identical
fingerprints.

           S   V   S (hv) V

4. Some identical twins look almost exactly alike, so it can be very difficult to
tell them apart.

           S   V   S (hv) V

5. Identical twins are always the same sex, but fraternal twins can be the
same or different sex.

           S (hv) V   S (hv) V

6. Fraternal twins can be two girls or two boys, or they can be a girl
and a boy.

           S (hv)   V   S   V

7. Fraternal twins may not look very much alike, for they are actually the
same as other sisters or brothers.

Exercise 2

                 S   (hv)   V

1. __CS__ Psychologists have studied children according to their birth order,

               S (hv)   V

and they have discovered the following general results.

               S   V   V

2. __SS__ First-born children often have strong personalities and like
to be leaders.

               S   V   S   V

3. __CS__ They usually get high grades in school, but they also get angry
more easily than other children.

               S   V

4. __CS__ Middle children are usually satisfied with their place in the family,

               S   V

and they are quite flexible.

               S   V   S (hv) V

5. __CS__ Middle children generally follow the rules, so they don't get into
trouble very much.

(Concluded)

6. __SS__ $\overset{S}{}$ $\overset{V}{}$ The youngest children in the family like to get along with other people and to try new things.

7. __CS__   Only children often need their parents, but they are also self-confident.

8. __CS__   These descriptions may fit your family well, or they may not

    describe the children in your family.

9. __CS__   Each family is different, so no description of birth order is perfect.

Exercise 3

Suggested answer:

Christine and Lyle wanted to have another baby, <u>but</u> Christine was not able to get pregnant. She had an operation to help her get pregnant, <u>and</u> it worked. Seven months later, Christine gave birth to quadruplets, <u>and</u> / <u>so</u> Aili, Daisey, Max, and Nathan joined the family. At first, Christine panicked at the babies' crying, <u>but</u> after a few months, she learned to help one and say "just a minute" to the others. Having four babies is a lot of work, <u>so</u> / <u>but</u> Christine has learned to ask for help from friends and neighbors. Nine-year-old brother Benjamin is good at changing diapers, <u>and</u> / <u>for</u> he likes making faces at the babies and watching them smile.

PART 2 WRITING FOCUS

CHAPTER 3

Holidays

More Formal Compound Sentences

Quick Facts   **Holidays**

- Even though the same holidays are observed in many different countries around the world, there is a variety of ways in which people celebrate them.

- Here are the main holidays in Canada and the United States:

Canada		United States	
New Year's Day*	January 1st	New Year's Day*	January 1st
		Martin Luther King Day*	3rd Monday in January
Valentine's Day	February 14th	Valentine's Day	February 14th
Easter Sunday	late March or early April	Presidents' Day*	3rd Monday in February
Easter Monday	Monday after Easter	Easter Sunday	late March or early April
Victoria Day*	3rd Monday in May	Memorial Day*	last Monday in May
Canada Day*	July 1st	Independence Day*	July 4th
Labour Day*	1st Monday in September	Labor Day*	1st Monday in September
Halloween	October 31st	Halloween	October 31st
Thanksgiving Day*	2nd Monday in October	Veterans Day	November 11th
Remembrance Day*	November 11th	Thanksgiving Day*	4th Thursday in November
Christmas Day*	December 25th	Christmas Day*	December 25th
Boxing Day*	December 26th		

* National holiday: most government offices and schools are closed.

And You?

- Of the holidays above or of holidays in your native culture, what is your favorite holiday? Why?

  What is your least favorite holiday? Why?

Form

In this chapter you will study compound sentences that use a semicolon (;) and usually a transition word (sometimes called a "conjunctive adverb"). These sentences are very similar to compound sentences with connecting words, but they are more formal.

More formal compound sentences look like this:

S V	; transition word,	S V	
(SENTENCE		SENTENCE)	

; in addition,
; moreover,   (similar meaning to *and*)
; furthermore,

; however,   (similar meaning to *but*)
; nevertheless,

; otherwise,   (*or* + result)

; therefore,
; consequently,   (similar meaning to *so*)
; as a result,

Compound sentences can also look like this:

S V	;	S V
(SENTENCE	;	SENTENCE)

Example Sentences

Transition words are often used at the beginning of a sentence. They are usually simple sentences. The transition word introduces the second sentence.

> My family always gets together with our relatives at Christmas. In addition, we have a big family picnic on the Fourth of July.

If the connection between the two sentences is very strong, the writer may want to combine the sentences together with a semicolon and a transition word. Here are compound sentences about holidays. Note the subjects, verbs, and transition words in each sentence.

S = subject
V = verb
hv = helping verb
trans = transition word

                                        S   V
1. On Independence Day, Americans meet with their friends and family for

                             trans   S   V
barbecues and picnics; in addition, most cities have big fireworks displays.

Note: The transition words *in addition, furthermore,* and *moreover* show similarity, almost the same as *and.* Often the idea in the second part of the sentence is stronger than in the first.

2. On some holidays, such as Veteran's Day and President's Day, all banks,
            S   S   hv   V   trans

schools, and U.S. government offices are closed; however, most private
     S   S   V

offices and stores remain open.

Note: The transition words *however* and *nevertheless* show difference or unexpected result. They mean almost the same as *but.*

    S V   trans   S   hv V

3. It's good to know about Halloween; otherwise, you will be surprised by
people in strange costumes.

Note: The transition word *otherwise* means *if not + result.* It is similar to *or* plus a result.

                    S   V

4. Many Americans wanted to make a day to celebrate the life of
                             trans   S   hv

Martin Luther King, Jr.; therefore, Martin Luther King Day was
     V

established in 1989.

Note: The transition words *therefore, consequently,* and *as a result* show a result. They mean almost the same as *so.*

If sentences are closely related, only a semicolon can be used. This is possible, but less common in English.

                              S   V   V

5. On New Year's Eve, many people go to parties and stay up
              S   V

until midnight; they like to greet the New Year with friends.

Watch Out For . . .

A   If there is no punctuation between two complete sentences, it is a run-on sentence. *See Run-ons on page 105 for more information.*

                      S V   S   V

No: In Canada, July first is Canada Day the first Monday in August is Civic Holiday in some areas.

B   Two complete sentences cannot be joined by only a comma. This is called a comma splice. *See Comma Splice on page 113 for more information.*

                      S V   S   V

No: In Canada, July first is Canada Day, the first Monday in August is Civic Holiday in some areas.

There are many ways to fix run-on and comma splice sentences:

Yes: In Canada, July first is Canada Day, and the first Monday in August is Civic Holiday in some areas.

Yes: In Canada, July first is Canada Day; in addition, the first Monday in August is Civic Holiday in some areas.

Yes: In Canada, July first is Canada Day. In addition, the first Monday in August is Civic Holiday in some areas.

Yes: In Canada, July first is Canada Day. The first Monday in August is Civic Holiday in some areas.

Yes: In Canada, July first is Canada Day; the first Monday in August is Civic Holiday in some areas.

Sentence Practice

Exercise 1

Write **S** over the subject(s) and **V** over the verb(s). Then write *and, but, so,* or *or* above the transition word to show its meaning. The first sentence is done for you.

Thanksgiving

Americans have a Thanksgiving holiday every fall; in addition, Canadians celebrate Thanksgiving in the fall. Canadians celebrate Thanksgiving on the second Monday in October; however, in the U.S. Thanksgiving is celebrated on the fourth Thursday in November. Long ago, the early European settlers survived a hard winter and had successful crops; therefore, they prepared a big meal together with their Indian neighbors and friends to thank God. Nowadays, people in both countries get together with their families and friends to eat a big dinner with traditional foods, such as turkey, potatoes, and pumpkin pie; moreover, they use this day to express their thankfulness for life. On Thanksgiving Day, we should not eat too much; otherwise, we may feel sick.

Write **S** over the subject(s) and **V** over the verb(s) in the following simple and compound sentences. Then write **C** in the blank if the sentence is correct. Write **I** if there is any mistake in punctuation and change the sentence to make it correct. The first sentence is done for you.

May Day

1. __C__   May 1st is a holiday in many countries; it is a day for workers.

2. __I__   May 1st is a big holiday in Europe however in North America, Labor Day is in September.

3. __C__   May 1st in the U.S. is called "May Day," and it is a kind of celebration for spring.

4. __I__   In the past, children danced around a Maypole on this day, moreover, people made May flower baskets to bring to their neighbors.

5. __C__   Usually a child put a basket on the neighbor's porch, rang the doorbell, and ran away.

6. __I__   The neighbor answered the door and found the basket, she (w) was surprised.

7. __C__   May Day used to be a very common celebration and an exciting day. However, not many Americans celebrate May Day today.

On another piece of paper, combine the following sentences using transition words.

Valentine's Day

1. On Valentine's Day, people in the United States and Canada often give cards to their loved ones. In addition,

   They may give their sweetheart flowers, candy, or other gifts.

2. Most people think the holiday was named for Saint Valentine. However,

   The holiday is probably based on a much earlier Roman custom.

3. Much later, in England, birds were thought to choose their mates on Valentine's Day. *therefore*

    It became known as a day for love.

4. Now elementary schoolchildren often buy or make Valentine's Day cards to exchange with their classmates. *moreover*

    Many classes have a Valentine's Day party and eat heart-shaped cookies.

5. Girlfriends, boyfriends, husbands, and wives expect to receive some kind of Valentine's card or gift. *otherwise*

    They may feel disappointed or angry.

6. Chocolate is a romantic gift. *as a result*

    Americans and Canadians buy and give more chocolate around Valentine's Day than any other time of the year.

Writing Practice (Optional)

Write Ten Perfect Compound Sentences with transition words. Use a variety of transition words. You may want to write about a holiday (or holidays) you enjoy or about another topic your teacher suggests. *(See pages 30–32 for instructions and examples.)*

Writing Topics

Your teacher may ask you to write a paragraph or essay on one of the following topics:

1. Describe a holiday from your culture.

    (Description)

2. Compare the celebration of the same holiday in two different places. For example, compare how Near Year's Day is celebrated in China and Canada.

    (Comparison)

3. Create a new holiday. Make up a new holiday, such as Students' Day or Yellow Day. Describe when, how, and why someone should celebrate it.

    (Description / Reasons)

Exercise 1

                        S   V   **and**   S

Americans have a Thanksgiving holiday every fall; in addition, Canadians

V   S   V

celebrate Thanksgiving in the fall. Canadians celebrate Thanksgiving on the

                        but   S   (hv)   V

second Monday in October; however, in the U.S. Thanksgiving is celebrated

                                                S

on the fourth Thursday in November. Long ago, the early European settlers

V   V   **so**   S   V

survived a hard winter and had successful crops; therefore, they prepared a

big meal together with their Indian neighbors and friends to thank God.

                S   V

Nowadays, people in both countries get together with their families and

friends to eat a big dinner with traditional foods, such as turkey, potatoes,

               and   S   V

and pumpkin pie; moreover, they use this day to express their thankfulness

                                S   (hv)   V   **or**

for life. On Thanksgiving Day, we should not eat too much; otherwise,

S   (hv) V

we may feel sick.

Exercise 2

                     S V   S V

1. __C__   May 1st is a holiday in many countries; it is a day for workers.

                     S V

2. __I__   May 1st is a big holiday in Europe; however, in North America,

                     S V

         Labor Day is in September.

                     S   (hv) V   S V

3. __C__   May 1st in the U.S. is called "May Day," and it is a kind of
         celebration for spring.

                     S   V

4. __I__   In the past, children danced around a Maypole on this day;

                     S   V

         moreover, people made flower baskets to bring to their

         neighbors.

(Concluded)

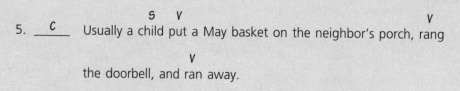

5. __C__   Usually a child put a May basket on the neighbor's porch, rang
the doorbell, and ran away.

6. __I__   The neighbor answered the door and found the basket;
she was surprised.

7. __C__   May Day used to be a very common celebration and an exciting
day. However, not many Americans celebrate May Day today.

Exercise 3

Suggested answer:

On Valentine's Day, people in the United States and Canada often give cards to their loved ones; in addition, they may give their sweetheart flowers, candy, or other gifts. Most people think the holiday was named for Saint Valentine; however, the holiday is probably based on a much earlier Roman custom. Much later, in England, birds were thought to choose their mates on Valentine's Day; therefore, it became known as a day for love. Now elementary schoolchildren often buy or make Valentine's Day cards to exchange with their classmates; moreover, many classes have a Valentine's Day party and eat heart-shaped cookies. Girlfriends, boyfriends, husbands, and wives expect to receive some kind of Valentine's card or gift; otherwise, they may feel disappointed or angry. Chocolate is a romantic gift; as a result, Americans and Canadians buy and give more chocolate around Valentine's Day than any other time of the year.

Note: There could be more than one transition word if the meaning makes sense; for example, *in addition, moreover,* and *furthermore* all mean *and.*

CHAPTER 4

In the Sky

Complex Sentences: Adverb Clauses

Quick Facts   **In the Sky**

- In the most northern areas of North America, including the Yukon Territory, the Northwest Territories, the Arctic Islands, and Alaska, the sun never sets in the summer. This is called the "midnight sun." There are several months of darkness, with no sunshine, in the winter.

- From 1990 to 1995, there were more than 1,000 tornadoes in North America each year.

- The rainiest spot in North America is Kauai, Hawaii: 460 inches (1,168 cm) of rain per year.

- The driest spot in North America is Death Valley, California: 1.63 inches (4.14 cm) of rain per year.

Words to Know

meteorology   The study of weather.

astrology   The study of the positions of the stars, planets, sun, and moon in the belief that they affect human lives.

Leap Year   A year that has an extra day on February 29.

And You?

- What kind of weather is typical in the area (or areas) you have lived?

  What is your astrological sign in the Eastern and Western systems? (*See page 56.*)

  Do you believe in astrology? Why or why not?

Form

A complex sentence with an adverb clause has two parts: a simple sentence (independent clause) and a dependent adverb clause (adverb clause marker + subject and verb). It is a complex sentence because it has an independent clause and a dependent clause. The dependent clause is like an adverb because it describes or explains the main clause verb.

These sentences look like this:

S   V   marker + s v
(SENTENCE   adverb clause)

Marker + s v,   S   V
(adverb clause,   SENTENCE)

Common Adverb Clause Markers

Cause	Condition	Contrast	Time
because	if	although	after
since		even though	before
		though	when
		while	since
			while
			the next time
			whenever

Note: Adverb clause markers are sometimes called *subordinating conjunctions.*

Example Sentences

Note the adverb clause markers, subjects, and verbs in the following adverb clause sentences about a snowstorm.

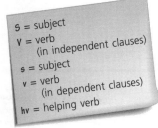

s = subject
v = verb
    (in independent clauses)
s = subject
v = verb
    (in dependent clauses)
hv = helping verb

         S   V   marker s   v
1. Many students were late for class because it snowed this morning.
   (cause)

marker s v   S   hv hv   V
2. If it snows a lot tomorrow, classes may be canceled.
   (condition)

     marker   s   v   S   hv   V
3. Although the snow was a problem, classes were held as usual.
   (contrast—unexpected result)

     S   hv   V   V
4. Students should listen to the radio or watch TV for a school closing report

marker s v
when it snows.
(time)

Note: Use a comma to separate the clauses if the adverb clause comes at the beginning of the sentence. If the adverb clause is second, there is usually no comma.

A In formal written English, the adverb clause cannot stand alone. It is a fragment, which is an incomplete sentence.

No: James was late for class. Because his car got stuck in the snow.

Yes: James was late for class because his car got stuck in the snow.

B Use a compound sentence or an adverb clause complex sentence, but not both!

No: Although the weather was horrible, but classes were held as usual.

Yes: The weather was horrible, but classes were held as usual.

Yes: Although the weather was horrible, classes were held as usual.

Yes: Classes were held as usual although the weather was horrible.

C Use *although, even though,* or *though* to show contrast (unexpected result). Do not use *even* by itself.

No: Even it was snowing, classes were held as usual.

Yes: Even though it was snowing, classes were held as usual.

Yes: Though it was snowing, classes were held as usual.

Yes: Although it was snowing, classes were held as usual.

Notice

1. Several adverb clause markers can have two meanings.

I've loved snow **since** I was a child. (*since* = time)

It can be hard to drive in a snowstorm **since** it's difficult to see. (*since* = reason)

While I was walking to school, I slipped and fell on the ice. (*while* = time)

While winters in Montreal are very snowy, winters in Victoria are usually rainy. (*while* = different or opposite)

2. Some adverb clause markers can also be prepositions (prep).

      S hv hv   V   marker s v
Yes: It's been snowing since I got up this morning.
(adverb clause sentence)

      S hv hv   V   prep
Yes: It's been snowing since 3:00. *(simple sentence)*

      S V   marker s   v
Yes: I plan to put snow tires on my car before I drive to work.
(adverb clause sentence)

      S V   prep
Yes: I plan to put snow tires on my car before Monday.
(simple sentence)

Sentence Practice

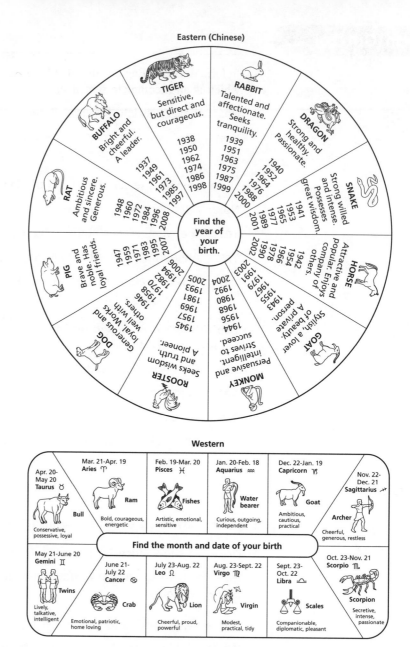

Eastern (Chinese)

Western

Find the month and date of your birth

In the following paragraph, underline the adverb clauses and write what kind of clause it is: time, cause, condition, or contrast. Then mark the subjects and verbs in the sentences. The first sentence is done for you.

Astrology, East and West

Since people began looking in the sky, they have wondered about the influence of stars. According to astrology, a person's future life depends on the position of the stars and planets when he or she was born. While the Western system of astrology is based on twelve "signs" according to the date of birth, the Eastern system of astrology is based on the year of birth. For example, if a girl is born on March 15, 2003, she will be a "Pisces" in Western astrology. When you look at the Eastern system, she will be a "sheep." Many people read their horoscope in the daily newspaper because they believe in astrology. Other people read their horoscope even though they don't believe the predictions. They do it because it is entertaining.

Exercise 2

Join sentences together to fix the fragments in the following paragraph. The first one is done for you.

Tornadoes

A tornado (also called a *twister* or *cyclone*) is a dark, narrow, round wind storm. Tornadoes usually occur in the flat middle part of the United States and Canada. When there is a mixture of warm, low wet air and cooler, drier air at high levels, A tornado could form. Tornadoes can have circular winds up to 320 to 480 kilometers (200–300 miles) per hour. Tornadoes can be very dangerous and can destroy buildings and trees. If they touch the ground.

Whenever there is a tornado, You should go to the basement or the cellar in a house or building. You should lie flat on the ground. If you are outside during a tornado. Although there can be many tornadoes in a year. Most of them do not cause any damage.

Exercise 3
_____

On another piece of paper, combine the following groups of sentences using adverb clauses. Use *if, when, because* (two times), *since, though,* and *although.* Think carefully about the meaning and the punctuation.

Leap Year

1. It takes the Earth 365 1/4 days to travel around the sun.
   The modern Western calendar has only 365 days per year.

2. We have Leap Year Day on February 29.
   It helps our calendar fit in the extra time.

3. The year can be divided by the number 4.*
   We add an extra day on February 29.

4. Leap Year occurs only every fourth year.
   People with birthdays or anniversaries on Leap Day have an unusual situation.

5. My friend Sara was born on February 29.
   She celebrates a birthday once every four years.

6. Sara has celebrated only five birthdays.
   She has actually lived for twenty years.

7. People ask Sara about her age.
   She answers, "five or twenty."

* *Note:* We do not add a Leap Day in years that end in 00 (such as 100) if they cannot be divided by 4. There is no Leap Year Day in the year 2100, 2300, or 2500, for example.

Writing Practice (Optional)

Write Ten Perfect Adverb Clause Complex Sentences. Use a variety of adverbs and types of adverb clause sentences (time, reason, condition, contrast). You may want to write about the weather in places you have lived, the traditional calendar in some part of the world, or about another topic your teacher suggests. *(See pages 30–32 for more instructions and examples.)*

Writing Topics

Your teacher may ask you to write a paragraph or essay on one of the following topics.

1. Describe a feature of the climate in a place you have lived. This could include the midnight sun, sandstorms, very cold winters, soft rains, hurricanes, perfect spring days, and so on.

   (Description)

2. Astrology is one way to predict the future. Describe any other ways you know to predict the future or to predict good or bad luck. Do you believe in these?

   (Description / Reasons)

3. Find descriptions of your personality according to Western and / or Eastern astrology. Do the descriptions seem to fit your sense of yourself. Why or why not?

   (Reasons)

Exercise 1

  s   v   S   (hv)   V
Since people began looking in the sky, they have wondered about the
                          time

                                                              S   V
influence of stars. According to astrology, a person's future life depends on

                                                    s   s   (hv) v
the position of the stars and planets when he or she was born. While the
                                                              time   contrast

           s   (hv)   v
Western system of astrology is based on twelve "signs" according to the date

                                                    S   (hv)   V
of birth, the Eastern or Chinese system of astrology is based on the year of

                          s (hv) v   S   (hv)   V
birth. For example, if a girl is born on March 15, 2003, she will be a "Pisces"
                                          condition

                          s   v   S   (hv)   V
in Western astrology. When you look at the Eastern system, she will be a
                                          time

                    S   V
"sheep." Many people read their horoscope in the daily newspaper because
                                                                                    cause

  s   v   S   V   s
they believe in astrology. Other people read their horoscope even though they
                                                                                    contrast

  (hv)   v   S   V   s   v
don't believe the predictions. They do it because it is entertaining.
                                                              cause

---

Exercise 2

A tornado (also called a *twister* or *cyclone*) is a dark, narrow, round wind storm. Tornadoes usually occur in the flat middle part of the United States and Canada. When there is a mixture of warm, low wet air and cooler, drier air at high levels, a tornado could form. Tornadoes can have circular winds up to 320 to 480 kilometers (200–300 miles) per hour. Tornadoes can be very dangerous and can destroy buildings and trees if they touch the ground. Whenever there is a tornado, you should go to the basement or the cellar in a house or building. You should lie flat on the ground if you are outside during a tornado. Although there can be many tornadoes in a year, most of them do not cause any damage.

(Concluded)

Exercise 3

<u>Although</u> / <u>Though</u> it takes the Earth 365 1/4 days to travel around the sun, the modern Western calendar has only 365 days per year. We have Leap Year Day on February 29 <u>because</u> / <u>since</u> it helps our calendar fit in the extra time. <u>If</u> / <u>When</u> the year can be divided by the number 4, we add an extra day on February 29. <u>Because</u> / <u>Since</u> Leap Year occurs only every fourth year, people with birthdays or anniversaries on Leap Day have an unusual situation. <u>Since</u> / <u>Because</u> my friend Sara was born on February 29, she celebrates a birthday once every four years. Sara has celebrated only five birthdays <u>though</u> / <u>although</u> she has actually lived for twenty years. <u>When</u> / <u>If</u> people ask Sara about her age, she answers, "five or twenty."

CHAPTER 5

Places

Complex Sentences: Adjective Clauses

Quick Facts   Places

	Canada	U.S.
Capital city:	Ottawa, Ontario	Washington, D.C.
Three largest cities:	Toronto, Ontario	New York, New York
	Montreal, Quebec	Los Angeles, California
	Vancouver, British Columbia	Chicago, Illinois
Popular tourist areas:	Quebec City, Quebec	Orlando, Florida
	Victoria, British Columbia	The Grand Canyon
	Banff National Park	Yellowstone National Park

And You?

- Have you visited or lived in any of these places?
- What places in North America would you like to visit?
- What do you like or not like about the neighborhood or city where you live now?

Form

A complex sentence with an adjective clause has two parts: a main independent clause and a dependent clause. The dependent clause describes a noun in the main clause, so it works like an adjective. The adjective clause can come after the subject or the object of the main clause.

Adjective clauses often look like this:

S, who (s) v, V

S V O, where s v

Adjective clauses use the following relative pronouns:

who	for the subject of the clause when it is a person
whom	for the object of the clause when it is a person (formal—not usually used in everyday American English)
which	for the subject or object of the clause when it is not a person
that	for the subject or object of the clause for a person, animal, or thing
where	for a place
when	for a time
whose	for a possessive noun or pronoun (belongs to) for a person, animal, or thing

Example Sentences

Note the adjective clauses and the subjects and verbs in the following sentences about a neighborhood. An arrow shows the word the adjective clause describes.

s = subject
v = verb
   (in independent clauses)
s = subject
v = verb
   (in dependent clauses)

1. The people who live across the street from me are very friendly.

2. The man who I talk to at the bus stop works downtown.

   (*whom* = correct, but for formal English)

3. The convenience store which is on the corner is open 24 hours a day.

4. The apartment building that is on the corner has an apartment for rent.

5. The park where I take walks isn't far from my house.

6. March was the month when I moved to my house.

7. I met the woman whose daughter lives next door to me.

Notice

Use commas to separate the dependent clause only if it is extra information. If the information is necessary, then don't use commas.

Examples:

1. Use a comma (or commas) when the adjective clause describes a name or someone (something) the reader knows.

   Paul Novotny, who is my neighbor, is on the city council.
   (name)

   My neighbor is moving to **South Dakota,** where the rest of her family lives. (name)

   My parents, who live nearby, come over for dinner often.
   (The reader knows it's your parents, not somebody else's parents.)

2. Do not use commas if the information in the adjective clause is necessary.

   The neighbor who lives across the street from me has a big dog.
   (Which neighbor has a big dog? The reader doesn't know which one. The neighbor who lives across the street from me.)

   I often stop at the **coffee bar that is on 15th Avenue.**
   (Which coffee bar? The coffee bar that is on 15th Avenue.)

3. Note the difference in meaning in the following sentences.

   My daughter, who lives in Toronto, will visit me soon.
   (My daughter will visit me soon. I have one daughter. She lives in Toronto. = extra information)

   My daughter who lives in Toronto will visit me soon.
   (Which daughter? My daughter who lives in Toronto. I have more than one daughter. The Toronto daughter will visit me. The other daughter or daughters live in other places and will not visit me.)

Watch Out For . . .

A The adjective clause part of the sentence cannot stand alone. It's a fragment, not a complete sentence.

   No: My sister who is a doctor.

   Yes: My sister, who is a doctor, lives nearby.

   Yes: My sister is a doctor.

No: The neighbor whose sister is a singer.

Yes: The neighbor whose sister is a singer got us some free tickets to the concert.

Yes: The neighbor's sister is a singer.

B The adjective clause part of the sentence must have a subject and a verb.

No: The grocery store which in my neighborhood has a good bakery.

Yes: The grocery store which is in my neighborhood has a good bakery.

C The adjective clause must be next to the noun it describes.

No: The bus has a wheelchair lift which I take to school.
(You take the lift to school? No, you take the bus to school.)

Yes: The bus which I take to school has a wheelchair lift.

Note: Some prepositional phrases go between the adjective clause and the noun it describes. For example:

The students in this class who work very hard are learning a lot.

My uncle owns a farm in Iowa where he grows corn.

D Do not repeat a pronoun with an adjective clause.

No: The new neighbor who I met her teaches chemistry.

Yes: The new neighbor who (whom) I met teaches chemistry.

E You cannot use an adjective clause to describe a personal pronoun (*he, she, him, her,* etc.)

No: She, who comes from Japan, is my roommate.

Yes: Akiko, who comes from Japan, is my roommate.

Yes: A woman who comes from Japan is my roommate.

Note: Only a few special expressions do this. For example, "He who laughs last laughs loudest."

F If you want to use commas for an adjective clause in the middle of a sentence, you cannot use only one comma.

No: My father, who works at the local garage lives in this neighborhood.

Yes: My father, who works at the local garage, lives in this neighborhood.

G If you are describing something very simple, especially using one adjective, it is usually better to use only the adjective in front of the word. Otherwise, the sentence becomes wordy.

No: I live in a house which is big.

Yes: I live in a big house.

Sentence Practice

Underline the adjective clauses in the following sentences. Draw an arrow to the word the clause describes. The first one is done for you.

A Neighbor

I have some problems with the neighbor <u>who lives next door to me</u>. He has a dog that barks day and night. His friends and relatives, who visit frequently, usually park their cars in my driveway and in front of my house. I'll never forget the night when I had to park a block away from home. I think my neighbor has a daughter whose boyfriend plays in a rock band. The band practices at my neighbor's house until 1:00 or 2:00 A.M. My neighbor brings home old broken-down cars from the mechanic's garage where he works. Of course, his yard is a mess. One old Ford which has been in his yard for over a year is especially ugly.

Review the examples and the Watch Out For . . . section about adjective clauses. Then look carefully at the following sentences. Write C in the blank if it is a correct adjective clause. Write I if it is incorrect. Then correct the mistakes.

Washington, D.C.

1. _____ Several weeks ago, I went to Washington, D.C., who is a wonderful city.

2. _____ I stayed with my friend Alberto, who lives there now.

3. _____ We saw many fantastic museums, which I enjoyed them.

4. _____ We saw the White House, the Capitol Building, and the monuments, which very famous and impressive.

5. _____ I was fascinated by the Ford Theatre, where Abraham Lincoln was shot.

6. ___I___ Georgetown has many interesting shops and restaurants which is a neighborhood in Washington, D.C.

7. ___I___ The subway system which is fast and easy to use.

8. ___C___ D.C., which stands for "District of Columbia," is not a state.

Exercise 3

On another piece of paper, combine the following pairs of sentences into one sentence by making the second sentence an adjective clause.

Mazatlán

1. Mazatlán is a popular resort city.
   It is located on the Pacific Coast of Mexico.

2. Many of the tourists enjoy its warm climate and beautiful beaches.
   The tourists visit Mazatlán.

3. Many people from cold climates love to visit Mazatlán in the winter months.
   It is warm and sunny there.

4. In the center of the city is the Municipal Market.
   You can buy all kinds of food, goods, and souvenirs there.

5. Mazatlán is one of Mexico's major seaports.
   Mazatlán is an important fishing center.

6. My friend wants to go to Mazatlán next year.
   His favorite hobby is deep-sea fishing.

Adjective Clauses with *Where* or *Which*

Can you find the error in the following sentence?

No: I've never visited Victoria, where is the capital of British Columbia.

Yes: I've never visited Victoria, which is the capital of British Columbia.

- When you use an adjective clause to describe a place, you could use *where* or *which* depending on the meaning of your adjective clause.

- Use *where* if . . .

    1) you can replace *where* with the idea *there* when you have the ideas in two simple sentences.

    2) the adjective clause part of the sentence has a different subject (not the place).

    Examples:

    a. Chicago is a city where many of my relatives live.

       (Chicago is a city. Many of my relatives live *there*.
       There = Chicago.)

    b. Chicago, where the tallest building in North America is located, is the third largest city in the U.S.

       (Chicago is the third largest city in the U.S. The tallest building in North America is located *there*. *There* = Chicago.)

- Use *which* if . . .

    1) the adjective clause describes the place.

    2) the adjective clause uses the main verb *be* or *have*.

    Examples:

    c. Chicago, which is my hometown, has hot summers and cold winters.

       (Chicago has hot summers and cold winters. *It* [= Chicago] *is* my hometown.)

    d. Chicago, which has many wonderful museums, is a great city for tourists.

       (Chicago is a great city for tourists. *It* [= Chicago] *has* many wonderful museums.)

    e. Chicago, which is located on Lake Michigan, is called "the Windy City."

       (Chicago is called "the Windy City." *It* [= Chicago] *is* located on Lake Michigan.)

Exercise 4

Draw a line to match the city sentence on the left with the correct sentence on the right. Then combine the two simple sentences into a complex sentence with an adjective clause, using the sentence on the right as the adjective clause. Think carefully about using *where* or *which*. Write your new sentence on another piece of paper.

Some North American Cities

1. Atlanta is a fast-growing city. *Where*

2. Calgary has a big annual rodeo. *when*

3. New York City is a great cultural center.

4. Mexico City is the largest city in North America.

5. San Francisco has many steep hills.

6. Denver is called "the Mile High City."

7. Orlando is a popular tourist destination.

8. Montreal is the second largest French-speaking city in the world.

The Golden Gate Bridge is located there.

It is often called "the Big Apple."

Disneyworld, the Epcot Center, and Universal Studios are located there.

It is located near the foothills of the Rocky Mountains.

It is on the St. Lawrence River.

The 1996 Summer Olympics were held there.

It hosted the 1988 Winter Olympics.

It is the capital of Mexico.

Writing Practice (Optional)

Write Ten Perfect Adjective Clause Complex Sentences. Use a variety of relative pronouns *(who, which, that, whose, when, where)*. You may want to write about the places where you have lived or visited or about another topic your teacher suggests. *(See pages 30–32 for instructions and examples.)*

Writing Topics

Your teacher may ask you to write a paragraph or essay on one the following topics:

1. Write about a memorable person from your neighborhood or community.

   (Description)

2. Write about a place you love and why it is special. This could be a region, city, town, island, or beach.

   (Reasons)

3. Think of two places that you have lived in or visited. Discuss their similarities and / or differences in three of these areas: climate, size, economy, atmosphere, natural surroundings, people, or political situation.

   (Comparison / Contrast)

Exercise 1

I have some problems with the neighbor <u>who lives next door to me</u>. He has a dog <u>that barks day and night</u>. His friends and relatives, <u>who visit frequently</u>, usually park their cars in my driveway and in front of my house. I'll never forget the night <u>when I had to park a block away from home</u>. I think my neighbor has a daughter <u>whose boyfriend plays in a rock band</u>. The band practices at my neighbor's house until 1:00 or 2:00 A.M. My neighbor brings home old broken-down cars from the mechanic's garage <u>where he works</u>. Of course, his yard is a mess. One old Ford <u>which has been in his yard for over a year</u> is especially ugly.

Exercise 2

1. __I__ Several weeks ago, I went to Washington, D.C., <u>which</u> is a wonderful city.

2. __C__ I stayed with my friend Alberto, who lives there now.

3. __I__ We saw many fantastic museums, which I enjoyed. (Remove *them*.)

4. __I__ We saw the White House, the Capitol Building, and the monuments, which <u>were</u> very famous and impressive. (Add a verb in the adjective clause.)

5. __C__ I was fascinated by the Ford Theatre, where Abraham Lincoln was shot.

6. __I__ Georgetown<u>, which is a neighborhood in Washington, D.C.,</u> has many interesting shops and restaurants.

7. __I__ The subway system which is fast and easy to use <u>worked well for transportation.</u> (Add a verb.)

   or

   The subway system is fast and easy to use. (Change to a simple sentence.)

8. __C__ D.C., which stands for "District of Columbia," is not a state.

(Concluded)

Exercise 3

Suggested answer:

Mazatlán, which is located on the Pacific Coast of Mexico, is a popular resort city. (or "Mazatlán is a popular resort city which is located on the Pacific Coast of Mexico.") Many of the tourists who visit Mazatlán enjoy its warm climate and beautiful beaches. Many people from cold climates love to visit Mazatlán in the winter months when it is warm and sunny. In the center of the city is the Municipal Market, where you can buy all kinds of food, goods, and souvenirs. Mazatlán, which is an important fishing center, is one of Mexico's major seaports. My friend whose favorite hobby is deep-sea fishing wants to go to Mazatlán next year.

Exercise 4

1. Atlanta, <u>where</u> the 1996 Summer Olympics were held, is a fast-growing city.

2. Calgary, <u>which</u> hosted the 1988 Winter Olympics, has a big annual rodeo.

3. New York City, <u>which</u> is often called "the Big Apple," is a great cultural center.

4. Mexico City, <u>which</u> is the capital of Mexico, is the largest city in North America.

5. San Francisco, <u>where</u> the Golden Gate Bridge is located, has many steep hills.

6. Denver, <u>which</u> is located near the foothills of the Rocky Mountains, is called "the Mile High City."

7. Orlando, <u>where</u> Disneyworld, the Epcot Center, and Universal Studios are located, is a popular tourist destination.

8. Montreal, <u>which</u> is on the St. Lawrence River, is the second largest French-speaking city in the world.

CHAPTER 6

Sports

Combination Sentences

Quick Facts   Sports

- The top five sports activities of adult participants in the U.S.: fast walking, swimming, bicycle riding, exercising with equipment, camping

- The top five sports of adult participants in Canada: baseball/softball, hockey, downhill skiing, swimming, golf

- Doctors recommend at least twenty-five minutes of aerobic exercise three times a week to maintain good health.

- The best all-time professional teams in popular North American sports:

  Baseball team with the most World Series wins—New York Yankees

  Basketball team with most National Basketball Association titles—Boston Celtics

  Ice hockey team with most Stanley Cup wins—Montreal Canadians

  Canadian Football League team with most Grey Cup wins—Toronto Argonauts

  U.S. football team with most successful National Football League record—Dallas Cowboys

Words to Know

aerobic exercise   Any form of exercise, such as fast walking, jogging, or swimming, when the body does a continuous, physical action so that the heart and lungs need to work hard.

And You?

- What is your favorite sport?

  What sports or exercise do you do? Do you get aerobic exercise doing it?

Form

A combination sentence can be any of the sentences discussed in earlier chapters joined together with one or more additional clauses to help express a related idea. There are many possible combinations. Here are some possibilities:

- a complex sentence with an adjective clause and an adverb clause
- a complex sentence with an adjective clause and a compound sentence
- a complex sentence with an adverb clause and compound sentence
- two compound sentences

Example Sentences

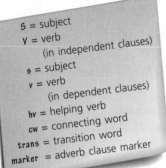

s = subject
v = verb
    (in independent clauses)
s = subject
v = verb
    (in dependent clauses)
hv = helping verb
cw = connecting word
trans = transition word
marker = adverb clause marker

Note the combination sentences in the examples below about sports.

1. Young people who participate in sports are usually in good health because
    they get so much exercise.
    (complex sentence with an adjective clause and an adverb clause)

2. Girls who play on school sports teams often have higher grades than other
    girls; in addition, they have more self-confidence and a better self-image.
    (compound sentence with an adjective clause)

3. Some sports, such as jogging and swimming, are good aerobic exercise
    because they give your heart steady, regular exercise, but other sports,
    such as bowling and weightlifting, do not exercise your heart so well.
    (compound sentence with an adverb clause)

4. According to scientists, it is not necessary to do a lot of heavy exercise
    every day; if you walk for a total of twenty-five minutes a day, you are
    probably getting enough exercise.
    (compound sentence with an adverb clause)

5. The game "football" to most of the world is called "soccer" in North
    America; in addition, football is popular in both Canada and the U.S., but
    there are some differences between Canadian and American football in
    the field size and certain rules.
    (two compound sentences)

Sentence Practice

Exercise 1

The following paragraph has many combination sentences. The subjects are marked with S in an independent clause and s in a dependent clause. First, mark the verbs with V in an independent clause or v in a dependent clause, and draw an arrow to their subjects. Then circle the connecting words and transition words. The first sentence is done for you.

The History of Soccer

Soccer, which is known throughout most of the world as "football," is the most popular sport in the world; in addition, it is a very old sport. The first soccer games that were written about took place in England; they were part of a festival to celebrate the victory of England over Rome in the year A.D. 217. The sport developed and remained popular in England as football; however, the beginning of another form of football, which became known as rugby, caused confusion in the 1800s. Because the two games were getting mixed up, the London Football Association was formed in 1863, and this association focused on soccer, which emphasized only the kicking of the ball. For many years the game was called "association football," and then the word "association" was abbreviated as "soccer," which is still the name of the sport in North America.

Exercise 2

Add commas and semicolons, where necessary. The first sentence is done for you.

The Spread of Soccer

After the game became popular in Europe, soccer spread to most countries in the world, where it is still known as "football." Soccer is played today in more than 140 countries however, soccer is not the most popular sport in North America because North Americans became more interested in football which developed from rugby. Even though traditional sports such as baseball, football, and basketball dominate professional sports, soccer is becoming more popular in the U.S. and millions of young people play on soccer teams throughout the country. Soccer has been more popular in Canada than in the U.S. but Canadian football, ice hockey, basketball, and baseball are bigger professional sports in Canada.

Exercise 3

On another piece of paper, combine each group of sentences into one combination sentence.

The Olympics

1. There are no written records of Olympic-style games until 776 B.C.
   Historians believe the Olympic games were started much earlier. and
   These games were a big part of ancient Greek culture.

2. The games were held every four years in Olympia.
   The games were played to honor Zeus.
   Zeus was a Greek god.

3. Women were not allowed to watch the Olympic games.
   Women were not allowed to participate in the Olympic games.
   Women held their own games.
   These games were called "Herea."

4. The ancient Olympic games were most popular around the fifth century B.C.
   The ancient Olympic games were stopped in the late 300s A.D.
   The Romans conquered Greece.

5. The modern Olympic games were first held in Athens in 1896. *Which*

   ~~The modern Olympic gam~~es were not very successful. *and*

   They were not well organized. *th*

   ~~Not many countri~~es were represented.

6. The first successful modern Olympic games were in London in 1908. *which*

   ~~The Olympic game~~s have been growing since then. *Besides,*

   ~~The Olympic games~~ now include women and winter sports.

Writing Practice (Optional)

Write Ten Perfect Combination Sentences. You may want to write about sports or about another topic your teacher suggests. (See pages 30–32 for instructions and examples.)

Writing Topics

1. Which sport or sports do you enjoy most? Why?

   (Reasons)

2. Discuss the benefits of participating in a team sport.

   (Effect)

3. Many professional athletes such as basketball, baseball, football, and hockey players have become stars who receive great attention and wealth in North America. Is this good or bad? Why?

   (Reasons)

Exercise 1

S   s (hv)   v   V
Soccer, which is known throughout most of the world as "football," is

                                                    S V
the most popular sport in the world; (in addition,) it is a very old sport. The

              S   s (hv)   v   V   S V
first soccer games that were written about took place in England; they were

part of a festival to celebrate the victory of England over Rome in the year

              S   V   V
A.D. 217. The sport developed and remained popular in England as football;

              S   s   v
(however,) the beginning of another form of football, which became known as

        V   s (hv)   v
rugby, caused confusion in the 1800s. Because the two games were getting

              S   (hv)   V
mixed up, the London Football Association was formed in 1863, (and) this

        S   V   s   v
association focused on soccer, which emphasized only the kicking of the ball.

                    S (hv)   V
For many years the game was called "association football," (and) then the

        S   (hv)   V   s v
word "association" was abbreviated as "soccer," which is still the name of

the sport in North America.

Exercise 2

After the game became popular in Europe, soccer spread to most countries in the world, where it is still known as "football." Soccer is played today in more than 140 countries; however, soccer is not the most popular sport in North America because North Americans became more interested in football which developed from rugby. Even though traditional sports such as baseball, football, and basketball dominate professional sports, soccer is becoming more popular in the U.S., and millions of young people play on soccer teams throughout the country. Soccer has been more popular in Canada than in the U.S., but Canadian football, ice hockey, basketball, and baseball are bigger professional sports in Canada.

Exercise 3

Suggested answer:

There are no written records of Olympic-styles games until 776 B.C., but (; however,) historians believe the Olympic games, which were a big part of ancient Greek culture, were started much earlier. The games were held every four years in Olympia and were played to honor Zeus, who was a Greek god. Because women were not allowed to watch or participate in the Olympic games, they held their own games, which were called "Herea." The ancient Olympic games were most popular around the 5th century B.C., but they were stopped in the late 300s A.D. when the Romans conquered Greece. The modern Olympic games were first held in Athens in 1896, but they were not very successful or well organized; in addition (, and) not many countries were represented. The first successful modern Olympic games were in London in 1908, and the Olympic games, which now include women and winter sports, have been growing since then.

Note: There could be more than one way to combine these sentences. Here are a few other possible sentences:

Although there are no written records of Olympic-style games until 776 B.C., historians . . .

Women were not allowed to watch or participate in the Olympic games, so (; therefore) they . . .

The modern Olympic games that were first held in Athens in 1896 were not very successful . . .

CHAPTER 7

Personal Stories

Sentence Variety

Which type of sentence is best? There is no answer to that question. Most good writing includes a variety of sentence types. Informal writing may have more simple and less formal compound sentences while formal or academic writing usually includes more formal compound sentences, complex sentences, and combination sentences.

If you write mostly simple and compound sentences, combine some of those ideas into more complicated sentences. You will show the relationships between the ideas, and your writing will have more variety. Your readers will enjoy the interesting combination of sentences. Be careful, though, not to create run-on sentences or comma splices.

Use

It may be difficult at first for you to know how to combine the sentences to write logical, correct sentences with more variety. As you read more English and notice the sentence types, you will write a variety of sentence types more naturally. This general description of how sentences are used may also be useful:

Simple sentences:	often used to introduce an idea or make a special point
Compound sentences:	used to join together two equal ideas
Adverb clauses:	usually give more information about when or why
Adjective clauses:	give more information about a noun

Examples

1. In the following paragraph, the student has written mostly simple sentences.

My Family

My family includes four people: my father, mother, younger brother, and me. We live in South Seoul. That area is known as a new part of Seoul. My father is a very nice person. He works at a university. He is an administrator. He is very proud of his job. My mother works at a cosmetics company. She is a successful businesswoman. She is a good wife. And she is a wonderful mother. She has an innocent mind, like a girl. She always laughs. My brother is a high school student. He has to take the entrance examination to go to university in November. He wants to spend time with his friends. But he needs to study a lot. The university exams are very difficult. I have been here for six months. I realize how important my family is to me. I miss them a lot.

The same paragraph could be revised to combine ideas together with more sentence variety. Notice the changes in the following revised paragraph.

My Family

My family includes four people: my father, mother, younger brother, and me. We live in south Seoul, which is a new part of the city. My father, who works as an administrator at a university, is a very nice person. He is very proud of his job. My mother works at a cosmetics company. She is a successful businesswoman, a good wife, and a wonderful mother. My mother has an innocent mind, like a young girl, and she always laughs. My brother is a high school student. In November, he has to take the university entrance exams, which are very difficult. He wants to spend time with his friends, but he needs to study a lot. Because I have been here for four months, I realize how important my family is to me, and I miss them a lot.

2. Read the following short essay. Notice how the writer has used a variety of sentences. The names of the types of sentences are given below the sentences.

Why I am Studying English

Like many students, it is often difficult for me to find the time to come

to class or do all of the homework; however, I realize that I need to study
compound sentence

English. I am studying English for three main reasons.
simple sentence

First, knowing English will help me in my personal life. For example,
simple sentence

when I go shopping or talk to my neighbors, I don't always understand
adverb clause (time)

native speakers since they talk so fast. In addition, every week I get
adverb clause (cause)

informative newsletters from my daughter's teacher and the school

principal; however, I can't read them well because they use special school
compound sentence   *adverb clause (cause)*

vocabulary that I don't understand. I also want to help my daughter with
adjective clause

her homework, but if the homework requires reading and writing, I can't
compound sentence with an adverb clause (condition)

help her. Knowing more English will allow me to get along better here.
simple sentence

Second, I need to know English to continue my education. I am trained
simple sentence

as a dental assistant in my country, but I need to take more classes here
compound sentence

to get certified in this country. When I know enough English, I'll be able
adverb clause (time)

to pass the placement exams and take the college classes that I need.
adjective clause

Then it will be easy for me to pass the test, in English, to be certified as a

dental assistant because I already understand the basic information.
adverb clause (cause)

Last, speaking English will help me get a good job. I am working as a
simple sentence

maid in a hotel, which is not a very rewarding job. After I learn English,
adjective clause   *adverb clause (time)*

take classes, and get my certification, I will be able to get a job in my

profession. Knowing English will help me get a good job in a dentist's

office, so I will use my skills to help people and earn more money.
compound sentence

I always remember these reasons for studying English. It is challenging,
simple sentence

but I know I will be successful if I work hard.
compound sentence   *adverb clause (condition)*

Sentence Practice

Exercise 1

The following paragraph has many simple sentences and several fragments. On another piece of paper, rewrite the paragraph to improve sentence variety and correctness.

The Happiest Day of My Life

I'll never forget the day. When my first child was born. My wife was so tired. She was so pregnant. The baby was two weeks late. My wife was very big. I was at work that day. When I got the telephone call at work. I stopped everything. I was very busy. I drove to our house as fast as possible. Then I helped my wife into the car. I drove her to the hospital. She got checked in. I kissed her. They took her away. I waited in a father's waiting room with several other men. They were also waiting for their wives. It seemed like days. It was only an hour later. A doctor called my name. He told me I was the father of a baby girl. She was big. She was healthy. A few minutes later I saw her. I cried. I was so happy. I had never felt such strong feelings of pure love in my life. I thanked my wife. She was very tired. She was also smiling as I had never seen. It was a very happy day.

Exercise 2

The following story has many simple sentences and several incorrect sentences, such as fragments and comma splices. On another piece of paper, rewrite the following story to improve the sentence variety and correctness.

My Host Mother

I came to San Antonio two years ago. I was on a one-month exchange program. I met a woman, her name was Marlene. She was my host mother. Marlene influenced my life a lot.

Marlene had many interesting life experiences. She was born in Germany. She grew up in Germany. She was sixteen years old. She left Germany with her boyfriend. She immigrated to the U.S. She graduated from high school in the U.S. She graduated from university in the U.S. She got good jobs. When I met her. Marlene taught German in college. She was an artist. Marlene always invited me to go to lectures, art exhibitions, book discussions, and parties. I didn't understand everything. I enjoyed meeting many different kinds of people. They had so many interests.

Before I met Marlene. I had been conservative. I had never wanted to live in another country. I wasn't interested in other cultures. I didn't have enough self-confidence to live abroad for a long time. Marlene taught me that I could do anything. If I tried my best. I wanted to try many new experiences. I wanted to meet new people. I wanted to meet different kinds of people.

Marlene encouraged me to come back to Texas. She encouraged me to study English at the university. I was able to come here to study and live for the last year. She helped me so much.

Sentence Variety in Your Writing

Your teacher may want you to look at the sentence variety in your writing. To see what kind of sentences you are using, use the Sentence Types Chart on page 365. (You can photocopy the chart for each writing assignment.)

Directions: After you complete your Error Chart and Progress Chart, you can also check your sentence variety in the writing assignment. Look at the first sentence. Decide which type of sentence you have written, and put a check in that row. It helps some students to mark the subjects and verbs on their sentences. If the sentence is one of the incorrect sentences (fragment, run-on, or comma splice), put a check in that row. When you are finished, add up the totals. If you used many simple sentences, you may want to combine some sentences together for your rewrite. If you had any incorrect sentences, be sure to correct them in your rewrite.

Here is an example of the Sentence Types Chart for "Why I Came to Canada" on page 21.

Sentence Types Chart

Name _____*Lily*_____ Writing # _____ Title _____

To check your sentence variety, look at each sentence in your writing. Decide which type of sentence it is. Then put a check in the row. Add up the totals and mark them on your Sentence Types Progress Chart.

Sentence Type		Total
Question		
Simple Sentence		
Compound Sentence	✓ ✓ ✓ ✓ ✓	6
Complex—Adverb Clause	✓	1
Complex—Adjective Clause		
Combination	✓	1
Incorrect Sentence (Fragment, Run-on, CS)		

Your teacher may also want you to keep a record of your sentence variety on the Sentence Types Progress Chart on page 367. Record the totals from the Sentence Types Chart onto the Sentence Types Progress Chart. That way you will be able to compare your sentence variety on several writing assignments.

Here is an example of a Sentence Types Progress Chart using "Why I Came to Canada" as the first writing assignment.

Sentence Types Progress Chart

Name _____

Record the totals from the Sentence Types Chart. You will see your sentence variety. If you use only a few types of sentences, you will see which types of sentences to try to include in future writing assignments.

Sentence Type	Writing	1	2	3	4	5	6	7	8	9	10
Question											
Simple Sentence		6									
Compound Sentence		1									
Complex—Adverb Clause		1									
Complex—Adjective Clause											
Combination		1									
Incorrect Sentence (Fragment, Run-on, CS)											

Title: Why I Came to Canada

PART **2** WRITING FOCUS

Exercise 1

Suggested answer:

I'll never forget the day when my first child was born. My wife was so tired, pregnant, and big because the baby was two weeks late. I was at work that day when I got the telephone call. I was very busy, but I stopped everything and drove to our house as fast as possible. Then I helped my wife into the car and drove her to the hospital. After she got checked in, I kissed her and they took her away. I waited in a fathers' waiting room with several other men who were also waiting for their wives. It seemed like days, but it was only an hour later when a doctor called my name. He told me I was the father of big, healthy baby girl. A few minutes later when I saw her, I cried. I was so happy. I had never felt such strong feelings of pure love in my life. I thanked my wife, who was very tired but also smiling as I had never seen. It was a very happy day.

Exercise 2

Suggested answer:

When I came to San Antonio two years ago on a one-month exchange program, I met a woman whose name was Marlene. She was my host mother. Marlene influenced my life a lot.

Marlene had many interesting life experiences. She was born and grew up in Germany. When she was sixteen years old, she left Germany with her boyfriend and immigrated to the U.S. After she graduated from high school and university in the U.S., she got good jobs. When I met her, Marlene taught German in college, and she was an artist. Marlene always invited me to go to lectures, art exhibitions, book discussions, and parties. I didn't understand everything, but I enjoyed meeting many different kinds of people who had so many interests.

Before I met Marlene, I had been very conservative. I had never wanted to live in another country, and I wasn't interested in other cultures. I didn't have enough self-confidence to live abroad for a long time. Marlene taught me that I could do anything if I tried my best. I wanted to try many new experiences; in addition, I wanted to meet new and different kinds of people.

Marlene encouraged me to come back to Texas to study English at the university. I was able to come here to study and live for the last year. She helped me so much.

Editing Focus

CHAPTER 1

Unclear Sentences and Translation Problems

This chapter will give you strategies rather than exercises for dealing with unclear sentences and translation problems. These kinds of problems are very individual, and the kinds of sentences one student writes may be very different from what you will write. The following information will help you understand what can cause unclear sentences and learn ways to avoid them.

When you write in English, you may try to use expressions from your own language. Usually it causes problems because most languages have different grammar patterns and vocabulary.

Sometimes students translate because they want to write at the same level as they do in their language. But learning to write fluently in another language can take many years, and students often need to write more simply than they do in their language.

Translation can be a big problem not only because it interrupts the flow of the writing but also because the reader may have no idea of what the writer is trying to say.

Here are some suggestions if you have problems with unclear sentences or translation:

1. Try to think in English, not in your own language. Don't analyze the grammar too much. When you learn a new phrase or grammar pattern, don't always try to find an exact translation for it. Often, there is no direct translation. This will help you develop a "feel" for the language. For example, when people meet one another, they often ask: *"How's it going?"* You know this is a greeting, and that it does not refer to cars or other kinds of transportation. Also, people don't say: *"How does it go?"* When you hear "How's it going?," you don't wonder why they use the present continuous. You have developed a "feel" for that phrase, and you know it means, "How are you?" You don't analyze it word for word to understand its use and meaning.

2. Check an English–English dictionary or an ESL dictionary. Sometimes students hear a phrase, and are not exactly sure about the correct words. A dictionary can often help you with the correct grammar of a phrase. For example, look at the following:

No: We played it ear.

Yes: We played it **by** ear. (= We didn't make plans.)

3. Read and listen to English as much as possible. It is very difficult to become a good writer if you don't hear and see particular expressions, idiomatic expressions, and vocabulary common to speaking and writing. After you hear and see something several times, you will begin to know in what contexts it can be used. You will know if something "sounds right," and your English will begin to sound more natural.

4. Ask native speakers. Remember that native speakers often can't tell you *why* a particular expression is used. That's OK. You don't always need to understand *why*. The more you work with and use the language, the more natural it will sound. This is another way you can help develop a "feel" for English.

5. Use phrases, grammar, and vocabulary you know, at the level you are studying in English. If you are in an intermediate level class, you probably won't be able to write at the higher level that you can in your language. Look at the following example:

Everybody has yearning in the U.S.

The student may have used "yearning'" because it works in his or her language. Or the student may think it sounds better to use a more difficult word. In any case, it results in a sentence where the reader has to guess at the meaning.

6. Study the Word Choice chapter. Often unclear sentences result from incorrect word choice. It can be difficult to know if a problem is translation or incorrect word choice.* Generally, the difference is that with a word choice problem, there is a problem with a word or a few words, but the reader knows what you are trying to say. "Unclear" means the reader is not really sure of the meaning, or an entire phrase really doesn't sound like English. Here are two examples of unclear sentences:

The police have to wear the mask because smell bad.

I hope to see my family next vacation because I have been one year I have never seen them.

The first sentence leaves the reader with questions. What smells bad? Is there air pollution? Is there another problem? The second sentence sounds very non-English. Probably the writer wants to say: "I hope to see my family next vacation because I haven't seen them for one year."

Here is a word choice error:

I hope I can find my goals.

The reader understands this sentence, but a better way to say it is "I hope I can *achieve* my goals" or "I hope I can *reach* my goals."

If you have this kind of problem, the word choice chapter will give you some helpful tips and exercises for choosing the correct vocabulary and phrases.

When you are working on unclear / translation, or word choice problems, keep a list of your mistakes on page 369 in the Appendix or in a notebook. If you see the same mistake more than once, study the problem and the correction. In this way, you will learn to avoid words and phrases that once sounded correct to you.

---

* Teachers may disagree as to whether a problem is unclear / translation or word choice. The distinction is not always 100% clear. Sometimes ESL / EFL teachers may be better able to guess the meaning of a phrase than readers who aren't as familiar with non-native writing, and may call a problem "word choice" rather than "unclear."

CHAPTER 2

Fragments

A fragment is an incomplete sentence. Some fragments, such as a sentence with no verb, are ESL errors. Other fragments, such as incomplete sentences that begin with the words *because* or *if* can be used in informal writing, but are not OK in formal writing. Native speakers of English can also have problems with these.

A Subjects

Look at these sentences. What is the difference between the correct and incorrect sentences?

No: I think is a plan that will succeed.

Yes: I think **it** is a plan that will succeed.

No: In my hometown, is a famous statue of my great grandfather.

Yes: In my hometown, **there** is a famous statue of my great grandfather.

- Every sentence and clause needs a subject (unless it is a command).
- Use *there* to introduce a noun that hasn't been mentioned yet.

Exercise 1

Check (✓) the sentences that have no mistakes.

Opinions about UFOs

1. _____   I think are real.

2. _____   In my opinion a fantasy.

3. _____   Is an interesting possibility.

4. _____ I hope are UFOs because life would be more interesting.

5. _____ I think is impossible that people live on other planets.

6. _____ If there are people from other planets, I hope are friendly.

B Subjects and Verbs

What is the difference between these correct and incorrect sentences?

s = subject
v = verb
hv = helping verb

No: My mother a wonderful woman.
         S

Yes: My mother **is** a wonderful woman.
        S   V

No: A time which I remember best.
      S   s v

Yes: A time which I remember best **was** with a group of friends.
     S   s v   V

No: The man standing in front of the telescope studying the scenery.
        S

Yes: The man standing in front of the telescope **is studying** the scenery.
        S   hv V

No: The papers sent by express mail.
         S

Yes: The papers **were sent** by express mail.
      S   hv   V

No: A growing child lots of support.
        S

Yes: A growing child **needs** lots of support.
       S   V

No: Studying for a final exam stressful.
      S

Yes: Studying for a final exam **is** stressful.
      S   V

- Every subject (S) needs a verb (V) to go with it. The verb must be complete.

Exercise 2   Write C for correct and I for incorrect. Then correct the mistakes and circle *yes* or *no*.

What's Your Opinion?

		Agree or disagree?	
1. _____	Learning to write English easy.	yes	no
2. _____	English spelling doesn't make sense.	yes	no
3. _____	Natural English spoken very quickly.	yes	no
4. _____	A British accent the easiest English accent to understand.	yes	no
5. _____	English can be learned well in less than a year.	yes	no

C Adverb Clauses

These words form dependent adverb clauses: *if, unless, before, after, when, while, since, because, although.* They do not form complete sentences.

Look at these sentences. Can you find the fragments?

No: If my dream comes true.

Yes: If my dream comes true, I will be shocked.

No: When I was a child in my country. I enjoyed playing baseball.

Yes: When I was a child in my country, I enjoyed playing baseball.

No: Because Chinese is the most spoken language in the world.

Yes: Because Chinese is the most spoken language in the world, I'd like to learn more about it.

No: I plan to study Chinese. Because it is the most spoken language in the world.

Yes: I plan to study Chinese because it is the most spoken language in the world.

• Dependent clauses need to be connected to another sentence.

Exercise 3

Check (✓) the sentences that are fragments.

What has been the happiest moment in your life so far?

1. _____ When my first child was born. I was amazed.

2. _____ I think my wedding day was the best time of my life. Because my husband and I were so in love.

3. _____ Although I don't remember it, my birth was probably the best day of my life. Because I am here now.

4. _____ While I was on the bus one day. I met an interesting man and he became my husband of forty years!

5. _____ The day after I graduated from college, I was offered an unbelievable job. I was amazed. Since I was so young.

6. _____ I think it is bad luck if I tell you.

D Reduced Clauses

Sometimes you can reduce clauses as follows:

> While he was watching the fans cheer, . . .

or   While watching the fans cheer, . . .

or   Watching the fans cheer, . . .

The reduced phrase must be connected to another sentence. It cannot be alone. If it is alone, it is a fragment.

No: Watching the fans cheer.

Yes: Watching the fans cheer, the man felt the excitement of the crowd.

E Prepositional Phrases, Infinitives, and Gerunds

Prepositional phrases, infinitives, and gerunds are fragments if they are alone in a sentence.

No: In the middle of the summer during a tense afternoon.

Yes: In the middle of the summer during a tense afternoon, I remembered the discussion we had.

No: To write an interesting journal for the teacher to read.

Yes: To write an interesting journal for the teacher to read, try writing about a personal experience.

No: Swimming ten laps in a cool pool in the early morning.

Yes: Swimming ten laps in a cool pool in the early morning is her favorite kind of exercise.

Exercise 4 Check (✓) the sentences that are fragments.

My Conversational Strengths

1. _____ Speaking to other people.

2. _____ In conversation with quiet people, I encourage them to talk more.

3. _____ When talking to my friends. I joke a lot.

4. _____ Helping people feel comfortable, especially shy people, is a strength I have.

5. _____ While listening carefully to other people.

6. _____ When participating in a conversation, I pay attention to what people say.

7. _____ To not interrupt other people when they are talking.

8. _____ With a large group of people who like to talk a lot.

F Especially, Such As, For Example

Look at these sentences. What is the difference between the correct and incorrect sentences?

No: She needs to study more. Especially grammar and vocabulary.

Yes: She needs to study more, especially grammar and vocabulary.

No: To improve your listening, I recommend practice. Such as listening to tapes and talking to native speakers.

Yes: To improve your listening, I recommend activities such as listening to tapes and talking to native speakers.

No: There are several causes of heart disease. For example, smoking and cholesterol.

Yes: There are several causes of heart disease, for example, smoking and cholesterol.

- *Especially, such as,* and *for example* cannot begin sentences unless they are followed by a subject and a verb (an independent clause).

Exercise 5

Correct the mistakes.

What was the most helpful advice your parents or grandparents gave you?

1. They taught me to be kind to others. Especially the poor, the sick and the elderly.

2. It is important to treat everyone well. For example, with respect and honesty.

3. My grandparents never allowed me to do dishonest things. Such as lie to them.

4. They gave me a lot of advice. For example, to be patient with others, try to understand their situation, and not judge them.

5. They always encouraged me to work hard. Especially when I didn't think I could be successful.

G Connecting Main Verbs

No: He came late, didn't study, got many absences.
No: He came late, and didn't study, and got many absences.
Yes: He came late, didn't study, and got many absences.

No: He's studying, working two jobs, taking care of his family.
Yes: He's studying, working two jobs, and taking care of his family.

- With three or more main verbs, use a connecting word (*and, or, but, so*) before the main verb.
- It is not necessary to repeat the same subject or *be* verb.

Exercise 6

Correct the mistakes.

What do you think about fast food restaurants?

1. There are too many and the food is unhealthy and they are expensive.

2. I love to eat hamburgers, drink milk shakes, not worry about calories.

3. I am used to buying fresh foods, cooking them myself, not eating

   fattening foods.

4. For me they are very convenient, cheap, fast.

5. I like them and go often, I don't think they are very healthy.

Chapter Review

Exercise 7

Check (✓) the sentences that are fragments. Then correct the mistakes.

Being Single vs. Being Married

What are some advantages to being single?

1. _____ You can do what you want. When you want.

2. _____ If you don't feel like cooking, you don't have to.

3. _____ Going out and meeting new people. It's easy.

4. _____ People who are single more freedom.

5. _____ When you are single. You can spend your money any way

   you want.

What are some advantages to being married?

6. _____ There always someone to do things with.

7. _____ I think that having a partner and not feeling lonely.

8. _____ If you have someone to help you, life is easier.

9. _____ I can think of two advantages. For example, having someone

   to care about and having someone to take care of you.

10. _____ The other person can cook. When you are tired.

Exercise 8

Write **C** for correct and **I** for incorrect. Then correct the mistakes.

Advice from Teenagers to Parents

1. _____ When you are angry and want to talk to your child. Wait until you calm down.

2. _____ Understanding how your teenager feels when he or she is upset.

3. _____ You don't have to be so serious just because you are the parent.

4. _____ I think it important to have patience.

5. _____ Try to remember how you felt when you a teenager.

6. _____ To have a close relationship with your kids, listen carefully.

7. _____ Teenagers wanting more freedom.

8. _____ The best advice is spending time with your children, listening to them, trying to understand the way they are feeling.

Exercise 9

Correct the mistakes.

Kinds of Movies I Like

My favorite kinds of movies are romance. Such as *Ghost* and *Pretty Woman.* When I was a teenager and chose books. I always wanted to read love stories, imagine a happy ending, dream about a life like that. I like it best. If the story has a happy ending. Other movies that I like mysteries. It exciting to try to figure out the ending. I also like action movies. If they are not too violent. I don't like a lot of guns and bombs. In this country are too many violent movies. One time sitting with my friends and watching an action movie. I covered my eyes because it was too violent. I think I missed most of the movie.

Exercise 1   All of the sentences have mistakes.

Exercise 2
1. __I__   Learning to write English <u>is</u> easy.
2. __C__   English spelling doesn't make sense.
3. __I__   Natural English <u>is</u> spoken very quickly.
4. __I__   A British accent <u>is</u> the easiest English accent to understand.
5. __C__   English can be learned well in less than a year.

Exercise 3
1. __✓__   When my first child was born. I was amazed.
2. __✓__   I think my wedding day was the best time of my life. Because my husband and I were so in love.
3. __✓__   Although I don't remember it, my birth was probably the best day of my life. Because I am here now.
4. __✓__   While I was on the bus one day. I met an interesting man and he became my husband of forty years!
5. __✓__   The day after I graduated from college, I was offered an unbelievable job. I was amazed. Since I was so young.
6. _____   I think it is bad luck if I tell you.

Exercise 4
1. __✓__   Speaking to other people.
2. _____   In conversation with quiet people, I encourage them to talk more.
3. __✓__   When talking to my friends. I joke a lot.
4. _____   Helping people feel comfortable, especially shy people, is a strength I have.
5. __✓__   While listening carefully to other people.
6. _____   When participating in a conversation, I pay attention to what people say.
7. __✓__   To not interrupt other people when they are talking.
8. __✓__   With a large group of people who like to talk a lot.

(Continued)

Exercise 5

1. They taught me to be kind to others, <u>especially</u> the poor, the sick and the elderly.

2. It is important to treat everyone well, <u>for</u> example with respect and honesty.

3. My grandparents never allowed me to do dishonest things, <u>such</u> as lie to them.

4. They gave me a lot of advice, <u>for</u> example, to be patient with others, try to understand their situation, and not judge them.

5. They always encouraged me to work hard, <u>especially</u> when I didn't think I could be successful.

Exercise 6

1. There are too many, the food is unhealthy, and they are expensive.

2. I love to eat hamburgers, drink milk shakes, <u>and</u> not worry about calories.

3. I am used to buying fresh foods, cooking them myself, <u>and</u> not eating fattening foods.

4. For me they are very convenient, cheap, <u>and</u> fast.

5. I like them and go often, <u>but</u> I don't think they are very healthy.

Exercise 7

1. ✓ You can do what you want <u>when</u> you want.
2. ___ If you don't feel like cooking, you don't have to.
3. ✓ Going out and meeting new people <u>is</u> easy.
4. ✓ People who are single <u>have</u> more freedom.
5. ✓ When you are single, <u>you</u> can spend your money any way you want.
6. ✓ There <u>is</u> always someone to do things with.
7. ✓ I think that having a partner and not feeling lonely <u>is</u> . . . (an advantage).
8. ___ If you have someone to help you, life is easier.
9. ✓ I can think of two advantages, <u>for</u> example, having someone to care about and having someone to take care of you.
10. ✓ The other person can cook <u>when</u> you are tired.

(Concluded)

Exercise 8

1. __I__   When you are angry and want to talk to your child, <u>wait</u> until you calm down.

2. __I__   Understanding how your teenager feels when he or she is upset <u>is</u> . . . (important).

3. __C__   You don't have to be so serious just because you are the parent.

4. __I__   I think it <u>is</u> important to have patience.

5. __I__   Try to remember how you felt when you <u>were</u> a teenager.

6. __C__   To have a close relationship with your kids, listen carefully.

7. __I__   Teenagers <u>want</u> more freedom.

8. __I__   The best advice is spending time with your children, listening to them, <u>and</u> trying to understand the way they are feeling.

Exercise 9

My favorite kinds of movies are romance, <u>such</u> as *Ghost* and *Pretty Woman*. When I was a teenager and chose books, I always wanted to read love stories, imagine a happy ending, <u>and</u> dream about a life like that. I like it <u>best if</u> the story has a happy ending. Other movies that I like <u>are</u> mysteries. It <u>is</u> exciting to try to figure out the ending. I also like action <u>movies if</u> they are not too violent. I don't like a lot of guns and bombs. In this country <u>there</u> are too many violent movies. One time sitting with my friends and watching an action movie, I covered my eyes because it was too violent. I think I missed most of the movie.

CHAPTER 3

Run-ons

A run-on sentence is a sentence that contains more than one sentence, but it is written as only one sentence. Many times the sentence is too long and should be divided into two or more shorter sentences. Native speakers of English also study this problem.

A Run-on Sentences

What is the difference between the correct and incorrect sentences?

	S	V	S	V
No: The runner went faster the crowd cheered.

| | S | V | S | V |
Yes: The runner went faster. The crowd cheered.

No: The movie was very sad many people in the audience cried.

Yes: The movie was very sad. Many people in the audience cried.

No: At first, I felt lonely then, I met some people.

Yes: At first, I felt lonely. Then, I met some people.

- A complete sentence has a subject and a verb. Run-on sentences are two complete sentences that are written as one sentence.

- One way to correct a run-on sentence is to put a period between the two complete sentences.

Exercise 1

Write **S** for subject and **V** for verb in each sentence.

S = subject
V = verb

Information about the Chinese Language

1. Chinese is the most spoken language in the world.
   (S over "Chinese", V over "is")

2. There are several Chinese dialects.
   (V over "are", S over "dialects")

3. The writing system uses about 4,000 characters.
   (S over "system", V over "uses")

4. Characters are usually not single words. They often represent

   single sounds.
   (S over "Characters", V over "are", S over "They", V over "represent")

5. The tone of a word sometimes changes to give a different meaning.
   (S over "tone", V over "changes")

6. Mandarin Chinese, for example, has four different tones.
   (S over "Chinese", V over "has")

Exercise 2

Check (✓) the sentences that are run-ons. (Remember, a run-on occurs when you have **S V S V** with no punctuation between them.) Then correct the sentences.

Reasons for Studying English

1. __✓__ It's an international language much of the business world

   speaks it.

2. _____ You can communicate with people from other cultures

   and countries.

3. _____ Learning another language helps you understand other ways

   of thinking.

4. __✓__ I want to study at a university in an English-speaking country

   my major is computer science.

5. _____ It's interesting it's fun.
   (✓ mark to the left)

B Correcting Run-on Sentences

There are other ways to correct run-on sentences:

1. Use a connecting word *(but, yet, and, so, or)* and a comma before it.

   No: I worked hard I didn't pass.

   Yes: I worked hard, **but** I didn't pass.   (contrast)

   Yes: I worked hard, **yet** I didn't pass.   (contrast)

   Yes: I worked hard, **and** I passed.   (addition)

   Yes: I worked hard, **so** I passed.   (result)

   Yes: I can work hard, **or** I can fail.   (choice)

2. Put a semicolon between the two sentences. A semicolon shows that the two sentences are closely related. A comma is not possible because it cannot be used between two sentences.

   No: The athletes trained for months they were in excellent condition.

   Yes: The athletes trained for months**;** they were in excellent condition.

3. Make one part of the sentence a dependent clause with words like *because, if, when, before, after*.

   No: He wanted his children to feel special each one got time alone with him.

   Yes: **Because** he wanted his children to feel special, each one got time alone with him.

Exercise 3

Correct the following run-ons using the word or punctuation in parentheses.

Did You Know?

1. The best time to buy shoes is at the end of the day your feet

   are bigger.   (because)

2. Shaking a young child is dangerous it can cause brain damage.   (;)

3. Wear pants when you fly on airplanes they will protect your legs if there

   is an accident.   (;)

4. Seahorses are different from other animals the males have

   the babies.   (because)

5. Only female bees are worker bees ~~,~~ *and* they are the ones that sting.   (, and)

6. Everyone dreams every night ⌃ some people don't remember

   their dreams.   (, but)

7. The cougar, mountain lion, and puma are the same animal they have

   different names in different places. ⌃   (, but)

8. It takes one month for the moon to go around the earth ; it takes 365 days

   for the earth to go around the sun.   (;)

Chapter Review

Exercise 4

Write C for correct and I for incorrect. Then correct the mistakes.

Internet History

1. __I__   The Internet began in 1969 it was an experiment by

   the U.S. government.

2. __C__   Originally, the Internet was planned so that academic and military

   people could communicate.

3. __C__   At the time, because the government was afraid of nuclear

   attack, it wanted a system that would work during an attack.

4. __C__   The government planned it without a main office that someone

   could bomb.

5. __C__   Since no one was in charge, it grew in many directions without

   rules or limits.

6. __C__   As a result, millions of users are now connected around

   the world.

Correct the run-ons.

My First Day in This Country

I arrived at 5:30 in the morning I was incredibly tired. My plane ride was 15 hours, and I didn't sleep at all during the flight. When I arrived, there was no one to meet me. My host family had car trouble they were about 15 minutes late. I was very scared, I cried a little and wondered why I left my country. Soon my host mother saw me and gave me a big smile, she was so kind. I felt better after I met her and her husband. They took me out to breakfast. The food was a little strange, and I didn't speak much English. But they were patient, and we communicated basic information. They wanted to show me a little of the city; however I was so tired I asked them if I could sleep first. They took me to their house. I went to bed and I slept for 17 hours!

Exercise 1

1. Chinese is the most spoken language in the world.
    (S) (V)

2. There are several Chinese dialects.
    (S) (V)

3. The writing system uses about 4,000 characters.
    (S) (V)

4. Characters are usually not single words. They often represent single sounds.
    (S) (V)   (S) (V)

5. The tone of a word sometimes changes to give a different meaning.
    (S) (V)

6. Mandarin Chinese, for example, has four different tones.
    (S) (V)

Exercise 2

1. ✓   It's an international language. Much of the business world speaks it.

2. _____   You can communicate with people from other cultures and countries.

3. _____   Learning another language helps you understand other ways of thinking.

4. ✓   I want to study at a university in an English-speaking country. My major is computer science.

5. ✓   It's interesting. It's fun.

Exercise 3

1. The best time to buy shoes is at the end of the day because your feet are bigger.

2. Shaking a young child is dangerous; it can cause brain damage.

3. Wear pants when you fly on airplanes; they will protect your legs if there is an accident.

4. Seahorses are different from other animals because the males have the babies.

5. Only female bees are worker bees, and they are the ones that sting.

6. Everyone dreams every night, but some people don't remember their dreams.

7. The cougar, mountain lion, and puma are the same animal, but they have different names in different places.

8. It takes one month for the moon to go around the earth; it takes 365 days for the earth to go around the sun.

(Concluded)

Exercise 4

1. __I__   The Internet began in 1969. It was an experiment by the U.S. government.

   or:

   The Internet began in 1969; it was an experiment by the U.S. government.

2. __C__   Originally, the Internet was planned so that academic and military people could communicate.

3. __C__   At the time, because the government was afraid of nuclear attack, it wanted a system that would work during an attack.

4. __C__   The government planned it without a main office that someone could bomb.

5. __C__   Since no one was in charge, it grew in many directions without rules or limits.

6. __C__   As a result, millions of users are now connected around the world.

Exercise 5

    I arrived at 5:30 in the morning. I was incredibly tired. My plane ride was 15 hours, and I didn't sleep at all during the flight. When I arrived, there was no one to meet me. My host family had car trouble. They were about 15 minutes late. I was very scared. I cried a little and wondered why I left my country. Soon my host mother saw me and gave me a big smile. She was so kind. I felt better after I met her and her husband. They took me out to breakfast. The food was a little strange, and I didn't speak much English. But they were patient, and we communicated basic information. They wanted to show me a little of the city; however, I was so tired I asked them if I could sleep first. They took me to their house. I went to bed. I slept for 17 hours!

Note: Connecting words can be used instead of periods: I went to bed <u>and</u> slept for 17 hours!

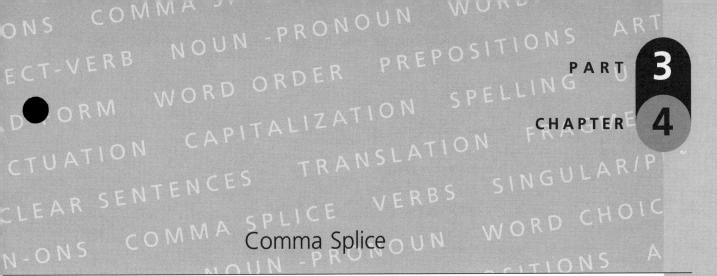

CHAPTER 4

Comma Splice

A comma splice is a type of run-on sentence. It contains two sentences connected by only a comma, but a comma is not strong enough to separate the two sentences. Native speakers of English also need to edit their writing to avoid comma splices.

A Basic Comma Splice

Can you discover the difference between the correct and incorrect sentences?

*hv = helping verb

　　　S hv* V　　　　　S hv V　　　　　S hv　 V
No:　We'll work together, we'll help each other, we'll succeed.

Yes:　We'll work together. We'll help each other. We'll succeed.

　　　S　V　　　　　S　 V
No:　I tried my best, there is nothing more I can do.

Yes:　I tried my best. There is nothing more I can do.

　　　S　V　　　　　S　V
No:　I studied really hard, I passed.

Yes:　I studied really hard. I passed.

- Two complete sentences cannot be separated by a comma. A complete sentence has a subject and a verb.

Exercise 1

Find the subject(s) and the verb(s) in each sentence. Write S for subject and V for verb.

Reggae Music

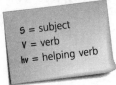

S = subject
V = verb
hv = helping verb

1. Reggae music comes from Jamaica.

2. It began in the 1960s.

3. The rhythm is slow and the beat is lively.

4. Bob Marley is probably the most famous reggae musician.

5. When he died, classic reggae also died.

Exercise 2

Write C for correct and I for incorrect. Correct the mistakes. Then mark if the sentence is true or false.

Animal Trivia: True or False?

True or false?

1. _____ Adult horses stand up when they sleep,

   they lie down when they are sick.   _____

2. _____ Alligators are supposed to be friendlier

   than crocodiles, they are still dangerous.   _____

3. _____ Butterflies can't fly in the mornings.

   Their wings are too heavy with dew.   _____

4. _____ People can be identified by their fingerprints,

   dogs can be identified by their nose prints. _____

5. _____ An eagle's nest is very large. It can weigh

   over 500 kilograms.   _____

6. _____ Female mosquitoes bite, male mosquitoes don't. _____

B Using Connecting Words

If you use a comma to separate two complete sentences, you also need one of the connecting words: *and, but, yet, so, or, for*.

No: We'll work together, we'll help each other.

Yes: We'll work together, **and** we'll help each other.   (and = addition)

Yes: We'll work together, **but** we may not succeed.   (but = contrast)

Yes: We'll work together, **yet** we may not succeed.   (yet = contrast)

Yes: We'll work together, **so** we can succeed.   (so = result)

Yes: We can work together, **or** we can fail.   (or = choice)

Yes: We'll work together, **for** we want to succeed.   (for = reason / because)

See Run-ons page 105 for other ways of correcting comma splices.

Exercise 3

Correct the sentences using one of the following: *and, but, yet, so, or, for*.

Do you think memorizing school material is a good way to learn?

1. It's useful, you might forget some things.

2. I have a good memory, it's a good method for me.

3. It's good for vocabulary, there are so many words.

4. It's not fun, it's important.

5. I wasn't a good student, I don't remember ever memorizing anything.

6. In school I had to memorize a lot of poetry. I still remember it,

   I guess it's useful.

7. I memorize speeches, I will forget them.

8. Some things you need to memorize, some things you can only

   learn by doing.

9. Important facts can be memorized, ideas should be discussed.

10. I memorize things that don't have many rules, like gerunds

    and infinitives, I will go crazy.

Chapter Review

Exercise 4

Correct the mistakes.

How have computers affected your life?

1. I used to send my family a lot of faxes, now I use e-mail because

   it's cheaper.

2. Actually, I don't know how to use them, I need to take some classes.

3. I only do word processing, it really helps me do my school work faster.

4. I love the Internet, instead of watching TV or playing video games,

   I spend a lot of time surfing the Internet.

5. Computers still seem complicated to me, I'm a little afraid of them.

6. I love the Spell Check, I save so much time because I don't need to always

   look in my dictionary when I write a paper.

Exercise 5

Correct the mistakes by putting periods (.) where necessary.

The Perfect Job for Me

There are several jobs I'm interested in, all of them allow me to work with my hands. I love to build things by hand. Sometimes I think about furniture making, I'm talking about regular furniture, I mean furniture made with beautiful woods, like cherry or oak. But that is probably a hard way to earn money to support a family. I am also interested in repairing antique cars, I love working with the engines and also making the outside of the car look beautiful again. Whatever job I choose, there is one thing that is very important to me. I don't want to work from 8:00 to 5:00, I want to decide my own hours. Maybe I will begin working at 11 A.M. and finish at midnight. Or I can wake up early with the birds and work until midday. My job needs to have a flexible schedule.

Exercise 1

1. Reggae music comes from Jamaica.
    S   V

2. It began in the 1960s.
  S V

3. The rhythm is slow, and the beat is lively.
    S   V   S   V

4. Bob Marley is probably the most famous reggae musician.
   S   V

5. When he died, classic reggae also died.
     S V   S   V

Exercise 2

1. __I__ Adult horses stand up when they sleep. They lie down when they are sick. (T)

2. __I__ Alligators are supposed to be friendlier than crocodiles. They are still dangerous. (T)

3. __C__ Butterflies can't fly in the mornings. Their wings are too heavy with dew. (T)

4. __I__ People can be identified by their fingerprints. Dogs can be identified by their nose prints. (T)

5. __C__ An eagle's nest is very large. It can weigh over 500 kilograms. (T)

6. __I__ Female mosquitoes bite. Male mosquitoes don't. (T)

Exercise 3

1. It's useful, but / yet you might forget some things.

2. I have a good memory, so it's a good method for me.

3. It's good for vocabulary, but / yet / for there are so many words.

4. It's not fun, but / yet it's important.

5. I wasn't a good student, so / and I don't remember ever memorizing anything.

6. In school I had to memorize a lot of poetry. I still remember it, so I guess it's useful.

7. I memorize speeches, or / but / yet / for I will forget them.

8. Some things you need to memorize, and / but / yet some things you can only learn by doing.

9. Important facts can be memorized, but / yet ideas should be discussed.

10. I memorize things that don't have many rules, like gerunds and infinitives, or I will go crazy.

(Concluded)

Exercise 4

1. I used to send my family a lot of faxes. <u>Now</u> I use e-mail because it's cheaper.

2. Actually, I don't know how to use them. <u>I</u> need to take some classes.

3. I only do word processing. <u>It</u> really helps me do my school work faster.

4. I love the Internet. <u>Instead</u> of watching TV or playing video games, I spend a lot of time surfing the Internet.

5. Computers still seem complicated to me. <u>I'm</u> a little afraid of them.

6. I love the Spell Check. <u>I</u> save so much time because I don't need to always look in my dictionary when I write a paper.

Note: Comma + connecting word can be used. A semicolon can also be used.

Exercise 5

    There are several jobs I'm interested in. <u>All</u> of them allow me to work with my hands. I love to build things by hand. Sometimes I think about furniture making. <u>I'm</u> talking about regular furniture. <u>I</u> mean furniture made with beautiful woods, like cherry or oak. But that is probably a hard way to earn money to support a family. I am also interested in repairing antique cars. <u>I</u> love working with the engines and also making the outside of the car look beautiful again. Whatever job I choose, there is one thing that is very important to me. I don't want to work from 8:00 to 5:00. <u>I</u> want to decide my own hours. Maybe I will begin working at 11 A.M. and finish at midnight. Or I can wake up early with the birds and work until midday. My job needs to have a flexible schedule.

Note: Comma + connecting word can also be used. A semicolon can also be used.

CHAPTER 5

Verbs

When students have problems with verbs, the sentence may be missing a verb or the student may have used the incorrect verb tense or verb form. Verb problems can be serious because the reader may not understand the meaning of the sentence.

A Verbs in a Sentence

Look at these sentences. What is the difference between the correct ones and the incorrect ones?

$$\text{S}$$
No: My father very tall.

$$\text{S} \quad \text{V}$$
Yes: My father **is** very tall.

$$\text{S}$$
No: My home city not very big.

$$\text{S} \quad \text{V}$$
Yes: My home city **is** not very big.

$$\text{S}$$
No: That why she transferred.

$$\text{S} \quad \text{V}$$
Yes: That **is** why she transferred.

- A complete sentence has a subject (S) and a verb (V).
- Make sure every sentence has a verb.

See Fragments on page 93 for more practice.

Exercise 1   Write C for correct and I for incorrect.

Famous Canadians

1. ___I___   Anne Murray a famous singer from Nova Scotia.

2. ___C___   Actor Michael J. Fox is originally from Ontario, Canada.

3. ___I___   A famous hockey player from Canada Wayne Gretzky.

4. ___C___   Alexander Graham Bell lived in Canada as a young man.

5. ___I___   Jazz musician Oscar Peterson in Montreal, Canada.

B Verb + Adjective

Look at these sentences. What is the difference between the correct ones and the incorrect ones?

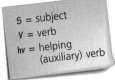

s = subject
V = verb
hv = helping (auxiliary) verb

        S
No: She absented school yesterday.

        S   V
Yes: She **was** absent from school yesterday.

      S
No: I will late to class tomorrow.

     S hv V
Yes: I **will be** late to class tomorrow.

      S
No: He very angry about the results.

      S   V
Yes: He **seemed** very angry about the results.

       S
No: They interested in studying English.

     S V
Yes: They **are** interested in studying English.

- Every sentence needs to have a complete verb. A helping verb needs a main verb.
- Some expressions have a form of *be* + an adjective (*absent, late, angry*).
- Other expressions have a form of *be* + a past participle that is used as an adjective (*interested, tired, surprised*)
- Make sure you have a *be* verb or another linking verb (*seem, look*) when you use these expressions.

See Word Form on page 207 for more information on participial (-ed / -ing) adjectives.

Common adjectives used with a verb	Examples
absent	Students should not **be absent** from class if they can come.
late	The sales representative **was late** for the staff meeting.
happy	The director **isn't happy** with her employees today.
angry	His mother **seemed angry** when Christopher spilled his milk.
sad	I **was sad** when my cat died.
sure	Tom **is sure** that he will pass the test.
confident	Joan **is confident** that she can handle it.
ready	The actors **are ready** to perform their play.

Exercise 2

These sentences are incorrect because they do not have a verb. Add *was* or *were* to each sentence to make it correct.

Yesterday's Class

1. Four students ~were~ absent yesterday.

2. One student ~was~ late to class.

3. The other students ~were~ ready to begin class on time.

4. The teacher ~was~ happy because the lesson went well.

5. The students ~were~ sure that they understood the lesson.

Participles used as adjectives	Examples
be tired	Tammy **is tired** of her job.
be surprised	I **will be surprised** if she stays in her current position.
be excited	She **is excited** about the possibility of a new job.
be confused	Some people **were confused** when another person got hired.
be interested in	I **am not interested in** changing jobs right now.

Exercise 3

Write C for correct and I for incorrect. Then correct the mistakes.

A New Computer

1. __I__ I very surprised when my parents bought a new computer.

2. __I__ The computer not very easy to set up.

3. __C__ At first, I was confused about how it worked.

4. __C__ Now we are very happy with the computer.

5. __I__ We excited about getting on the Internet and sending e-mail.

Exercise 4

There are five errors in the following postcard. Can you find and correct them?

A Postcard about School

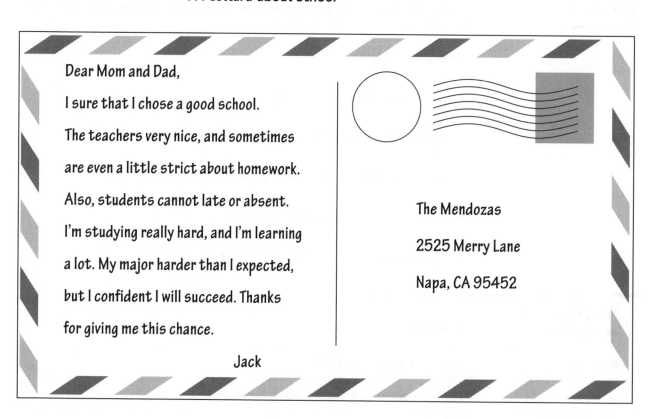

Dear Mom and Dad,

I sure that I chose a good school.
The teachers very nice, and sometimes
are even a little strict about homework.
Also, students cannot late or absent.
I'm studying really hard, and I'm learning
a lot. My major harder than I expected,
but I confident I will succeed. Thanks
for giving me this chance.

Jack

The Mendozas

2525 Merry Lane

Napa, CA 95452

C Present Time Verb Problems

1. Look at the following present time sentences. Can you find the verb tense problems?

    No: My friends and I are going to the library every afternoon.

    Yes: My friends and I **go** to the library every afternoon.

    No: I am always feeling nervous before I am taking a test.

    Yes: I always **feel** nervous before I **take** a test.

    No: I study ESL this quarter.

    Yes: I **am studying** ESL this quarter.

    - Use simple present tense for facts and habits.
    - Use the present continuous (also called present progressive) for an action happening now or in the current time period (*this quarter, this month, this year*).

Exercise 5

Write **C** for correct or **I** for incorrect. Then correct the mistakes.

Work Schedules

1. ___I___ In Japan most business people are working 10 or more

    hours a day.

2. ___C___ In Denmark, most people work 36 hours per week.

3. ___C___ In the Middle East, people don't work on Thursdays and Fridays.

4. ___C___ The average work week in North America is 40 hours.

5. ___I___ In Italy, people are working in the morning, taking a long break

    at lunch, and then working again until evening.

6. ___C___ In most of Latin America as in Italy, workers have a *siesta*, a

    break in the middle of the day to rest.

2. Can you discover the verb form problems in the following present time sentences?

> No: I am feel tired.
>
> Yes: I **am feeling** tired.

> No: They are need to learn English.
>
> Yes: They **need** to learn English.

> No: My brother is walk to school every day.
>
> Yes: My brother **walks** to school every day.

- In the present continuous, use a form of *be* + verb + ing.
- In the simple present tense, use the simple form of the verb; use verb + *s* for *he, she,* or *it.*

See Appendix 7 on page 345 to review spelling rules for verbs ending in -s.

See Subject–Verb Agreement on page 161 for more information and practice.

Exercise 6

Write **C** for correct and **I** for incorrect. Then correct the mistakes.

Family Schedules

1. ___/___ My mother is work as a hairdresser at a salon three days a week.

2. ___/___ My sister go to kindergarten every morning.

3. ___C___ My brother sells computers on weekends.

4. ___/___ My father helping my grandfather at his shop this summer.

5. ___/___ I am study English and work at a daycare center every day.

D **Past Time Verb Problems**

1. Can you find the past time verb problems in the following examples?

> No: I watch that movie.
>
> Yes: I **watched** that movie.

> No: While I watched TV, I heard a loud noise.
>
> Yes: While I **was watching** TV, I heard a loud noise.

No: When I came to Canada, I already met my Canadian relatives.

Yes: When I came to Canada, I **had** already **met** my Canadian relatives.

No: He had died in 1979.

Yes: He **died** in 1979.

- If something happened one time in the past, use simple past tense.
- Use the past continuous (progressive) to describe an action in progress at a specific time in the past.
- Use the past perfect to show that one past event happened before another past event, often with *already* or *by the time*.
- If you have one event in the past, use simple past tense, not past perfect.

Exercise 7

There are four past tense verb errors in the following story. Can you find and correct them?

My Pet Turtle

When I was a child, my grandparents were giving me a wonderful gift. It was a little turtle. I had loved that turtle so much. I made a home for the turtle out of a box. I fed the turtle every day. I talked to the turtle, and he became my friend. When the turtle get sick, I took care of him. I have that little turtle for eight years. He was a great pet.

D Past Time Verb Problems, continued

2. Can you discover the verb form problems in the following past time sentences?

No: He choosed the wrong number.

Yes: He **chose** the wrong number.

No: He didn't came.

Yes: He **didn't come.**

No: They didn't liked it.

Yes: They **didn't like** it.

No: They didn't be afraid.

Yes: They **weren't** afraid.

- Use the correct simple past form of irregular verbs.

  See Appendix 1 on page 325 for a list of irregular verbs and their simple past forms.

- To form the negative, use *didn't* + the simple form of the verb.

- Use the correct negative forms for the *be* verb. Don't use *did* with *be*.

- Here are the negative forms for the *be* verb:

I wasn't	We weren't
You weren't (*not* you wasn't)	You weren't
He wasn't	They weren't
She wasn't	
It wasn't	

Exercise 8

There are three past tense verb errors in the following story. Can you find and correct them?

A Frightening Experience

My brother-in-law told an interesting story. One summer he was in Southeast Asia. He was staying in a tent. One afternoon he went into the tent. He saw a long, long snake behind his bed, but he didn't be afraid. The snake was poisonous, so he killed it with a knife. Then he picked it up and throwed it outside the tent. It didn't bothered him at all.

D More Past Time Verb Problems

3. Life Events

Look at the following sentences that describe life events. Which sentences are correct? Check your knowledge by circling the letters of the correct expressions.

be born (One sentence is correct.)

a. I born in 1976.

b. I borned in 1976.

c. I was born in 1976.

graduate (Two sentences are correct.)

  a. I grew up there until graduate from high school.
  b. After graduate high school, I studied at college.
  ✓ c. After graduated from high school, I worked.
  ✓ d. After I graduated from high school, I worked.
  ✓ e. After graduating from high school, I worked.

marry (Three sentences are correct.)

  a. Her father marry another woman.
  b. Her father married to another woman.
  ✓ c. Her father married with another woman.
  d. Her father marriaged another woman.
  ✓ e. Her father got married to another woman.
  f. Her father married another woman.
  ✓ g. Her father is married.

die (One sentence is correct.)

  a. My father was died five years ago.
  b. My father dead five years ago.
  ✓ c. My father died five years ago.

(Correct answers: be born – c; graduate – d, e; marry – e, f, g; die – c.)

- Use the correct past tense expressions when describing life events with the verbs *be born, graduate, marry, die.*

Exercise 9

Guess when the following events happened. Fill in the blanks with the correct year. Then correct any verb errors in the sentences.

Use each year one time: 1847   1879   1945   1958   1973   1981   1984   1990

What Year Was It?

1. Thomas Edison ~~borned~~ *was* born in ___1847___.

2. Prince Charles got married to Princess Diana in ___1981___. (They were divorced in 1996.)

3. Albert Einstein born in ___1879___. *was*

4. Michael Jordan didn't graduate from college. After his junior year, he joined the Chicago Bulls professional basketball team in ___1984___.

5. After graduated from Yale Law School in ___1973___, Bill Clinton studied at Oxford University in England.

6. Anne Frank was died in ___1945___.

7. Madonna was born in ___1958___.

8. Tom Cruise married with Nicole Kidman in ___1990___.

E Problems with Present Perfect

1. Can you find the problems with the use of present perfect in these examples?

No: I study English since I was in elementary school.

Yes: I **have studied** English since I was in elementary school.

Yes: I **have been studying** English since I was in elementary school.

No: I live in New York for three years. (You live in New York now.)

Yes: I **have lived** in New York for three years.

Yes: I **have been living** in New York for three years.

No: She worked hard up to now.

Yes: She **has worked** hard up to now.

No: She is taking care of them for three years.

Yes: She **has been taking** care of them for three years.

No: I have been going to Texas three times.

Yes: I **have gone** to Texas three times.

No: Janice has been reading twenty pages of her book.

Yes: Janice **has read** twenty pages of her book.

No: I have graduated from high school in 1990.

Yes: I **graduated** from high school in 1990.

- Use the present perfect when you describe an action or situation that began in the past and continues now or until very recently.
- *Since, for three years,* or *up to now* are used with present perfect.
- Use present perfect continuous to emphasize an action that continues up to the present.
- When you describe a repeated action in the past (*three* times) or a completed task with a number (*twenty* pages) use present perfect.
- Remember: Use simple past tense to describe a finished event in the past.

Exercise 10

Write C for correct or I for incorrect. Then correct the mistakes.

Tiger Woods

1. _____ Tiger Woods played golf since he was a baby.

   [handwritten: has been playing]

2. _____ Tiger has appeared on *That's Incredible* TV show when he was

   five because of his golfing talent.

3. __C__ He has been a professional golfer since 1996.

4. __C__ Woods signed a deal with Nike for $40 million in 1997.

5. __/__ Woods has won the Master's in 1997 when he was twenty-one.

6. __C__ Woods has become the most famous new golfer since

Jack Nicklaus.

7. __/__ Tiger Woods has been winning three big tournaments recently.

8. __/__ Since Woods began playing professionally, many experts call him
have / has

a great athlete.

E Problems with Present Perfect, continued

2. Can you discover the verb form problems in these present perfect sentences?

No: My sister has go to New York three times.

Yes: My sister **has gone** to New York three times.

No: She has been read that book since Tuesday.

Yes: She **has been reading** that book since Tuesday.

No: I've been studying English since five months.

Yes: I've been studying English **for** five months.

- Use *have / has* + past participle for present perfect.
  See Appendix 1 on page 325 for a list of irregular verbs and their past participles.
- Use *have / has* + *been* + verb+*ing* for present perfect continuous.
- Use *since* with an exact time (*2:00, Monday, March, 1995*) and *for* with a duration of time (*two days, three months, several years*).

Exercise 11

Fill in the blanks with a time expression to answer the question. Then correct any verb errors.

How Long?

1. I have been ~~studied~~ studying English for _____ 5 years _____.

2. I have lived here since _____ last year _____.

3. My best friend has ~~know~~ known me since _____ I moved to Canada _____.

4. I've loved _____reading_____ (music, shopping, sports,

   reading, etc.) for _____a very long time_____.

5. I haven't ~~see~~ *seen* some of my friends since ___6 years ago___.

F Problems with Future Time

Most ESL students don't have problems with simple future tense (*will* + verb) or *be going to* + verb. However, a common problem occurs when two future times are used in the same sentence. Look at the following sentences. What happens to the verb tenses?

No: My brother will work for my father after he will finish school.

Yes: My brother will work for my father **after** he **finishes** school.

No: As soon as I will get a job, I'm going to buy a car.

Yes: **As soon as I get** a job, I'm going to buy a car.

- When you use two future times and a time word such as *when, before, after, as soon as,* or *if,* the time word clause is in simple present tense.
- Remember to use the *-s* present tense verb with *he, she,* or *it.*

Exercise 12

Write C for correct or I for incorrect. Then correct the mistakes.

Future Plans

1. __I__ My mother is taking classes to become a dental assistant. After

   she finish the course, her school will help her find a job in a

   dentist's office.

2. __C__ When my friend will come to visit us next summer, we will have

   a big party.

3. __C__ After my girlfriend and I get married, we will live with

   my parents.

4. __I__ If I will have enough money, I'm going to travel in Asia next year.

5. __C__ My best friend will go to graduate school as soon as she gets her

   bachelor's degree.

G Problems Using Two Verbs in the Same Time

Can you find the verb tense problems in the following sentences?

No: When I studied English, I learn many idioms.

Yes: When I **studied** English, I **learned** many idioms.

No: It's easy to pass this class, and many students did this.

Yes: It**'s** easy to pass this class, and many students **do** this.

No: I gave up my dreams because I found that it is impossible to keep studying.

Yes: I **gave up** my dreams because I **found** that it **was** impossible to keep studying.

- When you are describing two ideas in the same time, be sure to use the same verb tense.

Exercise 13

There is one verb tense error in each sentence. Can you find and correct each one?

My Diet

1. When I was a child, I like only a few vegetables.
   liked

2. Then, when I was a teenager, I become a vegetarian.
   became

3. I ate no meat for several years, and I feel really healthy at that time.
   felt

4. Now I eat mostly vegetables, but I also am having some chicken

   or fish occasionally.

5. I haven't eaten any red meat for ten years, and I didn't miss it.

H Problems with Passives

1. Can you discover the problems using active or passive in the following sentences?

   No: Someone built the cathedral in the 1700s.

   Yes: The cathedral **was built** in the 1700s.

   No: People buy thousands of computers every year.

   Yes: Thousands of computers **are sold** every year.

No: I was received a wonderful gift.

Yes: I **received** a wonderful gift.

No: A big change was happened.

Yes: A big change **happened.**

No: An accident was occurred.

Yes: An accident **occurred.**

No: My favorite pet was died.

Yes: My favorite pet **died.**

- Use the passive when the subject is unknown or unimportant.
- Intransitive verbs (*v.i.* in your dictionary) such as *happen, occur,* and *die* cannot be used in the passive form.

Exercise 14

Write C for correct or I for incorrect. Then correct the mistakes.

Did You Know?

1. ___C___ The *Mona Lisa* was painted by Leonardo da Vinci for the King of France to hang in his bathroom.

2. ___I___ The Globe Theatre in London, where Shakespeare's plays performed, had no roof. The performances canceled when it rained.

3. ___I___ In many theaters years ago, all of the women's parts were acted by boys.

4. ___I___ The first photograph took by Joseph Nicephore Niepce in France in the 1820s.

5. ___C___ The first children's books, such as *Alice in Wonderland,* wrote in the 1800s.

Exercise 15   Check your trivia knowledge and your grammar knowledge. Write T if the information in the statement is true, and write F if the information is false. Then correct any verb errors.

Trivia Quiz

1. _____ The movie *ET* directed by Steven Spielberg.

2. _____ Elvis Presley was died in 1977.

3. _____ Alaska is being the largest state in the U.S.

4. _____ The 1992 Summer Olympics were held in Seoul, Korea.

5. _____ The Kobe, Japan earthquake was occurred in 1996.

H Problems with Passives, continued

2. Can you find the problems using the passive form in the following sentences?

No: English is speaking all over the world.

Yes: English **is spoken** all over the world.

No: She was chosed as the class representative.

Yes: She **was chosen** as the class representative.

- Use the correct form of the passive.

Here are common active and passive forms:

	Active	**Passive**
Simple Present:	Thousands of immigrants **come** to North America every year.	ESL classes **are offered** at most schools in North America.
Simple Past:	An accident **happened** yesterday.	Fourteen people **were injured.**
Future:	We **will attend** the party.	The party **will be held** next week.
Present Continuous:	The crew **is working** overtime.	A bridge **is being built.**
Present Perfect:	We **have finished** three chapters.	Three chapters **have been completed** so far.

Exercise 16

Check your trivia knowledge and your grammar knowledge. Write **T** if the information in the statement is true, and write **F** if the information is false. Then correct any verb errors.

More Trivia

1. _____ *Romeo and Juliet* written by William Shakespeare.

2. _____ You can see the *Mona Lisa* in Rome, Italy.

3. _____ Abraham Lincoln was been elected the first U.S. President.

4. _____ Tom Hanks received the "Best Actor" academy award two years in a row.

5. _____ The Chicago Bulls won the NBA Championship in 1995, 1996, 1997, and 1998.

Exercise 17

Fill in the blanks with the correct form of the verb. (Use a past tense active or passive form.)

A Movie Review: The Fugitive

I really ___enjoied___ (enjoy) this movie. Harrison Ford ___played___ (play) Dr. Richard Kimble. Dr. Kimble's wife ___died___ (die). The police ___accused___ (accuse) Dr. Kimble of murdering his wife. He _____ (send) to jail. On the way to the jail, he _____ (escape). The movie was about his escape and how Sam Gerard, a special policeman, _____ (try) to catch him. Kimble _____ (chase) by Gerard and his team all over Illinois and Chicago. Finally, Kimble _____ (prove) that he was innocent when he _____ (catch) the real murderer. It _____ (be) a very exciting movie, and I recommend it.

Infinitive and Modal Forms

1. Can you find the errors using infinitives in the following sentences?

   No: They decided come home early.

   Yes: They decided **to come** home early.

   No: We need get jobs.

   Yes: We need **to get** jobs.

   No: If I want study, I will go to another country.

   Yes: If I want **to study,** I will go to another country.

   - Some verbs are followed by infinitives (*to* + verb).
   - The infinitive form uses the simple verb.

   See Word Form on page 201 for more practice.

2. Can you discover the modal problems in the following sentences?

   No: I couldn't to learn it.

   No: I couldn't learned it.

   Yes: **I couldn't learn** it.

   No: You must to follow the doctor's advice.

   Yes: You **must follow** the doctor's advice.

   - Simple modals (*can, must, should,* etc.) are followed by the simple form of the verb.
   - Don't use *to* or the past tense form of the verb after simple modals.

Exercise 18

There is one verb error in each sentence. Correct the mistakes and circle *yes* or *no*.

Advice

Agree or disagree?

1. If you want be a good student, you must study

   several hours every day.   yes   no

2. Young people should always to show respect

   to older people.   yes   no

3. You need get at least eight hours of sleep every night.   yes   no

4. If you couldn't succeeded the first time, try again.   yes   no

5. When you decide to start a project, you must to

    finish it.   yes   no

Chapter Review

Exercise 19

Write C for correct or I for incorrect. Then correct the mistakes.

My Grandmother's Life

1. _____   My grandmother borned in Taiwan in 1933.

2. _____   She had a very difficult life because her mother dead when

    she was a child.

3. _____   She got married and moved to a big city when she was about

    twenty years old.

4. _____   She is working at a big restaurant since her children grew up.

5. _____   When she will retire, she is going to learn to play the piano.

6. _____   She is a happy woman because she is surrounded by her family

    and friends.

Exercise 20

Fill in the blanks with the correct form of the verb.

The Best Weekend in My Life

Last year, I _____ (have) the best weekend in my life. I

_____ (travel) to Bali for three days. That weekend, a friend

_____ (stay) at the same hotel. We _____ (do) so

many things together. We both _____ (try) scuba diving, and we

_____ (see) some incredible fish. Then we _____

(walk) on the beach and _____ (swim). We _____(rent)

a sailboat and _____ (go) to some other beautiful beaches. Later

in the evening, we _____ (have) a quiet dinner under the stars.

But the best part was that I _____ (fall) in love with my friend,

and now we _____ (marry).

Exercise 21

Correct the verb errors.

My Early Life

I born in 1975. I lived in a small town until I six. Then I had moved to a

big city. I afraid because I didn't knew anyone. I went to a private school

because my parents want me to learn a lot of math and science, and this

school teached a lot of that. Unfortunately, I didn't was good in math, so I

wasn't do very well. But in my second year of elementary school, I begin

playing soccer. I really good, and other students admire me. I was be the

number one player for all of my elementary school years. As a result, I had

had a lot of friends.

Exercise 1

1. __I__   Anne Murray a famous singer from Nova Scotia.
2. __C__   Actor Michael J. Fox is originally from Ontario, Canada.
3. __I__   A famous hockey player from Canada Wayne Gretzky.
4. __C__   Alexander Graham Bell lived in Canada as a young man.
5. __I__   Jazz musician Oscar Peterson in Montreal, Canada.

Exercise 2

1. Four students <u>were</u> absent yesterday.
2. One student <u>was</u> late to class.
3. The other students <u>were</u> ready to begin class on time.
4. The teacher <u>was</u> happy because the lesson went well.
5. The students <u>were</u> sure that they understood the lesson.

Exercise 3

1. __I__   I <u>was</u> very surprised when my parents bought a new computer.
2. __I__   The computer <u>was</u> not very easy to set up.
3. __C__   At first, I was confused about how it worked.
4. __C__   Now we are very happy with the computer.
5. __I__   We <u>are</u> excited about getting on the Internet and sending e-mail.

Exercise 4

Dear Mom and Dad,

     I <u>am</u> sure that I chose a good school. The teachers <u>are</u> very nice, and sometimes are even a little strict about homework. Also, students cannot <u>be</u> late or absent. I'm studying really hard, and I'm learning a lot. My major <u>is</u> harder than I expected, but I <u>am</u> confident I will succeed. Thanks for giving me this chance.

     Jack

Exercise 5

1. __I__   In Japan most business people <u>work</u> 10 or more hours a day.
2. __C__   In Denmark, most people work 36 hours per week.
3. __C__   In the Middle East, people don't work on Thursdays and Fridays.
4. __C__   The average work week in North America is 40 hours.
5. __I__   In Italy, people <u>work</u> in the morning, <u>take</u> a long break at lunch, and then <u>work</u> again until evening.
6. __C__   In most of Latin America as in Italy, workers have a *siesta,* a break in the middle of the day to rest.

(Continued)

Exercise 6

1. ___I___ My mother <u>works</u> as a hairdresser at a salon three days a week.

2. ___I___ My sister <u>goes</u> to kindergarten every morning.

3. ___C___ My brother sells computers on weekends.

4. ___I___ My father <u>is</u> helping my grandfather at his shop this summer.

5. ___I___ I <u>study</u> English and work at a daycare center every day.

Exercise 7

When I was a child, my grandparents <u>gave</u> me a wonderful gift. It was a little turtle. I <u>loved</u> that turtle so much. I made a home for the turtle out of a box. I fed the turtle every day. I talked to the turtle, and he became my friend. When the turtle <u>got</u> sick, I took care of him. I <u>had</u> that little turtle for eight years. He was a great pet.

Exercise 8

My brother-in-law told an interesting story. One summer he was in Southeast Asia. He was staying in a tent. One afternoon he went into the tent. He saw a long, long snake behind his bed, but he <u>wasn't</u> afraid. The snake was poisonous, so he killed it with a knife. Then he picked it up and <u>threw</u> it outside the tent. It didn't <u>bother</u> him at all.

Exercise 9

1. Thomas Edison <u>was born</u> in <u>1847</u>.

2. Prince Charles got married to Princess Diana in <u>1981</u>. (They were divorced in 1996.)

3. Albert Einstein <u>was</u> born in <u>1879</u>.

4. Michael Jordan didn't graduate from college. After his junior year, he joined the Chicago Bulls professional basketball team in <u>1984</u>.

5. After <u>graduating</u> (*or* After <u>he graduated</u>) from Yale Law School in <u>1973</u>, Bill Clinton studied at Oxford University in England.

6. Anne Frank <u>died</u> in <u>1945</u>.

7. Madonna was born in <u>1958</u>.

8. Tom Cruise <u>married</u> (*or* <u>got married to</u>) Nicole Kidman in <u>1990</u>.

(Continued)

Exercise 10

1. ___I___ Tiger Woods <u>has played</u> golf since he was a baby.

2. ___I___ Tiger <u>appeared</u> on *That's Incredible* TV show when he was five because of his golfing talent.

3. ___C___ He has been a professional golfer since 1996.

4. ___C___ Woods signed a deal with Nike for $40 million in 1997.

5. ___I___ Woods <u>won</u> the Master's in 1997 when he was twenty-one.

6. ___C___ Woods has become the most famous new golfer since Jack Nicklaus.

7. ___I___ Tiger Woods <u>has won</u> three big tournaments recently.

8. ___I___ Since Woods began playing professionally, many experts <u>have called</u> him a great athlete.

Exercise 11

1. I <u>have been studying</u> English for _____. (one month, three years, etc.)

2. I have lived here since _____. (March, 1996, last year, etc.)

3. My best friend has <u>known</u> me since _____. (March, we were children, etc.)

4. I've loved _____ (*music, shopping, sports, reading,* etc.) for _____. (three years, many years, a long time, etc.)

5. I haven't <u>seen</u> some of my friends since _____. (last month, January, 1980, etc.)

Exercise 12

1. ___I___ My mother is taking classes to become a dental assistant. After she <u>finishes</u> the course, her school will help her find a job in a dentist's office.

2. ___I___ When my friend <u>comes</u> to visit us next summer, we will have a big party.

3. ___C___ After my girlfriend and I get married, we will live with my parents.

4. ___I___ If I <u>have</u> enough money, I'm going to travel in Asia next year.

5. ___C___ My best friend will go to graduate school as soon as she gets her bachelor's degree.

(Continued)

Exercise 13

1. When I was a child, I <u>liked</u> only a few vegetables.

2. Then, when I was a teenager, I <u>became</u> a vegetarian.

3. I ate no meat for several years, and I <u>felt</u> really healthy at that time.

4. Now I eat mostly vegetables, but I also <u>have</u> some chicken or fish occasionally.

5. I haven't eaten any red meat for ten years, and I <u>haven't missed</u> it.

Exercise 14

1. ___C___ The *Mona Lisa* was painted by Leonardo da Vinci for the King of France to hang in his bathroom.

2. ___I___ The Globe Theatre in London, where Shakespeare's plays <u>were performed</u>, had no roof. The performances <u>were canceled</u> when it rained.

3. ___C___ In many theaters years ago, all of the women's parts were acted by boys.

4. ___I___ The first photograph <u>was taken</u> by Joseph Nicephore Niepce in France in the 1820s.

5. ___I___ The first children's books, such as *Alice in Wonderland,* <u>were written</u> in the 1800s.

Exercise 15

1. ___T___ The movie *ET* <u>was directed</u> by Steven Spielberg.

2. ___T___ Elvis Presley <u>died</u> in 1977.

3. ___T___ Alaska <u>is</u> the largest state in the U.S.

4. ___F___ The 1992 Summer Olympics were held in Seoul, Korea. (Barcelona, Spain)

5. ___T___ The Kobe, Japan earthquake <u>occurred</u> in 1996.

Exercise 16

1. ___T___ *Romeo and Juliet* <u>was written</u> by William Shakespeare.

2. ___F___ You can see the *Mona Lisa* in Rome, Italy. (Paris, France)

3. ___F___ Abraham Lincoln <u>was elected</u> the first U.S. President. (George Washington)

4. ___T___ Tom Hanks received the "Best Actor" academy award two years in a row.

5. ___T___ The Chicago Bulls won the NBA Championship in 1995, 1996, 1997 and 1998.

(Concluded)

Exercise 17

    I really <u>enjoyed</u> (enjoy) this movie. Harrison Ford <u>played</u> (play) Dr. Richard Kimble. Dr. Kimble's wife <u>died</u> (die). The police <u>accused</u> (accuse) Dr. Kimble of murdering his wife. He <u>was sent</u> (send) to jail. On the way to the jail, he <u>escaped</u> (escape). The movie was about his escape, and how Sam Gerard, a special policeman, <u>tried</u> (try) to catch him. Kimble <u>was chased</u> (chase) by Gerard and his team all over Illinois and Chicago. Finally, Kimble <u>proved</u> (prove) that he was innocent when he <u>caught</u> (catch) the real murderer. It <u>was</u> (be) a very exciting movie, and I recommend it.

Exercise 18

1. If you want <u>to be</u> a good student, you must study several hours every day.

2. Young people <u>should always show</u> respect to older people.

3. You <u>need to get</u> at least eight hours of sleep every night.

4. If you <u>couldn't succeed</u> the first time, try again.

5. When you decide to start a project, you <u>must finish</u> it.

Exercise 19

1. __I__   My grandmother <u>was born</u> in Taiwan in 1933.

2. __I__   She had a very difficult life because her mother <u>died</u> when she was a child.

3. __C__   She got married and moved to a big city when she was about twenty years old.

4. __I__   She <u>has been working</u> at a big restaurant since her children grew up.

5. __I__   When she <u>retires</u>, she is going to learn to play the piano.

6. __C__   She is a happy woman because she is surrounded by her family and friends.

Exercise 20

    Last year, I <u>had</u> (have) the best weekend in my life. I <u>traveled</u> (travel) to Bali for three days. That weekend, a friend <u>stayed</u> (stay) at the same hotel. We <u>did</u> (do) so many things together. We both <u>tried</u> (try) scuba diving, and we <u>saw</u> (see) some incredible fish. Then we <u>walked</u> (walk) on the beach and <u>swam</u> (swim). We <u>rented</u> (rent) a sailboat and <u>went</u> (go) to some other beautiful beaches. Later in the evening, we <u>had</u> (have) a quiet dinner under the stars. But the best part was that I <u>fell</u> (fall) in love with my friend, and now we <u>are married</u> (marry).

Exercise 21

    I <u>was born</u> in 1975. I lived in a small town until I <u>was</u> six. Then I <u>moved</u> to a big city. I <u>was afraid</u> because I didn't <u>know</u> anyone. I went to a private school because my parents <u>wanted</u> me to learn a lot of math and science, and this school <u>taught</u> a lot of that. Unfortunately, I <u>wasn't</u> good in math, so I <u>didn't</u> do very well. But in my second year of elementary school, I <u>began</u> playing soccer. I <u>was</u> really good, and other students <u>admired</u> me. I <u>was</u> the number one player for all of my elementary school years. As a result, I <u>had</u> a lot of friends.

CHAPTER 6

Singular / Plural

Singular / plural problems include the following: not using the plural form to show that there is more than one, using the wrong plural form, or using a count or noncount noun incorrectly.

If you need extra review on nouns, count nouns, and noncount nouns, see Appendix 2 on page 329 before and as you work on this chapter.

A Count Nouns with Counting Words

The words *sister, brother, place, cow* and *sheep* are nouns that have a singular and plural form and can be counted. Can you find the problems in the following sentences?

No: I have three sister and two brother.

Yes: I have three sister**s** and two brother**s.**

No: When I went to Hawaii, I visited several beautiful place.

Yes: When I went to Hawaii, I visited several beautiful place**s.**

No: On our ride in the countryside, we saw many cows and sheeps.

Yes: On our ride in the countryside, we saw many cows and **sheep.**

- Counting words (*one, five, several, many, all,* etc.) with a count noun require the plural form of the noun.

  See Appendix 7 on page 345 to review spelling rules for nouns ending in -s.

- Use the correct form of irregular plurals.

  See Appendix 2 on page 329 for a list of common irregular count nouns and their plural forms.

Exercise 1

Change to the plural when necessary.

About My City

1. My city has many wonderful palace and temple.

2. My hometown has four season.

3. There are many great place to visit.

4. Many child love going to the ocean.

5. In the summer, we go swimming at several beach nearby.

Exercise 2

Write **C** for correct and **I** for incorrect. Then correct the mistakes.

At School

1. _____ I have three class every day.

2. _____ We use several books.

3. _____ There are about twenty students in my writing class.

4. _____ I have many friend at my school.

5. _____ Several man and woman in my class have been studying English

for many year.

Exercise 3

PART 3 EDITING FOCUS

There is one error in each sentence. Can you find and correct the mistakes?

The American Flag

1. The American flag has thirteen stripe.

2. The stripes represent the thirteen colony that made up the United States in 1776.

3. The first flag also had thirteen star arranged in a circle.

4. As more state joined the country, another star was added for each state.

5. The modern flag has fifty star, one for each state.

Exercise 4

Find and correct the irregular plural nouns. (*See Appendix 2 on page 329 for a list of common irregular count nouns.*)

About Animals

1. Some deers live in forests and fields near cities throughout North America.

2. Dogs and cats are more common, but some childs have mouses for pets.

3. Caterpillars, snails, and slugs often eat the leafs of plants in the garden.

4. All sharks have several rows of tooths. When one tooth falls out, another one replaces it.

5. Most sheeps are similar to goats, but sheeps are heavier, and male sheeps don't have beards.

B Count Nouns without Counting Words

Can you find the problems in the following sentences?

No: I have friend from Canada.

Yes: I have a friend from Canada.   (One friend)

Yes: I have friends from Canada.   (More than one friend)

No: My city has narrow road.

No: My city has a narrow road.   (Only one narrow road?)

Yes: My city has narrow roads.   (More than one road.)

No: I like apple.

No: I like an apple.   (This sentence is strange in English. You like only
                             one apple?)

Yes: I like apples.   (Apples = general. More than one apple.)

Yes: I like to eat an apple every day.   (Also OK, but it has a
                                             different meaning.)

- Count nouns can be singular or plural, depending on the meaning.
- A singular count noun needs an article.
- A plural count noun needs the plural form.
- In some sentences, only the plural form makes sense.

See Articles on page 257 for more information on articles with a singular count noun.

Exercise 5

Change to the plural where necessary. Each sentence has at least one mistake.

About School

1. The student in my class come from several country.

2. I have friend from Japan and Colombia.

3. I enjoy meeting new person at school.

4. Our writing class meets three day every week.

5. My writing and math teacher are from California and Arkansas.

Exercise 6

Check your history knowledge. See if you can answer the following questions. Then find and correct two mistakes in each sentence.

Where in History

1. The Vikings sailed in long wood boat to many country around 1000 A.D.

   Where were the Vikings from? _____

2. *Samurai* were great fighter. They worked for many lord who ruled from

    1185 to 1868.

    Where were *Samurai* from? _____

3. In one country, people preserved dead body as "mummies." They also

    built huge pyramid.

    Which country was this? _____

4. Around A.D. 1500, the Aztec Indians controlled a large area. They knew

    how to plant many crop and they worshipped several god.

    Which modern country was their home? _____

5. In 1450, Johannes Gutenberg invented a printing press that could print

    book much more easily and quickly. Before that time, all book were

    written by hand.

    Which country was he from? _____

C One of . . . , Some of . . .

Do *one of* and *some of* take a singular or plural count noun?

No: One of my classmate comes from Laos.

Yes: One of my classmate**s** comes from Laos.

No: Some of my friend are in my class.

Yes: Some of my friend**s** are in my class.

- *One of, some of,* and *many of* take a plural count noun.

Exercise 7   Change to the plural where necessary.

About My Job

1. Some of the worker in my office are bilingual.

2. It's very good because many of our customer live in different country.

3. One of my friend at work speaks three language.

4. We import and export special copy machine to most of the big city in Asia and Europe.

5. It's difficult to learn all of the tax law in various country.

D Special Count Nouns

Are words like *jeans* singular or plural?

No: I bought a new jean yesterday.

Yes: I bought some new jeans yesterday.

Yes: I bought a new pair of jeans yesterday.

- A few nouns in English such as *jeans* and *clothes* are always plural—there is no singular form.
- Many of these items (*jeans, glasses*) are made of two parts (two legs on the jeans, for example).
- To count these, we often use the expression *pair of.*
- Here are common plural count nouns:

  Clothing: jeans, pants, trousers, shorts, pajamas
  Items: glasses, scissors, pliers

Exercise 8   There are eight errors in the following message. Can you find and correct them?

An E-mail Message

Andreas,

I got your message asking what cloth to bring on the camping trip. Since we don't know what kind of weather to expect, I suggest the following: a good pair of jean, some short, several shirt, a warm jacket, and a raincoat. Oh, and bring a good pair of boot in case it rains, and some sunglass. If you have a good knife with a little pair of scissor, that might be helpful, too. Let me know if you have more question.

Elena

E   Noncount Nouns

Can you find the problems in the following sentences?

No: I hope I get some mails.
Yes: I hope I get some **mail.**

No: Please give me some informations.
Yes: Please give me some **information.**

- Noncount nouns are not counted and have no plural ending.
- Here are some common noncount nouns:

Nature:	rain, scenery, grass
Solids:	bread, ice cream, wood
Liquids:	water, soda, beer
Gases:	air, smog, pollution
Ideas:	time, life, happiness
Name of a group:	meat, mail, traffic
Sports:	football, baseball, swimming
School subjects:	English, psychology, biology

See Appendix 2 on page 329 for more noncount noun information.

Exercise 9	Change the count nouns to the plural where necessary. Do not change the noncount nouns.

At the Post Office

Clerk: May I help you?

Customer: Yes, I need to buy some stamp for these postcard

and this package.

Clerk: OK. The postage for all of this is $17.95. Anything else?

Customer: Yes. I need to place a hold on my mail and send

two registered letter.

Clerk: Fine. Just fill out these form.

Exercise 10	Change to the plural where necessary.

Transportation Problems

Brian: I was almost late. The traffic today was terrible.

Jean: I know. And when I got here all of the parking place

were taken.

Brian: Yeah, I had to park four block away.

Jean: When are they going to build more parking lot?

Brian: Or else improve the public transportation. There are no bus

or train I could take to get here.

F Confusing Count and Noncount Nouns

Why are these mistakes easy to make?

No: I like to learn words. I want to learn some new vocabularies.

Yes: I like to learn words. I want to learn some new **vocabulary.**

No: My friend doesn't have very much times.

Yes: My friend doesn't have very much **time.**

- Some count nouns have almost the same meaning as some noncount nouns.
- Some nouns can be count or noncount, depending on the meaning you want to express.

Here are some confusing noncount and count nouns:

Noncount (More general meaning)	Count (More specific meaning)
homework	an assignment, assignments
work	a job, jobs
vocabulary, slang	a word, words
information	a fact, facts
advice	a suggestion, suggestions
paper "Here is some paper"	a paper, papers = composition "I need to write a paper."
coffee "I like coffee." (also true for beer, wine, soda, etc.)	a coffee, coffees = cups of coffee "Two coffees, please."
fish "I like fish."	a fish, fish "We caught three fish." fishes = types of fish "The ocean has hundreds of fishes."
chicken "We eat a lot of chicken."	a chicken, chickens = animal "I have three chickens."
hamburger = meat "I need to buy a pound of hamburger."	a hamburger, hamburgers = sandwich "Two hamburgers, please."
light "The evening light is wonderful."	a light, lights "There are four lights in this room."
life "Life can be difficult."	a life, lives "The lifeguard has saved three lives."
time "I have some free time."	one time, times "I've been there three times."
crime "Crime is a big problem."	a crime, crimes "She has committed several serious crimes."
glass "The window is made of glass."	a glass, glasses "He had three glasses of water." glasses "I can't see well. I need glasses."
education "Education is important."	an education "I want to get a good education."

Exercise 11

Write C for correct and I for incorrect. Then correct the mistakes.

About School

1. _____   Our teacher assigns a lot of homework. We have at least

   three assignments every day.

2. _____   I need to go to the bookstore to buy some pencil, pen,

   and paper.

3. _____   The test had many question. I barely had enough time to finish.

4. _____   I read this page four times before I understood it.

5. _____   I need your advices. Do you have some suggestions for me

   to improve my reading?

Exercise 12

Change the count nouns to plural. Do not change the noncount nouns.

At a Restaurant

Joyce: Do you like fish?

Susan: No, I prefer chicken.

Joyce: Maybe I'll have a hamburger. Shall we order two beer with that?

Susan: We have to do a lot of work this afternoon. Maybe we should

   get two coffee, instead.

Joyce: OK. And two piece of pie, too.

Exercise 13

There are seven mistakes in the following letter. Can you find and correct them?

A Letter

Dear Johanna,

I love getting letter. Thanks! I'm enjoying my life here. I like studying English. I like my classmate, too. Once a week, we go to the computer lab. I'm enjoying learning about computer. In my free time, I see movie and go to shopping mall. There are a lot of fun activity at school, too. I have only two problem—not enough time or money. Write again soon.

Love,

Maria

Chapter Review

Exercise 14

There are thirteen mistakes in the following paragraph. Can you find and correct them?

A Big Problem in My Country

There are many big city in my country. Of course, each city has a lot of person, shop, school, and business. Also, most people have car. Since most people drive to work at the same time, this causes many traffic jam. When there is a lot of rain, the traffic is even worse. Sometimes it takes too much times to go somewhere. You can sit inside your car for two or three hour. Also, the traffic policeman have to wear mask because of the air pollution. I hope that the government will solve this problem by widening more road and adding more bus.

Exercise 15

Find and correct the mistakes.

The Biggest Problem in My Country

I think the biggest problem in my country is crime. For the last five year, crime has gotten much worse. For example, in my city in one night there can be eighteen murder. There are also a lot of drug dealer, and many young guy use drug. These person may break into house or rob innocent citizen to get more money for their drug. There aren't enough policeman on the street to protect us. Also, it seems that the government isn't doing enough to help stop the growing number of violent crime.

Exercise 16

Find and correct the mistakes.

What I Like about Living in Canada

I like many thing about living here. First of all, I can enjoy the beautiful nature in this area. There are so many more tree, bush, and flower here than in my city. All of the house have big yard, and many of them have wonderful flower garden and nice grass. Second, the air is clean and there is not so much pollution. Even though I don't like the rain, it makes the air very clear. I also like outdoor sport, so I can go camping, hiking, and so on. There are wonderful park nearby with spectacular lake and mountain. I sometimes see wild animal, such as deer and beaver. All in all, this is a nice place to live.

Exercise 1

1. My city has many wonderful <u>palaces</u> and <u>temples</u>.
2. My hometown has four <u>seasons</u>.
3. There are many great <u>places</u> to visit.
4. Many <u>children</u> love going to the ocean.
5. In the summer, we go swimming at several <u>beaches</u> nearby.

Exercise 2

1. __I__ I have three <u>classes</u> every day.
2. __C__ We use several books.
3. __C__ There are about twenty students in my writing class.
4. __I__ I have many <u>friends</u> at my school.
5. __I__ Several <u>men</u> and <u>women</u> in my class have been studying English for many <u>years</u>.

Exercise 3

1. The American flag has thirteen <u>stripes</u>.
2. The stripes represent the thirteen <u>colonies</u> that made up the United States in 1776.
3. The first flag also had thirteen <u>stars</u> arranged in a circle.
4. As more <u>states</u> joined the country, another star was added for each state.
5. The modern flag has fifty <u>stars</u>, one for each state.

Exercise 4

1. Some <u>deer</u> live in forests and fields near cities throughout North America.
2. Dogs and cats are more common, but some <u>children</u> have <u>mice</u> for pets.
3. Caterpillars, snails, and slugs often eat the <u>leaves</u> of plants in the garden.
4. All sharks have several rows of <u>teeth</u>. When one tooth falls out, another one replaces it.
5. Most <u>sheep</u> are similar to goats, but <u>sheep</u> are heavier, and male <u>sheep</u> don't have beards.

Exercise 5

1. The <u>students</u> in my class come from several <u>countries</u>.
2. I have <u>friends</u> from Japan and Colombia.
3. I enjoy meeting new <u>people</u> at school.
4. Our writing class meets three <u>days</u> every week.
5. My writing and math <u>teachers</u> are from California and Arkansas.

(Continued)

Exercise 6

1. The Vikings sailed in long wood <u>boats</u> to many <u>countries</u> around 1000 A.D.

   Where were the Vikings from? <u>Scandinavia: Denmark, Norway, and Sweden</u>

2. *Samurai* were great <u>fighters</u>. They worked for many <u>lords</u> who ruled from 1185 to 1868.

   Where were *Samurai* from? <u>Japan</u>

3. In one country, people preserved dead <u>bodies</u> as "mummies." They also built huge <u>pyramids</u>.

   Which country was this? <u>Egypt</u>

4. Around A.D. 1500, the Aztec Indians controlled a large area. They knew how to plant many <u>crops</u> and they worshipped several <u>gods</u>.

   Which modern country was their home? <u>Mexico</u>

5. In 1450 Johannes Gutenberg invented a printing press that could print <u>books</u> much more easily and quickly. Before that time, all <u>books</u> were written by hand.

   Which country was he from? <u>Germany</u>

Exercise 7

1. Some of the <u>workers</u> in my office are bilingual.

2. It's very good because many of our <u>customers</u> live in different <u>countries</u>.

3. One of my <u>friends</u> at work speaks three <u>languages</u>.

4. We import and export special copy <u>machines</u> to most of the big <u>cities</u> in Asia and Europe.

5. It's difficult to learn all of the tax <u>laws</u> in various <u>countries</u>.

Exercise 8

Andreas,

   I got your message asking what <u>clothes</u> to bring on the camping trip. Since we don't know what kind of weather to expect, I suggest the following: a good pair of <u>jeans</u>, some <u>shorts</u>, several <u>shirts</u>, a warm jacket, and a raincoat. Oh, and bring a good pair of <u>boots</u> in case it rains, and some <u>sunglasses</u>. If you have a good knife with a little pair of <u>scissors</u>, that might be helpful, too. Let me know if you have more <u>questions</u>.

Elena

(Continued)

Exercise 9

Clerk: May I help you?

Customer: Yes, I need to buy some <u>stamps</u> for these <u>postcards</u> and this package.

Clerk: OK. The postage for all of this is $17.95. Anything else?

Customer: Yes. I need to place a hold on my mail and send two registered <u>letters</u>.

Clerk: Fine. Just fill out these <u>forms</u>.

Exercise 10

Brian: I was almost late. The traffic today was terrible.

Jean: I know. And when I got here all of the parking <u>places</u> were taken.

Brian: Yeah, I had to park four <u>blocks</u> away.

Jean: When are they going to build more parking <u>lots</u>?

Brian: Or else improve the public transportation. There are no <u>buses</u> or <u>trains</u> I could take to get here.

Exercise 11

1. __C__ Our teacher assigns a lot of homework. We have at least three assignments every day.

2. __I__ I need to go to the bookstore to buy some <u>pencils</u>, <u>pens</u>, and paper.

3. __I__ The test had many <u>questions</u>. I barely had enough time to finish.

4. __C__ I read this page four times before I understood it.

5. __I__ I need your <u>advice</u>. Do you have some suggestions for me to improve my reading?

Exercise 12

Joyce: Do you like fish?

Susan: No, I prefer chicken.

Joyce: Maybe I'll have a hamburger. Shall we order two <u>beers</u> with that?

Susan: We have to do a lot of work this afternoon. Maybe we should get two <u>coffees</u>, instead.

Joyce: OK. And two <u>pieces</u> of pie, too.

(Concluded)

Exercise 13

Dear Johanna,

I love getting <u>letters</u>. Thanks! I'm enjoying my life here. I like studying English. I like my <u>classmates</u>, too. Once a week, we go to the computer lab. I'm enjoying learning about <u>computers</u>. In my free time, I see <u>movies</u> and go to shopping <u>malls</u>. There are a lot of fun <u>activities</u> at school, too. I have only two <u>problems</u>—not enough time or money. Write again soon.

Love,

Maria

Exercise 14

There are many big <u>cities</u> in my country. Of course, each city has a lot of <u>people</u>, <u>shops</u>, <u>schools</u>, and <u>businesses</u>. Also, most people have <u>cars</u>. Since most people drive to work at the same time, this causes many traffic <u>jams</u>. When there is a lot of rain, the traffic is even worse. Sometimes it takes too much <u>time</u> to go somewhere. You can sit inside your car for two or three <u>hours</u>. Also, the traffic <u>policemen</u> (or <u>police</u>) have to wear <u>masks</u> because of the air pollution. I hope that the government will solve this problem by widening more <u>roads</u> and adding more <u>buses</u>.

Exercise 15

I think the biggest problem in my country is crime. For the last five <u>years</u>, crime has gotten much worse. For example, in my city in one night there can be eighteen <u>murders</u>. There are also a lot of drug <u>dealers</u>, and many young <u>guys</u> use <u>drugs</u>. These <u>people</u> may break into <u>houses</u> or rob innocent <u>citizens</u> to get more money for their <u>drugs</u>. There aren't enough <u>policemen</u> (or <u>police</u>) on the street to protect us. Also, it seems that the government isn't doing enough to help stop the growing number of violent <u>crimes</u>.

Exercise 16

I like many <u>things</u> about living here. First of all, I can enjoy the beautiful nature in this area. There are so many more <u>trees</u>, <u>bushes</u>, and <u>flowers</u> here than in my city. All of the <u>houses</u> have big <u>yards</u>, and many of them have wonderful flower <u>gardens</u> and nice grass. Second, the air is clean and there is not so much pollution. Even though I don't like the rain, it makes the air very clear. I also like outdoor <u>sports</u>, so I can go camping, hiking, and so on. There are wonderful <u>parks</u> nearby with spectacular <u>lakes</u> and <u>mountains</u>. I sometimes see wild <u>animals</u>, such as deer and <u>beavers</u>. All in all, this is a nice place to live.

CHAPTER 7

Subject–Verb Agreement

A subject–verb agreement error occurs when the subject is singular, but the verb incorrectly has the plural form, or if the verb is singular and the subject is plural. Some errors, such as *he go,* are typical ESL problems, but other errors, such as *One of my friends are,* are also difficult areas for native speakers of English. Students with subject–verb agreement errors can improve their writing quickly if they learn the basic rules in this chapter.

A Third Person -*s*

Look at these sentences. What is the difference between the correct and incorrect ones?

No: She travel frequently.

Yes: She travel**s** frequently.

No: Dan doesn't works full-time.

Yes: Dan **doesn't work** full-time.

No: He can't works full-time.

Yes: He **can't work** full-time.

- *He, she, it,* and names of people (e.g., *Kim, Ahmed*) take -*s* in the simple present tense.
- With negatives (*don't, doesn't*) and modals (*can, must, shouldn't,* etc.), the main verb does not have -*s*.

Exercise 1

Fill in the blanks with the correct form of the verb.

Maria's First Impressions of This Country

Maria _____ (think) this country is so different from her own.

One thing she _____ (notice) is that the people smile so much.

She _____ (wonder) what they are smiling about! But she

_____ (like) it because they look very happy. Maria also

_____ (like) driving here. In her country, she _____

(drive) slow, but here she can _____ (go) fairly fast. There are a

lot of police so she _____ (have) to be careful and not go over

the speed limit. The food prices seem pretty cheap, but she doesn't

_____ (like) to buy clothes here. She doesn't _____

(think) they are as well made as in her country. Finally, this country doesn't

_____ (feel) crowded. She _____ (love) the space.

She _____ (hope) she can _____ (travel) a lot and really

_____ (get) to know this country and culture well.

B Some Confusing Nouns

Study the following nouns:

Singular	Plural
family	families
person	people
child	children
pair	glasses
fruit	jeans
pollution	shorts
information	clothes
fifteen minutes	police
100 miles	the elderly
major	the homeless
mathematics	the rich
physics	the poor
news	news stories
Japanese	the Japanese people

No: My major are not available at that school.

Yes: My major **is** not available at that school.

No: Physics are a challenging subject.

Yes: Physics **is** a challenging subject.

See Appendix 2 on page 329 for a longer list of regular and irregular nouns.

Exercise 2

Check (✓) the sentences that have no mistakes. Then circle *yes* or *no*.

What Do You Think?

Agree or disagree?

1. _____ Thirty minutes are enough time to do my homework.   yes   no

2. _____ Mathematics is a difficult subject for me.   yes   no

3. _____ French is similar to English.   yes   no

4. _____ In general, the police tries to be helpful. yes no

5. _____ The elderly should be taken care of by their children. yes no

6. _____ Twenty miles are a distance I can walk in a day. yes no

7. _____ My family is more important to me than my friends. yes no

C There Is / There Are

Which sentence is correct? Can you explain why?

a. There is several reasons why that happened.

b. There are several reasons why that happened.

- The answer is b. The verb *be* agrees with the noun that follows it.

Which sentence follows the above rule?

a. There is a lot of pollution in my country.

b. There are a lot of pollution in my country.

- The answer is a. *Pollution* is singular.

Exercise 3

Choose any city in the world that you know something about. Write the name below.

Then circle the correct verbs and circle *yes* or *no*. City: _____

What Do You Think?

Agree or disagree?

1. There (is / are) many traffic problems. yes no

2. There (is / are) a lot of pollution. yes no

3. There (is / are) great restaurants. yes no

4. There (is / are) beautiful parks. yes no

5. There (is / are) beautiful scenery. yes no

6. There (is / are) interesting tourist attractions. yes no

D One Of

Is *one of* singular or plural? How do you know?

No: One of my favorite memory involve my grandparents.

Yes: One of my favorite **memories involves** my grandparents.

- *One of* is singular and takes a singular verb. It is followed by a plural noun.

E Each, Every, and Any

Are *each, every,* and *any* singular or plural?

No: Each student have to buy a workbook.

Yes: Each student **has** to buy a workbook.

No: Every teacher give a course outline on the first day.

Yes: Every teacher **gives** a course outline on the first day.

No: Any student who have questions can come during office hours.

Yes: Any student who **has** questions can come during office hours.

- *Each, every,* and *any* are singular and take singular verbs.

F Subjects with *and*

Is a subject connected by *and* singular or plural?

No: Volleyball and soccer is my favorite sports.

Yes: Volleyball and soccer **are** my favorite sports.

- Subjects with *and* are plural and take plural verbs.

Exercise 4

Correct the mistakes.

What is the hardest part of learning English for you?

1. One of the hardest parts are speaking to native speakers.

2. Grammar and fast speech is the worst for me.

3. Spelling is difficult because each rule have an exception.

4. Any noun that need an article is so hard for me.

5. My neighbors and my boss doesn't understand my pronunciation very well.

6. In writing, every page I write have so many mistakes.

7. I think every student have problems with idioms.

8. One of my biggest problems are how to use *a* and *the* correctly.

G Gerunds and Infinitives

Are gerunds and infinitives singular or plural?

Yes: Winning an Olympic medal **is** a thrilling experience for an athlete.

Yes: To win an Olympic medal require**s** an athlete's complete dedication.

- Gerunds and infinitives are always singular and take a singular verb.

Exercise 5

Circle the correct verb.

What relaxes you?

1. Swimming (is / are) good because it makes my whole body tired.

2. Reading a good book (make / makes) me so sleepy and relaxed.

3. At the end of the day, to take a long hot bath (is / are) what I look forward to.

4. To lie outside on the grass on a sunny day and look up at the sky (is / are) very relaxing.

5. Doing anything physical (relax / relaxes) me.

6. To have a professional massage (work / works) best for me.

H More Than One Subject and Verb (Subject + Relative Clause)

Make sure you know which subjects and verbs go together. Study the following:

No: The articles that I read was complicated.

Yes: The (articles) that │I read│ (were) complicated.

No: The students who is studying English are friendly.

Yes: The (students) │who are studying│ English (are) friendly.

I Subject + Prepositional Phrase

The verb agrees with the subject of the sentence, not with the noun in the prepositional phrase.

No: The students in the class is loud.

Yes: The (students) in the class (are) loud.

No: My trip through the mountains were tiring.

Yes: My (trip) through the mountains (was) tiring.

Exercise 6

Circle the correct verb.

What is the best birthday present you have ever received?

1. A bracelet that my boyfriend gave me with both our names on it
   (was / were) the most memorable.

2. I think a video tape of my family telling me how much they appreciated
   me (was / were) the most special.

3. An airplane flight over the mountains in a private plane with my boyfriend
   (was / were) the best gift I've ever received.

4. A pair of cross-country skis (was / were) my favorite present because I
   use them all the time.

5. A year's supply of different flowers delivered every month (was / were)
   a wonderful surprise.

Chapter Review

Exercise 7

Put a checkmark (✓) next to the incorrect sentences. Then correct the mistakes.

Which do you like better: watching videos or going to the theater?

1. _____ Watching videos with my friends are cheaper.

2. _____ In a theater, people is able to watch the movie on a big screen.

3. _____ There are advantages to both watching videos and going

to a theater.

4. _____ Going to a theater for many families is too expensive.

5. _____ Two advantages of a movie theater are a big screen

and movie popcorn!

6. _____ One of my favorite activity are watching videos. It's fun and easy.

Exercise 8

Fill in the blanks with the correct form of the verb.

Culture Shock

I think I am experiencing a lot of culture shock now. One of my biggest

problems _____ (be) that I can't sleep very well. Sleeping _____

(have) always been a little hard for me, but now I can be awake all night. It's

really frustrating. Another problem _____ (be) that I don't like to go

out very much. In my country, I always did things with friends and there

_____ (be) so much to do. Here, I just want to stay home. My best

friend sometimes _____ (get) impatient with me, but I don't have the

energy to go out. My parents _____ (want) me to see a doctor, but I

think culture shock _____ (be) more psychological than physical.

Exercise 1

Maria <u>thinks</u> this country is so different from her own. One thing she <u>notices</u> is that the people smile so much. She <u>wonders</u> what they are smiling about! But she <u>likes</u> it because they look very happy. Maria also <u>likes</u> driving here. In her country, she <u>drives</u> slow, but here she can <u>go</u> fairly fast. There are a lot of police so she <u>has</u> to be careful and not go over the speed limit. The food prices seem pretty cheap, but she doesn't <u>like</u> to buy clothes here. She doesn't <u>think</u> they are as well made as in her country. Finally, this country doesn't <u>feel</u> crowded. She <u>loves</u> the space. She <u>hopes</u> she can <u>travel</u> a lot and really <u>get</u> to know this country and culture well.

Exercise 2

1. _____   Thirty minutes are enough time to do my homework.
2. ___✓___   Mathematics is a difficult subject for me.
3. ___✓___   French is similar to English.
4. _____   In general, the police tries to be helpful.
5. ___✓___   The elderly should be taken care of by their children.
6. _____   Twenty miles are a distance I can walk in a day.
7. ___✓___   My family is more important to me than my friends.

Exercise 3

1. There <u>are</u> many traffic problems.
2. There <u>is</u> a lot of pollution.
3. There <u>are</u> great restaurants.
4. There <u>are</u> beautiful parks.
5. There <u>is</u> beautiful scenery.
6. There <u>are</u> interesting tourist attractions.

Exercise 4

1. One of the hardest parts <u>is</u> speaking to native speakers.
2. Grammar and fast speech <u>are</u> the worst for me.
3. Spelling is difficult because each rule <u>has</u> an exception.
4. Any noun that <u>needs</u> an article is so hard for me.
5. My neighbors and my boss <u>don't</u> understand my pronunciation very well.
6. In writing, every page I write <u>has</u> so many mistakes.
7. I think every student <u>has</u> problems with idioms.
8. One of my biggest problems <u>is</u> how to use *a* and *the* correctly.

(Concluded)

Exercise 5

1. Swimming <u>is</u> good because it makes my whole body tired.

2. Reading a good book <u>makes</u> me so sleepy and relaxed.

3. At the end of the day, to take a long hot bath <u>is</u> what I look forward to.

4. To lie outside on the grass on a sunny day and look up at the sky <u>is</u> very relaxing.

5. Doing anything physical <u>relaxes</u> me.

6. To have a professional massage <u>works</u> best for me.

Exercise 6

1. A bracelet that my boyfriend gave me with both our names on it <u>was</u> the most memorable.

2. I think a video tape of my family telling me how much they appreciated me <u>was</u> the most special.

3. An airplane flight over the mountains in a private plane with my boyfriend <u>was</u> the best gift I've ever received.

4. A pair of cross-country skis <u>was</u> my favorite present because I use them all the time.

5. A year's supply of different flowers delivered every month <u>was</u> a wonderful surprise.

Exercise 7

1. ✓ Watching videos with my friends <u>is</u> cheaper.

2. ✓ In a theater, people <u>are</u> able to watch the movie on a big screen.

3. _____ There are advantages to both watching videos and going to a theater.

4. _____ Going to a theater for many families is too expensive.

5. _____ Two advantages of a movie theater are a big screen and movie popcorn!

6. ✓ One of my favorite activit<u>ies</u> <u>is</u> watching videos. It's fun and easy.

Exercise 8

I think I am experiencing a lot of culture shock now. One of my biggest problems <u>is</u> that I can't sleep very well. Sleeping <u>has</u> always been a little hard for me, but now I can be awake all night. It's really frustrating. Another problem <u>is</u> that I don't like to go out very much. In my country, I always did things with friends and there <u>was</u> so much to do. Here, I just want to stay home. My best friend sometimes <u>gets</u> impatient with me, but I don't have the energy to go out. My parents <u>want</u> me to see a doctor, but I think culture shock <u>is</u> more psychological than physical.

CHAPTER 8

Noun–Pronoun Agreement

A noun–pronoun agreement error occurs when a pronoun such as *he* or *them* doesn't match the noun it describes in number. Native speakers of English also need to edit for some types of noun–pronoun problems. This chapter provides some simple rules to follow.

A Repeating a Noun

Be careful not to repeat a noun with a subject pronoun in the same simple sentence.

No: My friend he likes to travel.

Yes: My friend **likes** to travel.

B Verb + Object Pronoun

Some verbs require an object pronoun such as *him, her, it, us,* or *them.*

No: It was a great movie. I saw four times.

Yes: It was a great movie. I saw **it** four times.

No: I enjoyed very much.

Yes: I enjoyed **it** very much.

No: The police couldn't control.

Yes: The police couldn't control **them.**

- Some common verbs that require an object pronoun are *see, watch, like, enjoy, want, discuss, talk about, recommend, kill, control,* and *arrest.*

Exercise 1

Write C for correct and I for incorrect. Then correct the mistakes, and circle *yes* or *no*.

What's Your Opinion?

Agree or disagree?

1. _____ Women they should stay home and not work.   yes   no

2. _____ Smoking on all airplanes it should be stopped.   yes   no

3. _____ If sick people want to die, a friend or doctor

         should be able to help them without the

         government arresting.   yes   no

4. _____ People should be allowed to smoke marijuana

         if they enjoy.   yes   no

5. _____ Children need to know about AIDS, and

         parents should discuss with their children.   yes   no

Exercise 2

Fill in the blanks with *it* or nothing.

Student Interview: Popular Movies

Here are some questions you can ask another student in class about a popular movie. If the person answers *no* to number 1, ask another person. Then write the answer.

_____

(name of popular movie)

1. Did you see _____?   _____

2. Did you enjoy _____? Why or why not? _____

    _____

    _____

3. How many times did you watch _____? _____

4. Would you recommend _____?   _____

C Possessive Pronouns

The pronouns *my, your, his, her, our* and *their* are sometimes used instead of the article *the* (or no article). This is especially true when referring to parts of the body and things that belong to you.

No: I'm tired of the life.

Yes: I'm tired of **my** life.

No: I looked at the surprise on the face.

Yes: I looked at the surprise on **his** face.

D Using *Own*

Own is generally used with personal adjectives: *my own, your own, his own, her own, our own* and *their own*.

No: They have own opinions.

Yes: They have **their** own opinions.

No: His parents each bought own car.

Yes: His parents each bought **their** own car.

Exercise 3

Correct the mistakes. Then circle *yes* or *no*.

What's Your Opinion?

Agree or disagree?

1. It is impolite to touch a person on head.   yes   no

2. People should solve own problems by themselves.   yes   no

3. If you don't like the life, it's OK to commit suicide.   yes   no

4. Kids should get own home when they become eighteen.   yes   no

5. What happens in the life is decided before you are born.   yes   no

6. It is OK for parents to physically punish the children.   yes   no

E Pronoun Agreement

The pronoun must agree with the noun it replaces.

No: My paragraphs had many mistakes, so my teacher told me to write it again.

Yes: My (paragraphs) had many mistakes, so my teacher told me to write **them** again.

No: I don't plan to visit my country soon because I don't miss them yet.

Yes: I don't plan to visit my (country) soon because I don't miss **it** yet.

F Each / Every / Any / No One

Each, every, any and *no one* are singular.

No: Each teacher had a different grading system for their students.*

Yes: Each teacher had a different grading system for **his** students.

Yes: Each teacher had a different grading system for **her** students.

No: Every student should buy their books.

Yes: Every student should buy **his** books.

Yes: Every student should buy **her** books.

No: Any student can drop a class they don't like.

Yes: Any student can drop a class **he** doesn't like.

Yes: Any student can drop a class **she** doesn't like.

No: No one can drop their class after the fifth week of the term.

Yes: No one can drop **his** class after the fifth week of the term.

Yes: No one can drop **her** class after the fifth week of the term.

---

*Note: To avoid using *he* to talk about all people, the plural form *their* is becoming common, especially in conversation. It is grammatically incorrect. Sometimes people use *his or her* instead:

Each teacher has a different grading system for **his or her** students.

Exercise 4

Correct the mistakes.

What are some rules for life that people should follow?

1. Everybody should take responsibility for their actions.

2. People should respect others and his property.

3. Every person should pay their bills on time.

4. Don't lie to anyone. They may not trust you after that.

5. Each person should spend their money wisely and save a little every day.

6. It's best to follow all the advice you give others. They will have more respect for them.

7. You should decide on a few important ones and then follow it so you set a good example.

8. When you talk to a person, look directly at them. You will be more believable.

Chapter Review

Exercise 5

Correct the mistakes.

How do you deal with unpleasant feelings?

1. Everybody should pay attention to their feelings in the life, especially negative ones. I watch own feelings very carefully.

2. I discuss with my friends.

3. My sister and my friends they help me when I feel sad or depressed.

4. I have own system. I write about them in my journal.

5. I notice all my dreams because it gives me a picture of what I am feeling.

Exercise 6

Correct the mistakes.

If there were one thing about your physical appearance you could change, what would it be?

I would change eye color. I know this sounds silly and unimportant, but here is the reason why. Everyone in family has blue eyes. Mine are green. They are not a pretty green, but a strange green. People are always asking me what color they are. Sisters and brother have deep blue eyes. The color catches your attention. I look as if I belong to a different family when I am with them. I don't think anyone is completely happy with their looks, and this is own small problem.

Exercise 7

There are five errors in the following paragraph. Correct the mistakes.

Nelson Mandela

Nelson Mandela he is a hero to many people in the world, especially black South Africans. He helped country fight against apartheid. In 1964, the government arrested for antigovernment activities. He was sentenced to prison for the rest of life. In 1990, the government released him because of international pressure. He became the voice for the antiapartheid movement, and was elected president of country in South Africa's first free election.

Exercise 1

1. __I__   <u>Women should</u> stay home and not work.
2. __I__   Smoking on all <u>airplanes should</u> be stopped.
3. __I__   If sick people want to die, a friend or doctor should be able to help them without the government arresting <u>them</u>.
4. __I__   People should be allowed to smoke marijuana if they enjoy <u>it</u>.
5. __I__   Children need to know about AIDS, and parents should discuss <u>it</u> with their children.

Exercise 2

1. Did you see <u>it</u>?
2. Did you enjoy <u>it</u>? Why or why not?
3. How many times did you watch <u>it</u>?
4. Would you recommend <u>it</u>?

Exercise 3

1. It is impolite to touch a person on <u>his</u> / <u>her</u> head.
2. People should solve <u>their</u> own problems by themselves.
3. If you don't like <u>your</u> life, it's OK to commit suicide.
4. Kids should get <u>their</u> own home when they become eighteen.
5. What happens in <u>your</u> life is decided before you are born.
6. It is OK for parents to physically punish <u>their</u> children.

Exercise 4

1. Everybody should take responsibility for <u>his</u> / <u>her</u> actions.
2. People should respect others and <u>their</u> property.
3. Every person should pay <u>his</u> / <u>her</u> bills on time.
4. Don't lie to anyone. <u>He</u> / <u>she</u> may not trust you after that.
5. Each person should spend <u>his</u> / <u>her</u> money wisely and save a little every day.
6. It's best to follow all the advice you give others. They will have more respect for <u>you</u>.
7. You should decide on a few important ones and then follow <u>them</u> so you set a good example.
8. When you talk to a person, look directly at <u>him</u> / <u>her</u>. You will be more believable.

(Concluded)

Exercise 5

1. Everybody should pay attention to <u>his</u> / <u>her</u> feelings in <u>his</u> / <u>her</u> life, especially negative ones. I watch <u>my</u> own feelings very carefully.

2. I discuss <u>them</u> with my friends.

3. My sister and my <u>friends help</u> me when I feel sad or depressed.

4. I have <u>my</u> own system. I write about them in my journal.

5. I notice all my dreams because <u>they give</u> me a picture of what I am feeling.

Exercise 6

I would change <u>my</u> eye color. I know this sounds silly and unimportant, but here is the reason why. Everyone in <u>my</u> family has blue eyes. Mine are green. They are not a pretty green, but a strange green. People are always asking me what color they are. <u>My</u> sisters and brother have deep blue eyes. The color catches your attention. I look like I belong to a different family when I am with them. I don't think anyone is completely happy with <u>his</u> / <u>her</u> looks, and this is <u>my</u> own small problem.

Exercise 7

Nelson <u>Mandela is</u> a hero to many people in the world, especially black South Africans. He helped <u>his</u> country fight against apartheid. In 1964, the government arrested <u>him</u> for antigovernment activities. He was sentenced to prison for the rest of <u>his</u> life. In 1990, the government released him because of international pressure. He became the voice for the antiapartheid movement, and was elected president of <u>his</u> country in South Africa's first free election.

CHAPTER 9

Word Choice

All ESL students have problems with word choice. Native speakers who read your sentence with a word choice error can guess what you mean, but they wouldn't use that word in that situation. (If native speakers can't understand the meaning, it would be problem number 1, "unclear.") You can improve your word choice by listening to and reading English often. Notice the expressions that native English speakers use. Second, keep a record of your word choice mistakes. You will see which ones occur again and again. These are the problems you want to focus on. At the back of this book on page 371, there is a place for you to write down your word choice errors.

This chapter focuses on some of the more common word choice errors. The organization is different from other chapters. For each section, first take the quick multiple choice test. If you miss any items, study the explanations that follow. If you get the answers right the first time, move on to the next section. The exercises at the end of the chapter will give you extra practice with common word choice problems.

Check Your Knowledge — Time Expressions

Do you have problems with time expressions? Choose the correct expression for each group. Only one answer in each is correct.

1. a. I came here three years ago.

    b. I came here before three years.

    c. I came here in three years.

2. a. I didn't learn that until now.

    b. I haven't studied that until to now.

    c. I haven't studied that up to now.

3. a. They bought a house. They moved in three weeks after.

    b. They bought a house. They moved in three weeks later.

    c. They bought a house after they moved in.

4. a. She took driving lessons. After, she got her driver's license.

    b. She took driving lessons after she got her driver's license.

    c. She took driving lessons. Afterwards, she got her driver's license.

5. a. At first, I enjoyed the people here, but now I don't.

    b. At first, I enjoy it.

    c. At first, I enjoy the people.

6. a. Then, I really like the lifestyle here.

    b. I moved to Boston. Then, I found an apartment.

    c. I moved to Boston then I found an apartment.

Check your answers: *1. a, 2. c, 3. b, 4. c, 5. a, 6. b.* If you have any mistakes, study the next section.

A Time Expressions

1. *ago*

    For an event that happened in the past, use *ago* with the simple past.

    No: I started classes three days before.

    No: I started classes before three days.

    Yes: I started classes three days **ago.**

2. *up to now*

    To talk about events that began in the past and continue in the present, use the phrase *up to now* with the present perfect.

    No: Until now, I haven't met many new friends.

    Yes: **Up to now,** I haven't met many new friends.

3. *After / later*

    After cannot follow two events that are combined in a sentence.

    No: We got engaged and then got married one year after.

    Yes: We got married one year **after** we got engaged.

    Yes: **After** we got engaged, we got married.

    Later is an adverb that goes after both events.

    Yes: We got engaged and then got married one year **later.**

4. *after / afterwards*

After is used before the first event to join two complete sentences. If you use a simple sentence and the meaning is *after that*, use *afterwards*.

No: I played tennis. After, I had an ice-cream cone.

Yes: I played tennis. **After that,** I had an ice-cream cone.

Yes: I played tennis. **Afterwards,** I had an ice-cream cone.

Yes: **After** I played tennis, I had an ice-cream cone.

Yes: I had an ice-cream cone **after** I played tennis.

5. *first / at first*

To list number one in a series, use *first. At first* means *in the beginning.* It is commonly used with the simple past.

No: At first, living here is cheaper than in my country. Second, there is less pollution.

Yes: **First,** living here is cheaper than in my country. Second, there is less pollution.

Yes: **At first,** I was surprised by the cheap prices here. Now, I'm used to them.

6. *then / next*

Then and *next* are overused. Use them at the beginning of a sentence only if you are referring to the order of events, not reasons. Do not use *then* between two sentences unless you have a period (.) before it.

No: First, I called the company, then I asked for a job application.

Yes: First, I called the company. **Then,** I asked for a job application.

Yes: First, I called the company. **Next,** I asked for a job application.

No: Then, I chose this college because of its convenient location.

No: Next, I chose this college because of its convenient location.

Yes: **Second,** I chose this college because of its convenient location.

Exercise 1

Check (✔) the sentences that have no mistakes.

Thoughts about My Life

1. _____   Until now, I have had a lot of success.

2. _____   After I finish college, I will go to graduate school.

3. _____   I am a good student because, at first, I work hard.

4. _____ I don't give up. Then, I have a positive attitude.

5. _____ Before five years I didn't have money or a job. Now I have both.

6. _____ I set a goal. Then, I work towards it.

7. _____ If I make a mistake, I accept it. I don't feel bad after.

8. _____ I have a good job. Next, I enjoy my family.

Check Your Knowledge — Verbs for Travel and Activities

Do you have problems with these verbs? Choose the correct expression for each group. Only one answer in each is correct.

1. a. I played at skiing.
   b. I went skiing.
   c. I play skiing.

2. a. We want to travel to Paris.
   b. We want to take trip to Paris.
   c. We want to trip to Paris.

3. a. I spent a very nice time here.
   b. I've had a very nice time here.
   c. I enjoy a nice time here.

4. a. They really enjoyed it.
   b. They very enjoyed it.
   c. They was really enjoy it.

5. a. When I was in Mexico for two weeks, I lived in a nice hotel.
   b. When I was in Mexico for two weeks, I stayed a nice hotel.
   c. When I was in Mexico for two weeks, I stayed in a nice hotel.

Check your answers: *1. b, 2. a, 3. b, 4. a, 5. c.* If you have mistakes, study the next section.

B Verbs for Travel and Activities

1. *play*

    In English, *play* is used for children playing together or for teenagers or adults playing specific games, such as baseball or Ping-Pong. It sounds strange to say adults *play* with their friends.

    No: I always like to play with my friends.

    Yes: I always like to **spend time with** my friends.

    Play is used with organized sports in teams or competitions.

    No: I played bowling.

    No: I'll play skiing.

    Yes: **play** golf, tennis, baseball, basketball, volleyball, soccer, football

    Yes: **go** skiing, skating, bowling, dancing, camping, swimming, running

2. *travel / take a trip*

    Trip can only be used as a noun when talking about traveling. For the verb form, use *travel* or *take a trip*.

    No: During vacation, I will trip to California.

    Yes: During vacation, I will **travel** to California.

    Yes: During vacation, I will **take a trip** to California.

3. *spend*

    Use *spend* with *time* or *money*.

    Yes: I **spent** a lot of time playing basketball when I was young.

    Yes: I went to the mall and **spent** a lot of money.

    The verb *have* is used with an adjective + *time*, such as *good time, fun time, bad time*. (Do the same with *vacation* and *stay*.)

    No: I spend a good time meeting people from other countries.

    Yes: I **have a good time** meeting people from other countries.

    No: I spent a great vacation.

    Yes: I **had a great** vacation.

    No: I spent an enjoyable stay here.

    Yes: I had **an enjoyable** stay here.

    Also possible:

    Yes: I **enjoyed** my stay here.

4. *enjoy*

Note how *enjoy* is used with *very much* or *really.*

No: I was very enjoyed it.

Yes: I **enjoyed** it **very much.**

No: I very enjoyed it.

Yes: I **really enjoyed** it.

5. *stay*

When you are vacationing for a short time, use *stay,* not *live.*

No: I lived in a romantic hotel for two weeks.

Yes: I **stayed** in a romantic hotel for two weeks.

Exercise 2

Check (✓) the sentences that have no mistakes.

What do you enjoy doing when you travel?

1. _____   I spend a lot of time talking to native speakers, not other tourists.

2. _____   For at least one night of my trip, I like to live in an expensive hotel. Then, I move to a cheaper one.

3. _____   I prefer to camp rather than stay in hotels. One thing I like about that is that I meet other people. I can play sports such as soccer and beach volleyball.

4. _____   I very enjoy sitting in cafes, drinking coffee, and watching people.

5. _____   I spend a good time walking in the early morning and watching the cities begin their day.

6. _____   I like to travel in groups because I always have someone to do something with.

7. _____   No matter where I am, I always go running first thing in the morning.

Do you have problems with these verbs? Choose the correct expression for each group. Only one answer in each is correct.

1. a. She studied German because she wanted to learn about the culture.
   b. She studied German because she wanted to know the culture.
   c. She studied German because she wanted to learn the culture.

2. a. I was break my car on the freeway.
   b. My car broke down on the freeway.
   c. My car was broken on the freeway.

3. a. I took some medicine.
   b. I drank some medicine.
   c. I ate some medicine.

4. a. I wish I can pass.
   b. I hope I can pass.
   c. I wish I will pass.

5. a. My friend told to me the answer.
   b. My friend said me the answer.
   c. My friend told me the answer.

6. a. We couldn't speak or hear English at all.
   b. We couldn't speak or listen English at all.
   c. We couldn't speak or understand English at all.

7. a. He made a company when he was twenty-one years old.
   b. He was make a company when he was twenty-one years old.
   c. He started a company when he was twenty-one years old.

8. a. I plan to study math class.
   b. I plan to take a math class.
   c. I plan to learn a math class.

9. a. People share their ideas with each other.
   b. People open mind each other.
   c. People are open mind each other.

Check your answers: *1. a, 2. b, 3. a, 4. b, 5. c, 6. c, 7. c, 8. b, 9. a.* If you have mistakes, study the next section.

C Other Verbs

1. *to learn or know about a subject*

   When you are talking about getting more information about a subject, you need to use *about* with *learn* or *know*.

   No: They want to learn Chinese culture.

   No: They want to know Chinese culture.

   Yes: They want to **learn about** Chinese culture.

   Yes: They want to **know about** Chinese culture.

2. *break / work / break down*

   No: My car was broken.

   Yes: My car wasn't **working.** (It didn't go.)

   Yes: My car **broke down.** (It suddenly quit working.)

3. *eat / take*

   Eat is used for meals. *Take* is used for medicines.

   No: I took breakfast with my family.

   Yes: I **ate** breakfast with my family.

   (Note: *Have* is also possible: I **had** breakfast with my family.)

   No: I ate some aspirin.

   Yes: I **took** some aspirin.

   No: I drank some cough medicine.

   Yes: I **took** some cough medicine.

4. *wish / hope*

   Hope is used with *can* and *will* to express a possible event. *Wish* is used with *could* and *would* to express an impossible event.

   No: I wish I can go there.

   Yes: I **hope** I **can** go there.

   Yes: I **wish** I **could** go there.

   No: I wish everything will be OK.

   Yes: I **hope** everything **will** be OK.

   Yes: I **wish** everything **would** be OK.

5. *say / tell*

When *say* is used with an indirect object such as *me,* you need to use *to.* Or, you can use *tell* without *to.*

No: My father said me that he was going to come.

Yes: My father **said to me** that he was going to come.

Yes: My father **told me** that he was going to come.

Tell is used with *tell a joke, tell a secret, tell a story.*

No: My grandmother said to me a story.

Yes: My grandmother **told me a story.**

6. *hear / listen / understand*

Hear means your ear recognizes a sound. *Listen* means you pay attention to what you hear. *Hear* and *listen* don't mean you understand. You need to use the verb *understand.*

No: I couldn't speak or hear English at all.

No: I couldn't speak or listen English at all.

Yes: I couldn't speak or **understand** English at all.

7. *make / cause*

The use of *make* is idiomatic. In these cases, the specific verb is used instead.

No: I want to make a company.

Yes: I want to **start** a company.

No: I made my own company.

Yes: I **started** my own company.

No: Cars make a lot of air pollution.

Yes: Cars **cause** a lot of air pollution.

8. *take / study*

Take is used when referring to a *class. Study* is used with a specific subject.

Yes: I want to **take an English class.**

Yes: I want to **study English.** (the subject, not a class)

9. *mind*

Mind is not used as a verb except in the sense of *care* (e.g., *Do you mind if I sit here? = Do you care if I sit here?)* *Open-minded* can be used as an adjective.

No: People are open mind each other.

Yes: People can share their feelings (or their ideas) with each other.

Yes: She is open-minded.

Check (✓) the sentences that have no mistakes.

My Grandmother's Plans

1. _____ She wants to go on an Alaskan cruise and study some nature classes.

2. _____ She plans to buy a used car, but will be careful not to get a broken one.

3. _____ She said me that her biggest dream is to have a family reunion.

4. _____ She would like to know flower arranging.

5. _____ She wishes she can meet all her great-grandchildren before she dies.

6. _____ She can read French but she can't hear it so she wants to visit a French-speaking country.

7. _____ She wants to share her feelings more honestly with her children.

8. _____ She plans to give her son some money so he can make a new company.

9. _____ Most important, she is going to get new glasses so she doesn't drink the wrong medicine.

Check Your Knowledge Common Expressions

Do you have problems with these common expressions? Choose the correct expression for each group. Only one answer in each is correct.

1. a. In the other words, I am really happy to be here.

    b. In other words, I am really happy to be here.

    c. Another words, I am really happy to be here.

2. a. In other hand, living with a host family has several advantages.

    b. On another hand, living with a host family has several advantages.

    c. On the other hand, living with a host family has several advantages.

3. a. Other countries' people do not have the same customs.

    b. Another countries' people do not have the same customs.

    c. People from other countries do not have the same customs.

4. a. English is spoken around the world.

   b. English is spoken all the world.

   c. English is spoken in the world.

5. a. I read to find out about other cultures.

   b. I read for finding out about other cultures.

   c. I read for find out about other cultures.

Check your answers: *1. b, 2. c, 3. c, 4. a, 5. a.* If you have mistakes, study the next section.

D Common Expressions

1. *in other words / on the other hand*

   Make sure when using idiomatic expressions that you have the exact words. You cannot use similar sounding words.

   No: Another words, it was great.

   Yes: **In other words,** it was great.

   No: I had a bad time. In other hand, my friends had a great time.

   Yes: I had a bad time. **On the other hand,** my friends had a great time.

2. *all over the world / around the world*

   When you are talking about something that happens all over the world, use the phrase *all over the world* or *around the world.*

   No: English is useful in the world.

   Yes: English is useful **all over the world.**

   Yes: English is useful **around the world.**

   With superlatives (*the biggest, the most . . .* , etc.) use *in the world.*

   Yes: The tallest building **in the world** is in Malaysia.

   Note how *in the world* is used:

   No: People in the world drink coffee.

   Yes: Some people **in the world** drink coffee.

   Yes: Most people **in the world** drink tea.

   Yes: People **around the world** drink coffee.

3. *people from other countries*

   When talking about people from other countries, you cannot make it possessive.

   No: I like to meet other countries' people.

   Yes: I like to meet **people from other countries.**

4. *to / in order to*

In order to is used to express purpose. You can use the complete phrase *in order to* or you can use *to* + the simple form of a verb.

No: I watched TV for learning English.

Yes: I watched TV **to learn** English.

Yes: I watched TV **in order to learn** English.

Exercise 4

There are five mistakes in this paragraph. Can you find and correct them?

Why People Visit Here

Other countries' people really enjoy the scenery. The mountains are breathtaking. A lot of people come here for hike and climb. One of the most beautiful lakes around the world is here. Although it is very calm and has the color of emeralds, it is extremely cold all year round. Another words, people don't come here to swim in it. They would rather relax on the beach or enjoy the view from the lodge. I, in other hand, climb the mountains for the best view.

Check Your Knowledge   **Other Common Word Choice Problems**

Here are some other common word choice problems. Choose the correct expression for each group. Only one answer in each is correct.

1. a. He repeated what I said.

    b. He repeated that I said.

    c. He repeated I said.

2. a. Even my friend has to work sixty hours a week, she enjoys it.

    b. My friend enjoys her job even she has to work sixty hours a week.

    c. Even if my friend has to work sixty hours a week, she enjoys it.

3. a. I need more speaking practice with Native Americans.

    b. I need more speaking practice with native speakers.

    c. I need more speaking practice with natives.

4. a. I'm studying for my master degree.

   b. I'm studying for my master's.

   c. I'm studying for my master.

Check your answers: *1. a, 2. c, 3. b, 4. b.* If you have mistakes, study the next section.

E Other Common Word Choice Problems

1. *what / that*

   What and *that* are used to begin noun clauses. *What* introduces a reported question. *That* introduces a reported statement.

   Yes: She asked me **what** I wanted.   ("What do you want?")

   Yes: She told me **that** she wanted some new clothes.   ("I want some new clothes.")

   That or *who* is used to begin an adjective clause. An adjective clause describes a noun.

   No: She was a person what helped me a lot.

   Yes: She was a person **that** helped me a lot.

   Yes: She was a person **who** helped me a lot.

2. *in our life / in the life*
   for my future / for my future life

   These phrases are very general. Try to be more specific. One way to do this is to write about yourself or your situation.

   No: It is important to succeed in our life.   (general)

   No: It is important to succeed in the life.   (general)

   Yes: I want to **have a successful life.**

   Yes: I want to **succeed in life.**

   No: I need English for my future.   (unclear)

   No: I need English for my future life.   (unclear)

   Yes: I need to know English **for my future job.**

3. *even if*

   Use *even if* to express an unexpected result.

   No: I want to take more ESL classes even I get a high TOEFL test score.

   Yes: I want to take more ESL classes **even if** I get a high TOEFL test score.

4. *Native Americans*

In the United States, *Native Americans* is used to describe American Indians.

No: When I talk with Native Americans, I can practice my English.
(not correct unless you are speaking about American Indians)

No: When I talk with natives, I can practice my English.

Yes: When I talk with **Americans,** I can practice my English.

Yes: When I talk with **native speakers,** I can practice my English.

5. *bachelor's degree, master's degree*

These expressions use the possessive form.

No: I'm going to study for a master.

Yes: I'm going to study for a **master's degree.**

No: My brother received his bachelor degree.

Yes: My brother received his **bachelor's degree.**

Yes: My brother received his **bachelor's.**

Exercise 5

Write C for correct and I for incorrect. Then correct the mistakes, and circle *yes* or *no.*

What's Your Opinion?

Agree or disagree?

1. _____ Talking with natives will help my

speaking / listening skills.   yes   no

2. _____ I need to have a master's degree.   yes   no

3. _____ Even I study English for five years, I won't

speak fluently.   yes   no

4. _____ It is easy to get a bachelors' degree.   yes   no

5. _____ I like to speak English even I make mistakes.   yes   no

6. _____ English will help my future.   yes   no

7. _____ It is more important for me to be successful

at work than at home.   yes   no

8. _____ Happiness is that I want most in life.   yes   no

Chapter Review

Exercise 6

Write C for correct or I for incorrect. Then correct the mistakes.

Why are you studying English?

1. _____ I know that English is very useful in the world.

2. _____ I'm studying English for passing the university entrance exam.

3. _____ Knowing English will help me to speak to people from

   other countries.

4. _____ I want to be able to understand movies what are in English.

5. _____ In my work I need to talk to native people.

6. _____ Of course I need English because I live in an

   English-speaking country.

7. _____ I want to talk to the children my daughter plays with.

8. _____ It's fun to study an English class.

9. _____ I'm going to get a master degree in business.

10. _____ I want to travel and talk to other country's people.

Exercise 7

Write C for correct and I for incorrect. Then correct the mistakes.

My Father

1. _____ My father came here before three years.

2. _____ He moved here in January and four months after, he found a job

   as a mechanic.

3. _____ Up to now, he has enjoyed living here.

4. _____ He wants to stay here for about five more years. After, he plans

to return to his hometown.

5. _____ He hopes to retire and spend the rest of his life with his friends

and family in his native country.

6. _____ Even my father goes back to his native country, he will continue

to visit me here.

Exercise 8

Write **C** for correct and **I** for incorrect. Then correct the mistakes.

A Bad Experience

1. _____ My worst experience was when my car was broken in the desert.

2. _____ When I was a child, a friend said to all of my classmates my

biggest secret.

3. _____ I was on a basketball team. At first, we did pretty well, but then

we lost the rest of our games.

4. _____ I didn't listen English well, so I couldn't talk to anyone my first

time in England.

5. _____ When I traveled to another country, I lost my passport.

6. _____ I broke my leg when I played skiing.

7. _____ There was a big war in my country. I haven't forgotten it

until now.

8. _____ I didn't like my teacher in school. I didn't understand that

she said.

Exercise 9

Correct the mistakes.

A Good Vacation

I had a very good vacation last year. A friend and I tripped to northern Mexico. We lived in a hotel at the beach for a week. I got to play waterskiing for the first time. I was very enjoyed it. Unfortunately, my friend and I knew only a little Spanish, so when we were shopping in town, we couldn't hear what most Mexican people said. Luckily, some Mexicans spoke English. It showed me that English is useful in the world. The best part of the trip was learning Mexican culture. We went to a "fiesta," which is a Mexican party. We played dancing and tried to break a "piñata," a type of Mexican game. The only bad part of the trip was that I got sick. I ate some medicine, which helped me feel better. I hope I could go back to Mexico again someday.

Exercise 1

1. _____ Until now, I have had a lot of success.
2. ✓ After I finish college, I will go to graduate school.
3. _____ I am a good student because, at first, I work hard.
4. _____ I don't give up. Then, I have a positive attitude.
5. _____ Before five years I didn't have money or a job. Now I have both.
6. ✓ I set a goal. Then, I work towards it.
7. _____ If I make a mistake, I accept it. I don't feel bad after.
8. _____ I have a good job. Next, I enjoy my family.

Exercise 2

1. ✓ I spend a lot of time talking to native speakers, not other tourists.
2. _____ For at least one night of my trip, I like to live in an expensive hotel. Then I move to a cheaper one.
3. ✓ I prefer to camp rather than stay in hotels. One thing I like about that is that I meet other people. I can play sports such as soccer and beach volleyball.
4. _____ I very enjoy sitting in cafes, drinking coffee, and watching people.
5. _____ I spend a good time walking in the early morning and watching the cities begin their day.
6. ✓ I like to travel in groups because I always have someone to do something with.
7. ✓ No matter where I am, I always go running first thing in the morning.

Exercise 3

1. _____ She wants to go on an Alaskan cruise and study some nature classes.
2. _____ She plans to buy a used car, but will be careful not to get a broken one.
3. _____ She said me that her biggest dream is to have a family reunion.
4. _____ She would like to know flower arranging.
5. _____ She wishes she can meet all her great-grandchildren before she dies.
6. _____ She can read French but she can't hear it so she wants to visit a French-speaking country.
7. ✓ She wants to share her feelings more honestly with her children.
8. _____ She plans to give her son some money so he can make a new company.
9. _____ Most important, she is going to get new glasses so she doesn't drink the wrong medicine.

Exercise 4

    <u>People from other countries</u> really enjoy the scenery. The mountains are breathtaking. A lot of people come here <u>to</u> hike and climb. One of the most beautiful lakes <u>in</u> the world is here. Although it is very calm and has the color of emeralds, it is extremely cold all year round. <u>In other</u> words, people don't come here to swim in it. They would rather relax on the beach or enjoy the view from the lodge. I, <u>on the</u> other hand, climb the mountains for the best view.

Exercise 5

1. __I__ Talking with <u>native speakers</u> will help my speaking / listening skills.
2. __C__ I need to have a master's degree.
3. __I__ Even <u>if</u> I study English for five years, I won't speak fluently.
4. __I__ It is easy to get a bachelor<u>'s</u> degree.
5. __I__ I like to speak English even <u>if</u> I make mistakes.
6. __I__ English will help my future <u>job</u> / <u>plans</u> / <u>etc</u>.
7. __C__ It is more important for me to be successful at work than at home.
8. __I__ Happiness is <u>what</u> I want most in life.

Exercise 6

1. __I__ I know that English is very useful <u>all over</u> / <u>around</u> the world.
2. __I__ I'm studying English <u>to pass</u> the university entrance exam.
3. __C__ Knowing English will help me to speak to people from other countries.
4. __I__ I want to be able to understand movies <u>that</u> are in English.
5. __I__ In my work I need to talk to native <u>speakers</u>.
6. __C__ Of course I need English because I live in an English-speaking country.
7. __C__ I want to talk to the children my daughter plays with.
8. __I__ It's fun to <u>take</u> an English class.
9. __I__ I'm going to get a <u>master's</u> degree in business.
10. __I__ I want to travel and talk to <u>people from other countries</u>.

(Concluded)

Exercise 7

1. ___I___ My father came here three years <u>ago</u>.

2. ___I___ He moved here in January and four months <u>later</u>, he found a job as a mechanic.

3. ___C___ Up to now, he has enjoyed living here.

4. ___I___ He wants to stay here for about five more years. <u>Afterwards</u>, he plans to return to his hometown.

5. ___C___ He hopes to retire and spend the rest of his life with his friends and family in his native country.

6. ___I___ Even <u>if</u> my father goes back to his native country, he will continue to visit me here.

Exercise 8

1. ___I___ My worst experience was when my car <u>broke down</u> in the desert.

2. ___I___ When I was a child, a friend <u>told</u> all of my classmates my biggest secret.

3. ___C___ I was on a basketball team. At first, we did pretty well, but then we lost the rest of our games.

4. ___I___ I didn't <u>understand</u> English well, so I couldn't talk to anyone my first time in England.

5. ___C___ When I traveled to another country, I lost my passport.

6. ___I___ I broke my leg when I <u>went</u> skiing.

7. ___I___ There was a big war in my country. I haven't forgotten it <u>up to now</u>.

8. ___I___ I didn't like my teacher in school. I didn't understand <u>what</u> she said.

Exercise 9

I had a very good vacation last year. A friend and I <u>took a trip</u> / traveled to northern Mexico. We <u>stayed</u> in a hotel at the beach for a week. I got to <u>go</u> waterskiing for the first time. I <u>really</u> enjoyed it. Unfortunately, my friend and I knew only a little Spanish, so when we were shopping in town, we couldn't <u>understand</u> what most Mexican people said. Luckily, some Mexicans spoke English. It showed me that English is useful <u>all over</u> / <u>around</u> the world. The best part of the trip was learning <u>about</u> Mexican culture. We went to a "fiesta," which is a Mexican party. We <u>went</u> dancing and tried to break a "piñata," a type of Mexican game. The only bad part of the trip was that I got sick. I <u>took</u> some medicine, which helped me feel better. I hope I <u>can</u> go back to Mexico again someday.

CHAPTER 10

Word Form

A word form error occurs when you have the correct word but the wrong form of that word. Sometimes a dictionary can help you find the correct word form. In other cases, you can memorize the common forms. You can also pay attention to word forms as you read or listen to English.

A Problems with Parts of Speech

Can you find the problems in these sentences?

No: I live in a freedom country.

Yes: I live in a **free** country.

No: I hope to be success in this class.

Yes: I hope to be **successful** in this class.

- Use the correct form of a word for its use in the sentence.

- Here are common uses of parts of speech (*noun, adjective, verb, adverb*) in sentences:

Nouns are people, animals, places, things, and ideas. They occur as the following:

Subject:	**Freedom** is an important idea for most people.
Object:	Most people want **freedom.**
After a possessive:	A person's **freedom** is very important.
Object of preposition:	I believe **in freedom.**
After a *be* verb:	An important idea is **freedom.** (**idea** = **freedom**)

Adjectives describe nouns. They come as follows:

Before a noun: We live in a **free** country.

After a *be* verb: This country is **free.**

(In this sentence, **free** describes **this country**)

Verbs describe actions or "being." They come as follows:

After a subject: The park rangers **freed** the captured animal.

In infinitive form: They chose **to free** the captured animal.

(after some verbs)

Adverbs describe verbs, adjectives, or other adverbs. They come as follows:

After a verb: Ms. Roth spoke **freely** about animal rights.

(**freely** describes **spoke**)

After a verb + object: She shared her opinions **freely.**

(**freely** describes **shared**)

Before an adjective: The **very** large crowd applauded after the speech.

(**very** describes **large**)

Before another adverb: She spoke **very** persuasively on the subject.

(**very** describes **persuasively**)

See Appendix 3 on page 333 for more information on word forms.

Exercise 1

Write the word form (*n, adj, v, adv*) above the underlined words. If you are not sure, check a dictionary.

From a Class Syllabus

n = noun
adj = adjective
v = verb
adv = adverb

1. Attendance is very important.
   n

2. It is the student's responsibility to do all of the assignments.
   n   *n*

3. Students are responsible for keeping a journal.
   adv

4. Any late homework should be made up quickly.
   adj

5. Students should participate in class discussions.
   v   *n*

Exercise 2

Have you ever read an advice column in a newspaper? This exercise is based on a letter to Marie and her letter back to the reader. First, study the chart below. Then fill in the blanks in the exercise with the correct form of the word in parentheses.

Verb	Noun	Adjective	Adverb
differ	difference	different	differently
xxxx	patience	patient	patiently
approve	approval	xxxx	xxxx
persuade	persuasion	persuasive	persuasively
advise	advice (noncount)	xxxx	xxxx
worry	worry	worried	xxxx
marry	marriage	married	xxxx
get married			

A "Dear Marie" Letter

Ask Marie

Dear Marie,

I have a big problem. I want to ____marry____ (marry) my boyfriend,

but my parents don't ____approve____ (approve). They don't like my

boyfriend because he was ____married____ (marry) before. They are very

____worried____ (worry) that our ____marriage____ (marry) will not last. I

love him very much. What can I do to ____persuade____ (persuade) my

parents to ____approve____ (approve) of my boyfriend? I need your

____advice____ (advise).

Sincerely,

Troubled

Dear Troubled,

You need to be _____patient_____ (patience). Perhaps you and your

parents have very _____different_____ (differ) ideas about the subject of

_____marriage_____ (marry). It's natural for your parents to _____worry_____

(worry) about you. I _____advise_____ (advise) you to let your parents get to

know your boyfriend well. Maybe then they will think _____differently_____

(differ) about him. If not, you will need to decide if you want to

_____marry_____ (marry) without your parents' _____approval_____ (approve).

Good luck!

Sincerely,

Marie

Exercise 3

First, fill in the chart with the correct form of the word. You may want to use your dictionary. Then, complete the sentences with the correct form of the word in parentheses.

Verb	Noun	Adjective	Adverb
xxxx	peace	peaceful	peacefully
xxxx	noise	noisy	noisily
xxxx	safeness	safe	safely
xxxx	health	healthy	xxxx
xxxx	danger	dangerous	dangerously

About My City

1. One thing I like about my city is that it is a very ___peaceful___ (peace)

   place to live.

2. When I'm downtown, it's ___noisy___ (noise), but I am

   ___safe___ (safety) even at night.

3. There may be some ___dangerous___ (danger) parts of town, but I've

   never seen them.

4. I often go jogging, even at night, because I want to stay

   ___healthy___ (health).

5. It's a wonderful feeling to live in ___peace___ (peace).

Exercise 4

First, fill in the chart with the correct form of the word. You may want to use your dictionary. Then, complete the sentences with the correct form of the word in parentheses.

Verb	Noun	Adjective	Adverb
suggest	suggestion	xxxx	xxxx
succeed	success	successful	successfully
agree	agreement	xxxx	xxxx
xxxx	homesickness	homesick	xxxx
xxxx	loneliness	lonely	xxxx

Suggestions for Schools with International Students

1. I have some ___suggestions___ (suggest) to help international students.

2. Of course, all students who are living far from home are _homesick_
(homesickness) and _lonely_ (loneliness) sometimes.

3. I _suggest_ (suggest) that we form a club, which will help
students deal with their _✓_ (loneliness).

4. If students have more friends, they will probably be _succeed_
(success) in classes, too.

5. We are in _agreement_ (agree) that most students want to
succeed (success) in school.

B Country / Nationality / Language

Can you find the errors in the following?

No: Young went to a Korea high school.
Yes: Young went to a **Korean** high school.

No: We had Mexico food last night.
Yes: We had **Mexican** food last night.

No: Caroline is from French.
Yes: Caroline is from **France.**

- Use the correct word form for a country, nationality, and language.
- Here is a list of common forms and some unusual forms:

Country (noun)	Nationality (adjective)	Language (noun)
Korea	Korean	Korean
Mexico	Mexican	
Vietnam	Vietnamese	Vietnamese
Poland	Polish	Polish
France	French	French
Germany	German	German
Greece	Greek	Greek
Switzerland	Swiss	

See Appendix 3C on pages 335–336 for a more complete list.

Exercise 5

First circle your answer to the question. Then correct the mistake in each answer.

Choices

1. Which food do you think is spicier: Vietnam or Korean? *[handwritten: Vietnamese]*

2. Which country would you prefer to visit: France or German? *[handwritten correction]*

3. Which nationality would you guess are the names "Polaski"

    and "Walenza:" Switzerland or Polish? *[handwritten: Swiss]*

4. Which language would you like to know: France or Vietnamese?

5. Which kind of restaurant are there more of in your area: Mexican

    or Greece?

C Verb-*ing* and Verb-*ed* as Adjectives

Look at these sentences. What is the difference between the correct ones and the incorrect ones?

No: I went to a very excited baseball game.

Yes: I went to a very **exciting** baseball game.

No: I loved the game. However, my friend was boring.

Yes: I loved the game. However, my friend was **bored.**

- Some expressions use verb-*ing* or verb-*ed* as an adjective. The difference in meaning depends on who or what causes or receives the action.

- Use the correct form (verb-*ing* or verb-*ed*) as in this example:

V
The math class **bores** me.

Adj   Adj
The math class is **boring.** ⟶ I am **bored.**
Cause ⟶ Effect

Here are some common participial adjectives:

To describe what causes the feeling:	To describe who has the feeling:
interesting	interested
exciting	excited
boring	bored
frightening	frightened
confusing	confused
tiring	tired
exhausting	exhausted (very, very tired)
embarrassing	embarrassed
depressing	depressed (very sad)

Exercise 6

Write C for correct or I for incorrect. Then correct the mistakes.

Book Reviews

1. __I__ I thought *Gone with the Wind* was really excited.

2. __I__ When I read *Anna Karenina,* I was confusing because there were so many characters.

3. __C__ When I was a child, I was depressed when Charlotte died in *Charlotte's Web.*

4. __I__ In high school, we read *The Old Man and the Sea.* I was really boring.

5. __C__ *Shogun* was really interesting. I couldn't put it down.

Exercise 7

How do you feel about the following? Consider your own ideas and the correct grammar. Then circle one answer for each sentence.

What's Your Opinion?

1. Watching a basketball game is (exciting)   boring   excited   bored.

2. When I watch a romantic movie, I am usually   interesting   boring   (interested)   bored.

3. After I exercise a lot, I usually feel   tiring   exhausting   (tired)   exhausted.

4. I think English grammar is   interesting   confusing   (interested)   confused.

5. Forgetting someone's name is   (embarrassing)   depressing   embarrassed   depressed.

D   Verb + Gerund or Infinitive?

Look at the following sentences. Which sentences are correct? Check your knowledge by circling the letter of the correct expressions.

like (Two sentences are correct.)
a. I like sleep late.
b. I like to sleep late.
c. I like sleeping late.

know
a. I want know more about this city.
b. I want to know more about this city.

tell
a. He told me to get a better dictionary.
b. He told to get a better dictionary.

finish
a. I finished to study for my test.
b. I finished studying for my test.

be interested
a. I am interested to study English.
b. I am interested in studying English.

be busy
a. I am busy to work on my lesson.
b. I am busy working on my lesson.

(Answers: like: b, c; know: b; tell: a; finish: b; be interested: b; be busy: b)

- When a main verb is followed directly by another verb, the second verb is in the gerund (verb + *ing*) or infinitive (*to* + verb) form. Use the correct gerund or infinitive form.

- A few verbs can take either a gerund or infinitive. Many verbs need a gerund. Other verbs need an infinitive.

- Some verbs need an object + infinitive: *He told **me to get** a better dictionary.*

- Some verbs need a preposition + gerund: *I am interested **in studying** English.*

- Here are some common verbs with gerund / infinitive forms after the verb:

    1. Verb + gerund or infinitive (both are OK and have the same meaning):

       love, like, dislike, hate, prefer, start, begin, continue

       Example: He hates discussing politics.

                        She hates to talk about sports.

    2. Verb + infinitive only:

       ask (for yourself), decide, expect, hope, need, plan, promise, want, would like

       Example: I asked to leave early.

                        Tom needs to plan his vacation.

    3. Verb + object (someone, person's name, me, him, her, them, etc.) + infinitive:

       advise, allow, ask (for another person), invite, let*, tell

       Example: I asked someone to open the window.

                        Sherry invited her class to come to a party.

       **Note:* with the verbs *let, help* or *make* use the bare infinitive (no *to*)

       Example: My parents **let me go** to college in another city.

    4. Verb + gerund only:

       enjoy, discuss, finish, give up, keep (on), quit

       Example: I enjoy going to outdoor concerts.

    5. Expression + preposition + gerund:

       be excited about, be worried about, complain about, talk about, apologize for, be responsible for, have a good reason for, thank you for, be interested in, be in charge of

       Example: I apologize for coming late.

    6. Other expressions + gerund only:

       have a difficult time, have difficulty, have a hard time, have trouble, have a good time, have fun, be busy

       Example: We had a good time making pies.

See Appendix 4 on page 337 for a more complete list of common verbs that can be followed by gerunds and / or infinitives.

Exercise 8   Fill in the blank with the correct gerund or infinitive form. You may also need to add a preposition or object.

My Ideal Profession

1. I've always wanted (try) __to try__ acting. I think I could be a good actor, but my parents never allowed (take) __me to take__ acting lessons.

2. As soon as I finish (study) __studing__ English, I want (open) __to open__ my own restaurant. I love (cook) __cooking__.

3. I enjoy (sing) __singing__. I hope (become) __to become__ an opera singer.

4. I plan (be) __To be__ a full-time mother. I think the parents are responsible (raise) __for raising__ their children. I could never ask (take care of) __someone to take care of__ my child.

5. I wanted (play) __to play__ professional baseball, but I gave up (play) __playing__ sports because of back problems. I have trouble (sit) __in sitting__ now, but maybe I could coach baseball. I would be excited (help) __about helping__ younger players.

E Almost / Most

Can you find the problems in these sentences?

No: Almost Americans have a TV.

Yes: **Almost all** Americans have a TV.

Yes: **Most** Americans have a TV.

- *Almost* means nearly or about 80 percent to 99 percent. It cannot be used directly before a noun. It is often used before the word *all*.

- *Almost* can come directly before adjectives or the pronouns *everyone* and *everybody* as in the following examples:

    My daughter is almost tall enough to reach the TV.

    It seems that almost everyone has a TV.

- Use *most* with a noun.

Exercise 9

Choose *almost* or *most* in the following sentences.

School Schedules

1. (Almost / Most) schools in North America begin in the fall and finish in the spring.

2. (Almost / Most) all schools in Japan begin the school year in April.

3. There is some kind of vacation around New Year's Day in (almost / most) countries.

4. In Korea, (almost / most) high school students study at school until 7 or 8 P.M.

5. (Almost / Most) everyone wants a break, but after a long vacation, students are (almost / most) ready to come back to school.

F ***This / These* and *Another / Other***

Can you find the problems in the following sentences?

No: This problems must be solved.

Yes: **These** problems must be solved.

No: There is other reason why I love baseball.

Yes: There is **another** reason why I love baseball.

Yes: There are **other** reasons why I love baseball.

No: I have another sisters living in Ohio.

Yes: I have **another** sister living in Ohio.

Yes: I have **other** sisters living in Ohio.

• Use the correct form of *this / these* and *another / other*.

Here are the correct forms:

this + singular noun	*these* + plural noun
another + singular noun (means "one more" or "a different one")	*other* + plural noun (means "two," "several," or "many more")

Exercise 10

Write **C** for correct and **I** for incorrect. Then correct the mistakes.

Sports Facts

1. ___C___ Baseball uses a bat. Another sport that uses a bat is cricket.

2. ___I___ In American football, you can make points with a touchdown and

    an extra point kick. Another ways to get points in these game are

    with a field goal or a safety.

3. ___I___ Volleyball uses a high net. Other sport that uses a high net is

    badminton.

4. ___C___ Soccer is very popular in Sweden. Other popular sports there are

    skiing, tennis, badminton, and table tennis.

5. ___I___ Golf is becoming more popular in the United States. Another

    sports gaining popularity are rollerblading and walking. You can

    do this sports alone or with a friend.

G Comparative and Superlative Adjectives

Can you discover the problems in these sentences?

No: It was the most happiest day of my life.

Yes: It was the **happiest** day of my life.

No: It was bad, more bad than last time.

Yes: It was **worse** than last time.

- Use the correct adjective forms when you compare two or more people, objects, or events.

Here are some comparative and superlative forms:

	Adjective	Comparing two	More than two
One syllable:	tall	taller than	the tallest
Ends in *y*:	happy	happier than	the happiest
Two or more syllables:	intelligent	more intelligent than	the most intelligent
Irregular:	good	better than	the best
	bad	worse than	the worst

Exercise 11

Correct the mistakes.

Exams

1. When I took the college entrance exam, it was the ~~most~~ difficult test in my life.

2. High school exams were more hard*er* than college exams.

3. The most big*gest* reason I hate exams is I forget the information.

4. The worse*t* test I ever took was a math test.

5. My last test was ~~easy, more~~ *easier* than the first one.

Chapter Review

Exercise 12

Write *C* for correct and I for incorrect. Then correct the mistakes.

Advice to Parents

1. __C__ I suggest that you keep your baby warm. Don't let her get

   too cold.

2. __I__ I think you should let your teenagers to have some freedom.

   Don't be too controlling.

3. __C__ You need to love and respect your children. Each one

   is different.

4. __I__ Almost parents need to talk to their children more often.

5. __I__ Don't allow your children to watch too much TV. Other problem

   is spending too much time on the computer.

6. __C__ Talk to your baby all the time. He'll learn to talk sooner.

7. ___I___ Make your house a safety place so your children won't get hurt.

8. ___C___ A good marriage is important for a healthy family.

9. ___I___ Babies don't sleep well when it is noise, so keep the house quiet during naps.

10. ___C___ If you promise to do something, be sure to do it!

Exercise 13

There are nine mistakes in the following paragraph. Can you find and correct them?

Fall

Fall is my favorite season. I enjoy to see [Seeing] the red, orange, and yellow leaves on the trees. The air is freshly [fresh] and cleanly [clean] after an autumn rain. All of the children are back in [to] school. They are so exciting [excited] as they walk to their classes to meet their new teacher and classmates. In these [this] country, there are also some interested [interesting] holidays in fall, such as Halloween and Thanksgiving. Of course, the weather becomes cold, more cold [colder] than in summer. For some people, cold weather is depressed [depressing] but I like it. You can see why fall is my most best [best] time of year.

Exercise 14

Correct the mistakes.

Advice to ESL Students

Learning English as a Second Language is difficult, but you can learn more quickly if you follow this suggestions. One way to help your English comprehension is by listening to fast English on the radio and television every day. Even if you don't understand everything, don't be worry. It will be more easy little by little. You just need to be patience. Other way to help your English is to talk a lot with native speakers of English. In these case, don't be shyness. You need talk in English, even if it is difficulty. When you try to speak English, don't be confusing. Just relax and use simple English. My last suggest is to think in English. When you are by yourself, try to think in English. It will become easier for you to use English vocabulary and sentences. If you begin thinking in your own language, don't give up. Keep on to use English. I hope you will follow my advise.

Exercise 1

1. <u>Attendance</u> = n
2. <u>responsibility</u> = n   <u>assignments</u> = n
3. <u>responsible</u> = adj
4. <u>quickly</u> = adv
5. <u>participate</u> = v   <u>discussions</u> = n

Exercise 2

Dear Marie,

I have a big problem. I want to <u>marry</u> (marry) my boyfriend, but my parents don't <u>approve</u> (approve). They don't like my boyfriend because he was <u>married</u> (marry) before. They are very <u>worried</u> (worry) that our <u>marriage</u> (marry) will not last. I love him very much. What can I do to <u>persuade</u> (persuade) my parents to <u>approve</u> (approve) of my boyfriend? I need your <u>advice</u> (advise).

Sincerely,
Troubled

Dear Troubled,

You need to be <u>patient</u> (patience). Perhaps you and your parents have very <u>different</u> (differ) ideas about the subject of <u>marriage</u> (marry). It's natural for your parents to <u>worry</u> (worry) about you. I <u>advise</u> (advise) you to let your parents get to know your boyfriend well. Maybe then they will think <u>differently</u> (differ) about him. If not, you will need to decide if you want to <u>get married</u> (marry) without your parents' <u>approval</u> (approve).

Sincerely,
Marie

Exercise 3

Verb	Noun	Adjective	Adverb
xxxx	peace	<u>peaceful</u>	<u>peacefully</u>
xxxx	noise	<u>noisy</u>	<u>noisily</u>
xxxx	<u>safety</u>	safe	<u>safely</u>
xxxx	health	<u>healthy</u>	xxxx
xxxx	danger	<u>dangerous</u>	<u>dangerously</u>

1. peaceful
2. noisy, safe
3. dangerous
4. healthy
5. peace

(Continued)

Exercise 4

Verb	Noun	Adjective	Adverb
suggest	suggestion	xxxx	xxxx
succeed	success	successful	successfully
agree	agreement	xxxx	xxxx
xxxx	homesickness	homesick	xxxx
xxxx	loneliness	lonely	xxxx

1. suggestions
2. homesick, lonely
3. suggest, loneliness
4. successful
5. agreement, succeed

Exercise 5

1. Vietnamese or Korean
2. France or Germany
3. Swiss or Polish
4. French or Vietnamese
5. Mexican or Greek

Exercise 6

1. __I__ I thought *Gone with the Wind* was really exciting.
2. __I__ When I read *Anna Karenina*, I was confused because there were so many characters.
3. __C__ When I was a child, I was depressed when Charlotte died in *Charlotte's Web*.
4. __I__ In high school, we read *The Old Man and the Sea*. I was really bored.
5. __C__ *Shogun* was really interesting. I couldn't put it down.

Exercise 7

1. exciting *or* boring
2. interested *or* bored
3. tired *or* exhausted
4. interesting *or* confusing
5. embarrassing *or* depressing

(Continued)

Exercise 8

1. to try, me to take
2. studying, to open, cooking / to cook
3. singing, to become
4. to be, for raising, someone to take care of
5. to play, playing, sitting, about helping

Exercise 9

1. <u>Most</u> schools . . .
2. <u>Almost</u> all schools in Japan . . .
3. . . . <u>most</u> countries.
4. . . . <u>most</u> high school students . . .
5. <u>Almost</u> everyone . . . <u>almost</u> ready . . .

Exercise 10

1. ___C___ Baseball uses a bat. Another sport that uses a bat is cricket.
2. ___I___ In American football, you can make points with a touchdown and an extra point kick. <u>Other</u> ways to get points in <u>this</u> game are with a field goal or a safety.
3. ___I___ Volleyball uses a high net. <u>Another</u> sport that uses a high net is badminton.
4. ___C___ Soccer is very popular in Sweden. Other popular sports there are skiing, tennis, badminton, and table tennis.
5. ___I___ Golf is becoming more popular in the United States. <u>Other</u> sports gaining popularity are rollerblading and walking. You can do <u>these</u> sports alone or with a friend.

Exercise 11

1. When I took the college entrance exam, it was the <u>most</u> difficult test in my life.
2. High school exams were <u>harder</u> than college exams.
3. The <u>biggest reason</u> I hate exams is I forget the information.
4. The <u>worst</u> test I ever took was a math test.
5. My last test was <u>easier than</u> the first one.

(Concluded)

Exercise 12

1. __C__ I suggest that you keep your baby warm. Don't let her get too cold.

2. __I__ I think you should <u>let your teenagers have</u> some freedom. Don't be too controlling.

3. __C__ You need to love and respect your children. Each one is different.

4. __I__ <u>Most</u> parents need to talk to their children more often.

5. __I__ Don't allow your children to watch too much TV. <u>Another</u> problem is spending too much time on the computer.

6. __C__ Talk to your baby all the time. He'll learn to talk sooner.

7. __I__ Make your house a <u>safe</u> place so your children won't get hurt.

8. __C__ A good marriage is important for a healthy family.

9. __I__ Babies don't sleep well when it is <u>noisy</u>, so keep the house quiet during naps.

10. __C__ If you promise to do something, be sure to do it!

Exercise 13

Fall is my favorite season. I enjoy <u>seeing</u> the red, orange, and yellow leaves on the trees. The air is <u>fresh</u> and <u>clean</u> after an autumn rain. All of the children are back in school. They are so <u>excited</u> as they walk to their classes to meet their new teacher and classmates. In <u>this</u> country, there are also some <u>interesting</u> holidays in fall, such as Halloween and Thanksgiving. Of course, the weather becomes <u>colder</u> than in summer. For some people, cold weather is <u>depressing</u>, but I like it. You can see why fall is my <u>best</u> time of year.

Exercise 14

Learning English as a Second Language is difficult, but you can learn more quickly if you follow <u>these</u> suggestions. One way to help your English comprehension is by listening to fast English on the radio and television every day. Even if you don't understand everything, don't be <u>worried</u>. It will be <u>easier</u> little by little. You just need to be <u>patient</u>. <u>Another</u> way to help your English is to talk a lot with native speakers of English. In <u>this</u> case, don't be <u>shy</u>. You need <u>to</u> talk in English, even if it is <u>difficult</u>. When you try to speak English, don't be <u>confused</u>. Just relax and use simple English. My last <u>suggestion</u> is to think in English. When you are by yourself, try to think in English. It will become easier for you to use English vocabulary and sentences. If you begin thinking in your own language, don't give up. Keep on <u>using</u> English. I hope you will follow my <u>advice</u>.

CHAPTER 11

Word Order

Word order problems occur when the words are correct but in the wrong place in a sentence. It can be difficult if your language has very different word order from English. This chapter will give you some basic rules to follow.

A Basic Word Order

The basic word order in English is subject + verb + object (SVO).

No: A book, which my friend gave me, I read.

Yes: I read a book which my friend gave me.

Exercise 1

Write **C** for correct and **I** for incorrect. Then correct the mistakes.

What is the best way to study for a test?

1. _____ A long sleep you need to get the night before.

2. _____ I write questions that I think the teacher might ask.

3. _____ Everything the teacher assigned you should always study.

4. _____ My notes I rewrite and review.

5. _____ All the important information I try to memorize.

B Time Expressions

Yesterday and specific times with *ago, since,* and *for* usually go at the beginning or the end of a sentence.

No: I spoke yesterday to my friend.

Yes: **Yesterday** I spoke to my friend.

Yes: I spoke to my friend **yesterday.**

No:	My friend three years ago came to this country.
Yes:	**Three years ago,** my friend came to this country.
Yes:	My friend came to this country **three years ago.**

No:	I have since 1997 been studying for my Ph.D.
Yes:	**Since 1997** I have been studying for my Ph.D.
Yes:	I have been studying for my Ph.D. **since 1997.**

No:	My family has for three months been traveling.
Yes:	**For three months** my family has been traveling.
Yes:	My family has been traveling **for three months.**

Exercise 2

Correct the mistakes.

What is the biggest success in your life so far?

1. I for three years have been working at the same company.

2. For me it was when I ten years ago had my child.

3. I yesterday found out I am going to graduate first in my class.

4. I have learned to appreciate and enjoy since I was a child life's gifts.

5. My husband and I have for thirty-five years stayed happily married.

C Always

Always comes before the main verb or after the *be* verb.

No:	Always my parents call me on Saturdays.
Yes:	My parents **always** call me on Saturdays.
Yes:	My parents are **always** at home on Saturdays.

D Especially and Really

Especially and *really* usually go before the word or words they describe.

No:	Especially I like this class.
Yes:	I **especially** like this class.

No: Really I was in the library last night.

Yes: I **really** was in the library last night.

No: Especially I tell my secrets to my best friend.

Yes: I tell my secrets **especially** to my best friend.

Exercise 3

Write **C** for correct and **I** for incorrect. Then correct the mistakes.

What is the best way to get a high grade in a class?

1. _____   Really you must be friendly to the teacher.

2. _____   Especially you need to sit in the front of the class.

3. _____   Always I raise my hand when the teacher asks a question.

4. _____   It helps always to study with friends.

5. _____   A teacher especially likes active students.

E   Order of Adjectives

1. Adjectives go before the noun they describe. If there is more than one adjective before a noun, use this guide:

   1   2   3   4   5
   number–size–shape–color–type   +   noun

2. Use commas between descriptive adjectives.

   No: I found five round, blue, big, stained-glass windows.

   Yes: I found **five big, round, blue, stained-glass** windows.

   No: She had brown, long hair.

   Yes: She had **long, brown** hair.

3. Ordinal numbers come before cardinal numbers.

   No: two first years

   Yes: **first two years**

Exercise 4

Correct the mistakes.

What are you afraid of?

1. I don't like snakes long.

2. I prefer not to fly in passenger small airplanes.

3. Once I went on one of those tall, big roller coasters and I thought I would die.

4. I guess my biggest fear is dentists. I went to a few dentists unfriendly when I was a child and had bad experiences.

5. I am uncomfortable in dark, small spaces because in the three first years of my life, my brother sometimes put me in a closet as a joke.

6. I don't like heights so when I am in a hotel, I always stay on the two first floors.

F Adjective Clauses

Adjective clauses need to go directly after the word they describe.

No: Tom Cruise was in the movie *Top Gun,* who I like very much.
Yes: Tom Cruise, **who I like very much,** was in the movie *Top Gun.*

Exercise 5

Write *C* for correct and I for incorrect. Then correct the mistakes.

What is important to you in a job?

1. _____ A job would be great that involves sports such as a soccer coach or ski instructor.

2. _____ Work is important where I can be outside.

3. _____ I would like to work at a place that is close to my home.

4. _____ I am more interested in work that I enjoy rather than a job where I make a lot of money.

5. _____ A boss I need who supports me and treats me with respect.

G Wh Clauses

Look at the following sentences. What happens to the word order in a *wh* clause?

No: I want to learn how can I make more progress.

                                      s   hv   v

Yes: I want to learn **how I can make** more progress.

No: I need to know where did he go.

                                      s   v

Yes: I need to know **where he went.**

- When you begin a clause with a *wh* word, use regular sentence word order (subject + verb). *Do* and *does* are not used.

Exercise 6

Look at each pair of sentences. In the *wh* clause, write **s** over the subject, **v** over the main verb, and **hv** over the helping verb. Then decide which one is correct in each pair and circle *a* or *b*.

What do your parents like to tell you again and again?

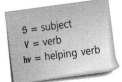

s = subject
v = verb
hv = helping verb

1. a. My parents often say, "Don't forget why you are studying here."

   b. My parents often say, "Don't forget why are you studying here."

2. a. They always tell me why I should work hard.

   b. They always tell me why should I work hard.

3. a. They want me to live where don't I have so much freedom.

   b. They want me to live where I don't have so much freedom.

4. a. I can't remember what they tell me.

   b. I can't remember what do they tell me.

5. a. They want me to meet people who can I practice my English with.

   b. They want me to meet people who I can practice my English with.

Chapter Review

Exercise 7

Correct the mistakes.

What are your impressions of this country?

1. Especially the people here are friendly.

2. The weather I'm not used to.

3. Really the food doesn't have much flavor.

4. I'm surprised by how big is this country.

5. I love the green, tall mountains.

Exercise 8

Correct the mistakes in the following paragraph.

Advice for a New ESL / EFL Teacher

Really, it is important to speak very clearly and slowly. You want your students to understand what are you saying. Kind and patient you want to be so that your students are not afraid of you. Learning English is scary, and students want a teacher friendly. Also, you need to explain English grammar well. The best way to do this is to explain simply and not to use a lot of grammar vocabulary. Students don't need all the grammar terms to know. If you do all of these things, your students will be more comfortable with you.

Exercise 1

1. ___I___ You need to get <u>a long sleep</u> the night before.

2. ___C___ I write questions that I think the teacher might ask.

3. ___I___ You should always study <u>everything the teacher assigned</u>.

4. ___I___ I rewrite and review <u>my notes</u>.

5. ___I___ I try to memorize <u>all the important information</u>.

Exercise 2

(Some sentences have two possible answers.)

1. I have been working at the same company <u>for three years</u>.

   <u>For three years</u>, I have been working at the same company.

2. For me it was when I had my child <u>ten years ago</u>.

3. I found out <u>yesterday</u> I am going to graduate first in my class.

   <u>Yesterday</u> I found out I am going to graduate first in my class.

4. I have learned to appreciate and enjoy life's gifts <u>since I was a child</u>.

   <u>Since I was a child</u>, I have learned to appreciate and enjoy life's gifts.

5. <u>For thirty-five years</u>, my husband and I have stayed happily married.

   My husband and I have stayed happily married <u>for thirty-five years</u>.

Exercise 3

1. ___I___ You must be <u>really</u> friendly to the teacher.

2. ___I___ You <u>especially</u> need to sit in the front of the class.

3. ___I___ I <u>always</u> raise my hand when the teacher asks a question.

4. ___I___ It <u>always</u> helps to study with friends.

5. ___C___ A teacher especially likes active students.

Exercise 4

1. I don't like <u>long</u> snakes.

2. I prefer not to fly in <u>small</u> passenger airplanes.

3. Once I went on one of those <u>big</u>, tall roller coasters and I thought I would die.

4. I guess my biggest fear is dentists. I went to a few <u>unfriendly</u> dentists when I was a child and had bad experiences.

5. I am uncomfortable in <u>small</u>, dark spaces because in the <u>first three</u> years of my life, my brother sometimes put me in a closet as a joke.

6. I don't like heights so when I am in a hotel, I always stay on the <u>first</u> two floors.

(Continued)

Exercise 5

1. ___I___   A job that involves sports such as a soccer coach or ski instructor <u>would be great</u>.

2. ___I___   Work where I can be outside <u>is important</u>.

3. ___C___   I would like to work at a place that is close to my home.

4. ___C___   I am more interested in work that I enjoy rather than a job where I make a lot of money.

5. ___I___   <u>I need</u> a boss who supports me and treats me with respect.

Exercise 6

1. (a.) My parents often say, "Don't forget why you^{s hv} are studying^v here."

    b. My parents often say, "Don't forget why are^{hv} you^s studying^v here."

2. (a.) They always tell me why I^s should^{hv} work^v hard.

    b. They always tell me why should^{hv} I^s work^v hard.

3. a. They want me to live where don't^{hv} I^s have^v so much freedom.

    (b.) They want me to live where I^s don't^{hv} have^v so much freedom.

4. (a.) I can't remember what they^s tell^v me.

    b. I can't remember what do^{hv} they^s tell^v me.

5. a. They want me to meet people who can^{hv} I^s practice^v my English with.

    (b.) They want me to meet people who I^s can^{hv} practice^v my English with.

Exercise 7

1. The people here are <u>especially</u> friendly.

2. I'm not used to <u>the weather</u>.

3. The food <u>really</u> doesn't have much flavor.

4. I'm surprised by how big this country <u>is</u>.

5. I love the <u>tall</u>, green mountains.

(Concluded)

Exercise 8

It is <u>really</u> important to speak very clearly and slowly. You want your students to understand what <u>you are</u> saying. You want to be <u>kind and patient</u> so that your students are not afraid of you. Learning English is scary, and students want a <u>friendly teacher</u>. Also, you need to explain English grammar well. The best way to do this is to explain simply and not to use a lot of grammar vocabulary. Students don't need <u>to know</u> all the grammar terms. If you do all of these things, your students will be more comfortable with you.

CHAPTER 12

Prepositions

Words such as *at, on, in, for, above, with,* and *during* are prepositions. They are very difficult for non-native speakers, and it can take many years of English experience to use prepositions naturally. Some prepositions follow rules that are easy to learn, but others simply must be memorized. For some students, it helps to make flashcards and practice them for a short time each day until they are learned. It is also important to learn the verbs and adverbs that do not take prepositions. This chapter will show you some of the most common uses of prepositions that you will need for your writing. It takes practice and time to improve a lot, but better preposition use makes your writing sound much more fluent.

A Common Verbs + Prepositions

Many preposition errors occur when a preposition is needed, but the writer doesn't use one. Look at the following examples. These verbs usually take a preposition. Check (✓) the ones you know. Study the ones you don't know.

	Yes	**No (Common Errors)**
agree with	I **agree with** her.	I agree her.
arrive at	I **arrived at** the airport on time. (for a specific place that is not a city or country)	I arrived to the airport on time.
arrive in	I **arrived in** Dallas yesterday. (for a city or country)	I arrived Dallas yesterday.
come to	He **came to** our house.	He came our house.
go to	We **went to** Spain.	We went Spain.
go back to	I **went back to** my country.	I went back my country.
graduate from	I **graduated from** high school.	I graduated high school.
knock on / at	He **knocked on (at)** the door.	He knocked the door.
listen to	I **listened to** some music.	I listened music.
live in	I **lived in** the house.	I lived the house.
move to	We **moved to** a new house.	We moved a new house.
stay with	We **stayed with** my friend.	We stayed my friend.
stay at	We **stayed at** my friend's house.	We stayed my friend's house.
work at / for	I **work at / for** Boeing.	I work in Boeing.
work in + city	I **work in Quebec.**	I work Quebec.

Exercise 1

Fill in the blanks with the correct preposition.

Tommy Lee Jones

Actor Tommy Lee Jones lived _____ Texas as a child. After he

graduated _____ high school, he went _____ Harvard University.

Then Jones moved _____ New York and began acting on Broadway.

Later, he moved _____ Los Angeles, where he became a movie star. After

becoming successful, he went back _____ Texas, where he bought a

ranch. Jones doesn't agree _____ movie stars who go _____ all of

the Hollywood parties and want a lot of media attention. He'd rather spend

his free time working on his ranch in Texas.

Exercise 2

Fill in the blanks with the correct preposition.

A Mix-up

My friend from out-of-town is staying _____ me this week. When she

arrived _____ the airport last night, I wasn't there to meet her because I

hadn't gotten the right flight information. She had to get a taxi to come

_____ my apartment. Then, when she knocked _____ my door, I didn't

hear her because I was listening _____ some music. She called me from a

pay phone. I'll be sure to take her to the airport when she goes back

_____ her country next week.

B Verbs without Prepositions

Another type of preposition error occurs when the verb does not need a preposition, but the writer adds one. Look at the following examples. These verbs do not usually take a preposition. Check (✓) the ones you know. Study the ones you don't know.

	Yes	No (Common Errors)
ask	I **asked** my friend.	I asked to my friend.
attend	I **attend** Central High School.	I attend at Central High School.
call	I **called** my friend.	I called to my friend. (telephone)
enter	I **entered** high school.	I entered to high school.
leave	I **left** the house.*	I left from the house.
teach	She **taught** the students.	She taught to the students.
tell	I **told** my friend.	I told to my friend.
visit	I **visited** the U.S.	I visited in the U.S.

* Note: There is another verb **leave for.** It means *depart:* Tomorrow I will **leave for** Hawaii.

Exercise 3

Fill in the blanks with the correct preposition or Ø, and the correct information about you.

A Typical Day

1. I leave _____ my home at _____.
   (time)

2. I go _____ _____.
   (place)

3. I am attending _____ _____.
   (name of school)

4. I arrive _____ my house at _____.
   (time)

5. Sometimes, I visit _____ my friends, _____ and
   (name)

   _____, and sometimes I call _____ them.
   (name)

C · Special Place Words

You have just learned that some verbs must have prepositions. However, there are some words that change that rule. When these words are used, there is no preposition. Look at the following examples. Check (✓) the ones you know. Study the ones you don't know.

	Yes	No (Common Errors)
here	I'm living **here.**	I'm living in here.
there	Let's go **there.**	Let's go to there.
everywhere	We went **everywhere.**	We went to everywhere.
somewhere	He went **somewhere.**	He went to somewhere.
downtown*	We went **downtown.**	We went to downtown.
home**	I'm going **home** soon.	I'm going to home.

* If you use the name of the city, use *to*: I went to downtown Baltimore.

** With non-action verbs like *stay* or *be,* the preposition *at* can be used: I'm staying at home. / I'm staying home.

Exercise 4

Here are some questions you can ask another student. Fill in the blanks with the correct preposition or Ø. Then ask the student and write his or her answers.

Student Interview: Your Neighborhood

Questions   *Answers*

1. What do you like about   _____

   living _____ here?   _____

2. How often do you   _____

   go _____ downtown?   _____

3. What do you   _____

   do _____ there?   _____

4. What do you like to do when

    you are _____ home?   _____

_____

5. I want to go _____

    somewhere interesting.   _____

    Can you suggest a place?   _____

Review: Parts A, B, C

Exercise 5

Write **C** for correct and **I** for incorrect. Then correct the mistakes.

Bill Gates

1. _____ Bill Gates, one of the richest men in the world, lived in Seattle

        as a child.

2. _____ He graduated from high school and then attended

        Harvard University.

3. _____ He left from Harvard after two years and moved New Mexico

        to start a computer software company.

4. _____ Gates went back to the Seattle area and asked several of his old

        friends to work at his company, Microsoft.

5. _____ Microsoft became a successful company, and you can find

        Microsoft products in everywhere.

Exercise 6

Correct the mistakes in the following paragraph. There are ten errors.

My Classmate

Young is my classmate. She is from Korea. She arrived Los Angeles three months ago. She came to here because she wants to live the United States. Now she is staying her uncle and aunt. She told to me that she is very happy here. She enjoys listening music and going to downtown in her free time. Young wants to visit to her friend in Texas. She hopes to go to there next summer. Young says learning English is very difficult, but useful. I agree her.

D Time Prepositions

1. Here are some time prepositions. They can show past or future time.

Longer Time	A Day	Specific Time
in	**on**	**at**
the twentieth century	Wednesday	3:00 P.M.
the nineties	July 3	noon
1993	Christmas Day	midnight
the summer	my birthday	night
August		
the morning		
the afternoon		
the evening		

No: My mother was born on July, 1944.
Yes: My mother was born **in** July, 1944.

No: I will be with my family and friends in New Year's.
Yes: I will be with my family and friends **on** New Year's.

No: She will graduate after three weeks.
Yes: She will graduate **in** three weeks.

Exercise 7   Fill in the blanks with the correct preposition and information about your birth. If you are not sure about some of the information, you can guess.

My First Birthday

I was born _____ _____
              (prep.)   (year)

_____ _____
   (prep.)   (date)

_____ _____
   (prep.)   (day of the week)

_____ _____
   (prep.)   (time of day: the morning / the afternoon / etc.)

_____ _____
   (prep.)   (clock time)

D Time Prepositions, continued

2. *In* and *on* are not used with phrases such as *this week, next year, last Thursday, everyday*.

   No: I am going to move in this week.
   Yes: I am going to move **this week.**

   No: In next year, I will change jobs.
   Yes: **Next year,** I will change jobs.

   No: My sister visited me on last Thursday.
   Yes: My sister visited me **last Thursday.**

3. *During* and *while* both describe a period of time. However, they are used differently in a sentence.

   No: I lived in a dormitory during I was in college.
   Yes: I lived in a dormitory **during** college.
   Yes: I lived in a dormitory **while I was** in college.

   - *During* is a preposition and is followed by a noun.
   - *While* is an adverb clause marker that must be followed by a subject and a verb.

Exercise 8   Fill in the blanks with *at, during, in,* or *Ø.*

A Hike

I'll never forget my hike to Crystal Lake. It was _____ last summer.

We got up early _____ the morning and hiked to the lake. We got

there late _____ the afternoon, had a picnic, and then went back.

_____ our walk, we had to climb over many large rocks and go up and

down some steep hills. We got home very late, almost _____ midnight.

I was very tired. Since that trip, I try to exercise _____ every day to get

in better shape. I'll be ready to go on another long hike _____ next year.

D More Time Prepositions

4. *By* and *until* have different meanings.

   No: I hope to graduate until June.

   Yes: I hope to graduate **by** June.

   (*in* June is also OK, but *by* means "the latest time")

   Yes: I will study here **until** June.

   (study, study, study, study until June = a long time)

   • Use *by* to describe an end time or the last possible time.

   • Use *until* to describe an action that continues up to a specific time.

5. *From* and *to* have different meanings.

   Yes: I worked for a computer company **from** 1994 **to** 1997.

   Yes: My classes meet **from** 10:00 **to** 3:00.

   Yes: I studied **from** January **to** March.

   • When you have two times, *from* is used for the beginning time, and *to* is used
     for the end time. (*Note:* Some people use *until* rather than *to*, but *to* is more
     common.)

Exercise 9

Fill in the blanks with *in, on, by, until,* or *Ø.*

Homework

I've been very busy _____ this quarter because I have a lot of

homework. For example, I have to turn in an essay _____ every Friday

in my writing class. I often work on my essay _____ very late Thursday

night. This week I'm really busy because I have a big science project that I

have to turn in _____ Monday at the latest. I'm not looking forward to

final exams _____ March. I don't remember having this much

homework _____ last year.

Exercise 10

Fill in the blanks with the correct prepositions. Use *at, by, from, to,* or *until.*

My Dream Schedule

Wake up _____ 10:00. Take a shower and get dressed.

Drink coffee, eat breakfast, and relax _____ 10:30 _____ 12:00.

Spend time with my friends and do sports _____ 6:00.

Eat dinner _____ 6:30 _____ 7:30.

Watch videos _____ 12:00.

Be in bed _____ 1:00 at the latest.

6. *Since* and *for* have different uses.

Yes: I have lived here **since** 1992.

Yes: I have lived here **for** six years.

- *Since* tells the beginning time.
- *For* tells how long.

Exercise 11

Sam   Steve   Jackie   Susan   Pat

Fill in the blanks with *since* or *for*.

Strange People

1. Sam has lived in a tent _____ ten years.

2. Steve has studied movie stars' garbage _____ 1988.

3. Jackie has been married to her ninth husband _____ one year.

4. Susan has been looking for her old glasses _____ 1991.

5. Pat has loved poisonous spiders _____ his birth.

6. Pat has loved poisonous spiders _____ all his life.

E Place Prepositions

1. in New York   on Broadway   at 225 Broadway

Yes: I live **in** New York.

Yes: I live **on** Broadway.

Yes: I live **at** 225 Broadway.

Exercise 12

Fill in the blanks with *in, on* or *at*.

My Best Friend

1. Presently, she lives _____ the city _____ 1st Street.

2. Her apartment is _____ 405 1st Street.

3. She's going to move to a house _____ 610 Lake Way.

4. She has always wanted to live _____ Lake Way.

E Place Prepositions, continued

2. *next to / far from / near / opposite*

Next to and *far from* take prepositions; *near* and *opposite* do not.

Examples: Sue lives **next to** the freeway.   Kim lives **near** the beach.

Jack lives **far from** the city.   Sara lives **opposite** the park.

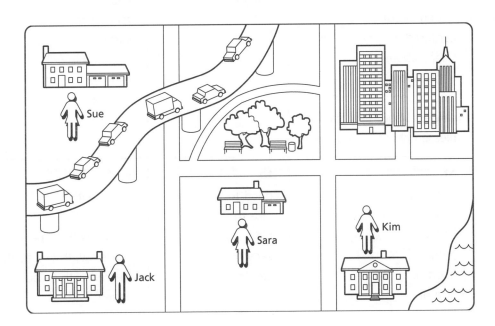

Exercise 13

Think about your classroom. Fill in the blanks with the correct preposition or Ø. Then answer the questions in complete sentences.

The Classroom

1. Who usually sits next _____ you?

   _____

2. Who usually sits far _____ the teacher?

   _____

3. Who usually sits near _____ the teacher?

   _____

4. Who usually sits opposite _____ you?

   _____

F Adjectives + Common Prepositions

Look at the following adjectives + prepositions. Check (✓) the ones you know. Then circle the ones that you think you may use in your writing. These are the ones you especially want to study.

about	at	for	in
worried about	angry at	thankful for	interested in
sorry about	good at	good for	
right about	bad at	bad for	
wrong about		famous for	
confused about		sorry for	
happy about		responsible for	
angry about		early for	
careful about (+ situation)		late for	
careless about (+ situation)			
pleased about (+ situation)			

of	to	with
afraid of	good to	bored with
tired of	nice to	angry with
sure of	mean to	careful with (+ people / things)
proud of	early to	careless with (+ people / things)
good of	late to	pleased with (+ people / things)
nice of		patient with

1. Some adjectives have different meanings when used with different prepositions:

   Dan is **good at** sports.   (talent or ability)

   Dan is **bad at** singing.   (talent or ability)

   Vegetables are **good for** your health.   (effect)

   Smoking is **bad for** your health.   (effect)

   He is **good to** his grandmother.   (behavior with a person)

   He is **mean to** his children.   (behavior with a person)

2. *Good, nice, kind, helpful,* etc. take different prepositions depending on the grammar. Look at these examples. The first one is more common. The second is more formal.

   You were **nice to** me.

   It was **nice of** you to help me.

3. *Angry at* and *angry with* have the same meaning. They are used with people. *Angry about* is used for a thing.

   Sara is **angry at** her teacher.

   Sara is **angry with** her teacher.

   Sara is **angry about** her grade.

Exercise 14
_____

Think about the leader of your country. Complete the sentences with the correct preposition and information that makes sense.

The Leader of My Country

I think he or she . . .

1. is worried   _____   _____

2. is thankful   _____   _____

3. is confused   _____   _____

4. is careful   _____   _____

5. is interested _____   _____

6. is tired   _____   _____

Exercise 15   Complete the questions and then give an answer for each.

Personal Questions

1. Who are you good _____?

   _____

2. What are you good _____?

   _____

3. Who have you been angry _____ in your life?

   _____

4. What have you been angry _____ in your life?

   _____

5. What are you pleased _____?

   _____

6. What are you bored _____?

   _____

G Idiomatic Expressions

Look at the following idiomatic expressions. Check (✓) the ones you know. Then circle the ones that you think you may use in your writing. These are the ones you especially want to study.

by	in	on	out	up
by mistake	in love with (really love)	on purpose (planned, not an accident)	out-of-date (old-fashioned)	up-to-date (modern)
by car, bus, plane train (to travel)	in a hurry (quickly, rushed, not much time)		out of work (no job)	
by hand (made with your hands)	in charge of (manage)		out of order (broken)	

| Exercise 16 | Fill in the blanks with the correct prepositions. |

The Love of Uncle Jack's Life

    Let me tell you a story about my uncle, Jack. He was in love _____

cars. He traveled everywhere he could _____ car, never _____

plane or train. When he was home, he made wooden cars _____ hand

for his children. His hobby was fixing really old cars. He didn't like new cars;

in fact, he said that they had no character. I remember one time he lost his

job and was _____ _____ work for a few weeks. But Jack didn't

care. He wasn't _____ a hurry to find a new job. He just had more

time to spend with the love of his life: cars.

H Nouns + Prepositions

Look at the following nouns with prepositions. Check (✓) the ones you know. Then circle the ones that you think you may use in your writing. These are the ones you especially want to study well.

in	**for**	**of**
rise in	reason for	cause of
increase in	need for	result of
fall in		price of
decrease in		cost of

| Exercise 17 | Fill in the first blank with the correct preposition. Then choose a noun from the list that makes sense to finish the phrase. |

Common Phrases

1. rise   _____ _____   a. food

2. need   _____ _____   b. war

3. price   _____ _____   c. prices

4. cause   _____ _____   d. population

5. reason   _____ _____   e. love

6. decrease _____ _____   f. crime

I More Verbs with Prepositions

In section A, you studied common verbs that need prepositions. These are very important to learn for your writing because they are so common. There are many more verbs in English that take prepositions.

Look at the following verbs with prepositions. Check (✓) the ones you know. Then circle the ones that you think you may use in your writing. These are the ones you especially want to study.

about	after	at	for
talk about	look after	look at	wait for
laugh about		laugh at	pay for
smile about		smile at	look for
think about		yell at	ask for
		shout at	

from	of	on	to
hear from	consist of	concentrate on	pay attention to
	think of	decide on	belong to
		depend on	happen to
		rely on	talk to
			yell to
			look forward to

As you can see in the chart, the same verb can take different prepositions. With these verbs, the meaning does change. Can you see the differences in meaning?

I was angry. I **yelled at** my friend.
   (yell at / shout at = feel angry)

My friend couldn't hear me. I **yelled to** her.
   (yell to / shout to = talk louder because someone can't hear you)

I just **looked at** my food instead of eating it because I wasn't hungry.
   (look at = watch, see)

I **looked after** my friend's child because she couldn't find a baby-sitter.
   (look after = take care of)

I spent all morning **looking for** my contact lens because I dropped it on the floor.
   (look for = try to find)

He told a great joke. We all **laughed at** his joke.
   (To laugh at a joke or story is polite.)

I wore one blue sock to school and one brown one. Everyone **laughed at** me.
   (laugh at someone = make fun of someone. It is impolite to laugh at someone.)

Luckily, I was in a good mood and we all **laughed about** my mistake.
   (laugh about something)

Exercise 18	Complete the questions and then give an answer for each.

Some More Personal Questions

1. What do you need to concentrate _____?

   I need to concentrate _____ _____.

2. How do you feel if you are laughed _____?

   If I am laughed _____, I feel _____.

3. Who do you depend _____?

   I depend _____ _____.

4. What would cause you to yell _____ someone?

   I would yell _____ someone if she or he _____.

5. What do you need to pay attention _____?

   I need to pay attention _____ _____.

Chapter Review

Exercise 19	Write C for correct and I for incorrect. Correct the mistakes. Then mark if the sentence is true or false.

What's Your Opinion?

True or false?

1. _____ Usually, people look forward in their death. _____

2. _____ People like other people to laugh at their jokes. _____

3. _____ It's polite to yell at someone. _____

4. _____ A student feels proud in good grades. _____

5. _____ A rise on prices usually makes people happy. _____

6. _____ When growing up, children usually depend

to their parents. _____

7. _____ A four-year-old child can look after a teenager. _____

8. _____ A four-year-old child can look for a teenager. _____

9. _____ Glass consists sand and water. _____

Exercise 20

Fill in the blanks with the correct preposition. Then answer the questions in complete sentences.

Modern Conveniences

a. copy machines
b. cordless phones
c. computers

d. cell phones
e. answering machines
f. fax machines

g. e-mail
h. the Internet
i. Post-it notes

1. Which ones belong _____ you?

   _____

2. Which ones do you rely _____?

   _____

3. Which ones become _____ of-date most quickly?

   _____

4. Which ones do you not have but are interested _____ having?

   _____

5. Which ones can you learn to use _____ a hurry?

   _____

6. Are any of them bad _____ society? Why?

   _____

Exercise 21

Write **C** for correct and **I** for incorrect. Then correct the mistakes.

What are your goals for the next few months?

1. _____ I want to concentrate in my studies.

2. _____ I hope to be less angry at my children and more patient

with them.

3. _____ We need to move a new apartment that is closer to our jobs.

4. _____ I want to finish knitting a sweater with hand

for my granddaughter.

5. _____ I want to finish my ESL classes by the end of the quarter.

6. _____ My parents are in Miami now, so I want to go to there

to visit them.

7. _____ I'll go back my country soon.

8. _____ I want to slow down and not be in a hurry all of the time.

9. _____ I'm looking for another job. I need an increase in salary.

10. _____ I can't decide for any goals.

Exercise 22

Fill in the blanks with the correct preposition or Ø.

My Brother

My brother has always been interested _____ airplanes. While

growing up, he loved to go _____ the airport to look _____ all

of the planes. _____ his twenties, he graduated _____ college

and worked _____ a bank _____ several years, but he became

bored _____ that job and got a job as a flight attendant. He's glad he is not responsible _____ flying the plane. He loves his work because he

enjoys talking _____ people. Passengers laugh _____ his jokes,

especially when he calls himself a "stewardess," which is an _____–

_____– date word used years ago when only women could have his

job. He's not worried _____ accidents because statistics show that it is

safer to travel _____ plane than _____ car. He also gets to visit

_____ his friends all over the country because he can fly for free. My

brother has been a flight attendant _____ 1985, and he is still

_____love _____ airplanes.

Exercise 23

There are ten mistakes in the following paragraph. Can you find and correct them?

Tattoos

Several of my friends have gotten tattoos on their bodies at a tattoo

parlor near to our dormitory. I agree my friends that tattoos look cool, but I'm

afraid in getting one. My best friend laughed to me because of that, so I got

angry to her and I told to her that she wasn't being nice to me. I guess I'm

confused with tattoos, and I want to be sure in myself before I get one.

Maybe in this weekend I will go to downtown to get my ears pierced instead.

Exercise 1

Actor Tommy Lee Jones lived <u>in</u> Texas as a child. After he graduated <u>from</u> high school, he went <u>to</u> Harvard University. Then Jones moved <u>to</u> New York and began acting on Broadway. Later, he moved <u>to</u> Los Angeles, where he became a movie star. After becoming successful, he went back <u>to</u> Texas, where he bought a ranch. Jones doesn't agree <u>with</u> movie stars who go <u>to</u> all of the Hollywood parties and want a lot of media attention. He'd rather spend his free time working on his ranch in Texas.

Exercise 2

My friend from out-of-town is staying <u>with</u> me this week. When she arrived <u>at</u> the airport last night, I wasn't there to meet her because I hadn't gotten the right flight information. She had to get a taxi to come <u>to</u> my apartment. Then, when she knocked <u>on</u>/<u>at</u> my door, I didn't hear her because I was listening <u>to</u> some music. She called me from a pay phone. I'll be sure to take her to the airport when she goes back <u>to</u> her country next week.

Exercise 3

1. I leave *Ø* my home at . . .
2. I go <u>to</u> . . .
3. I am attending *Ø* . . .
4. I arrive <u>at</u> my house at . . .
5. Sometimes, I visit *Ø* my friends, . . . and sometimes I call *Ø* them.

Exercise 4

1. What do you like about living *Ø* here?
2. How often do you go *Ø* downtown?
3. What do you do *Ø* there?
4. What do you like to do when you are <u>at</u> home?
5. I want to go *Ø* somewhere interesting.

Exercise 5

1. __C__ Bill Gates, one of the richest men in the world, lived in Seattle as a child.
2. __C__ He graduated from high school and then attended Harvard University.
3. __I__ He <u>left Harvard</u> after two years and moved <u>to</u> New Mexico to start a computer software company.
4. __C__ Gates went back to the Seattle area and asked several of his old friends to work at his company, Microsoft.
5. __I__ Microsoft became a successful company, and you can find Microsoft products <u>everywhere</u>.

(Continued)

Exercise 6

       Young is my classmate. She is from Korea. She arrived <u>in</u> Los Angeles three months ago. She came <u>here</u> because she wants to live <u>in</u> the United States. Now she is staying <u>with</u> her uncle and aunt. She told <u>me</u> that she is very happy here. She enjoys listening <u>to</u> music and going <u>downtown</u> in her free time. Young wants to visit <u>her</u> friend in Texas. She hopes to go <u>there</u> next summer. Young says learning English is very difficult, but useful. I agree <u>with</u> her.

Exercise 7

I was born   <u>in</u>   (year)

                     <u>on</u>   (date)

                     <u>on</u>   (day of the week)

                     <u>in</u>   (time of day: the morning / the afternoon / etc.)

                     <u>at</u>   (clock time)

Exercise 8

       I'll never forget my hike to Crystal Lake. It was Ø last summer. We got up early <u>in</u> the morning and hiked to the lake. We got there late <u>in</u> the afternoon, had a picnic, and then went back. <u>During</u> our walk, we had to climb over many large rocks and go up and down some steep hills. We got home very late, almost <u>at</u> midnight. I was very tired. Since that trip, I try to exercise Ø every day to get in better shape. I'll be ready to go on another long hike Ø next year.

Exercise 9

       I've been very busy Ø this quarter because I have a lot of homework. For example, I have to turn in an essay Ø every Friday in my writing class. I often work on my essay <u>until</u> very late Thursday night. This week I'm really busy because I have a big science project that I have to turn in <u>by</u> Monday at the latest. I'm not looking forward to final exams <u>in</u> March. I don't remember having this much homework Ø last year.

Exercise 10

Wake up <u>at</u> 10:00. Take a shower and get dressed.

Drink coffee, eat breakfast, and relax <u>from</u> 10:30 <u>to</u> / <u>until</u> 12:00.

Spend time with my friends and do sports <u>until</u> 6:00.

Eat dinner <u>from</u> 6:30 <u>to</u> / <u>until</u> 7:30.

Watch videos <u>until</u> 12:00.

Be in bed <u>by</u> 1:00 at the latest.

(Continued)

Exercise 11

1. Sam has lived in a tent <u>for</u> ten years.
2. Steve has studied movie stars' garbage <u>since</u> 1988.
3. Jackie has been married to her ninth husband <u>for</u> one year.
4. Susan has been looking for her old glasses <u>since</u> 1991.
5. Pat has loved poisonous spiders <u>since</u> his birth.
6. Pat has loved poisonous spiders <u>for</u> all his life.

Exercise 12

1. Presently, she lives <u>in</u> the city <u>on</u> 1st Street.
2. Her apartment is <u>at</u> 405 1st Street.
3. She's going to move to a house <u>at</u> 610 Lake Way.
4. She has always wanted to live <u>on</u> Lake Way.

Exercise 13

1. Who usually sits next <u>to</u> you?
2. Who usually sits far <u>from</u> the teacher?
3. Who usually sits near <u>Ø</u> the teacher?
4. Who usually sits opposite <u>Ø</u> you?

Exercise 14

1. . . . is worried <u>about</u>
2. . . . is thankful <u>for</u>
3. . . . is confused <u>about</u>
4. . . . is careful <u>with</u> / <u>about</u>
5. . . . is interested <u>in</u>
6. . . . is tired <u>of</u>

Exercise 15

1. Who are you good <u>to</u>?
2. What are you good <u>at</u>?
3. Who have you been angry <u>at</u> / <u>with</u> in your life?
4. What have you been angry <u>about</u> in your life?
5. What are you pleased <u>with</u> / <u>about</u>?
6. What are you bored <u>with</u>?

(Continued)

Exercise 16

Let me tell you a story about my uncle, Jack. He was in love <u>with</u> cars. He traveled everywhere he could <u>by</u> car, never <u>by</u> plane or train. When he was home, he made wooden cars <u>by</u> hand for his children. His hobby was fixing really old cars. He didn't like new cars; in fact, he said that they had no character. I remember one time he lost his job and was <u>out of</u> work for a few weeks. But Jack didn't care. He wasn't <u>in</u> a hurry to find a new job. He just had more time to spend with the love of his life: cars.

Exercise 17

1. rise <u>in</u> prices / population / crime
2. need <u>for</u> love / food
3. price <u>of</u> food
4. cause <u>of</u> war / crime
5. reason <u>for</u> war / crime
6. decrease <u>in</u> population / crime / prices

Exercise 18

1. What do you need to concentrate <u>on</u>?
2. How do you feel if you are laughed <u>at</u>?
3. Who do you depend <u>on</u>?
4. What would cause you to yell <u>at</u> someone?
   What would cause you to yell <u>to</u> someone?
5. What do you need to pay attention <u>to</u>?

Exercise 19

1. __I__ Usually, people look forward <u>to</u> their death.   (F)
2. __C__ People like other people to laugh at their jokes.   (T)
3. __C__ It's polite to yell at someone.   (F)
4. __I__ A student feels proud <u>of</u> good grades.   (T)
5. __I__ A rise <u>in</u> prices usually makes people happy.   (F)
6. __I__ When growing up, children usually depend <u>on</u> their parents.   (T)
7. __C__ A four-year-old child can look after a teenager.   (F)
8. __C__ A four-year-old child can look for a teenager.   (T)
9. __I__ Glass consists <u>of</u> sand and water.   (T)

(Concluded)

Exercise 20

1. Which ones belong <u>to</u> you?

2. Which ones do you rely <u>on</u>?

3. Which ones become <u>out</u>-of-date most quickly?

4. Which ones do you not have but are interested <u>in</u> having?

5. Which ones can you learn to use <u>in</u> a hurry?

6. Are any of them bad <u>for</u> society?

Exercise 21

1. __I__   I want to concentrate <u>on</u> my studies.

2. __C__   I hope to be less angry at my children and more patient with them.

3. __I__   We need to move <u>to</u> a new apartment that is closer to our jobs.

4. __I__   I want to finish knitting a sweater <u>by</u> hand for my granddaughter.

5. __C__   I want to finish my ESL classes by the end of the quarter.

6. __I__   My parents are in Miami now, so I want to go <u>there</u> to visit them.

7. __I__   I'll go back <u>to</u> my country soon.

8. __C__   I want to slow down and not be in a hurry all of the time.

9. __C__   I'm looking for another job. I need an increase in salary.

10. __I__   I can't decide <u>on</u> any goals.

Exercise 22

My brother has always been interested <u>in</u> airplanes. While growing up, he loved to go <u>to</u> the airport to look <u>at</u> all of the planes. <u>During</u>* his twenties, he graduated <u>from</u> college and worked <u>at</u>/<u>for</u> a bank <u>for</u> several years, but he became bored <u>with</u> that job and got a job as a flight attendant. He's glad he is not responsible <u>for</u> flying the plane. He loves his work because he enjoys talking <u>to</u> people. Passengers laugh <u>at</u> his jokes, especially when he calls himself a "stewardess," which is an <u>out-of</u>-date word used years ago when only women could have his job. He's not worried <u>about</u> accidents because statistics show that it is safer to travel <u>by</u> plane than <u>by</u> car. He also gets to visit <u>Ø</u> his friends all over the country because he can fly for free. My brother has been a flight attendant <u>since</u> 1985, and he is still <u>in</u> love <u>with</u> airplanes.

* "In" is also possible.

Exercise 23

Several of my friends have gotten tattoos on their bodies at a tattoo parlor <u>near our</u> dormitory. I agree <u>with</u> my friends that tattoos look cool, but I'm afraid <u>of</u> getting one. My best friend laughed <u>at</u> me because of that, so I got angry <u>at</u>/<u>with</u> her and I <u>told her</u> that she wasn't being nice to me. I guess I'm confused <u>about</u> tattoos, and I want to be sure <u>of</u> myself before I get one. Maybe <u>this</u> weekend I will <u>go downtown</u> to get my ears pierced instead.

CHAPTER 13

Articles

Is it "United States" or "the United States"? Is it "Mexico" or "the Mexico"? The words *a, an,* and *the* are articles. Using articles correctly can be very difficult for non-native speakers. While the incorrect use of articles is not considered a big problem, it can prevent your writing from seeming fluent or native-like. With attention and practice, ESL students can improve their use of articles greatly.

Part 1 Articles with Proper Nouns

There is usually no article with names of people, cities, streets, states, and provinces. Some rules for geographical names follow.

A Geographical Names

1. Use *the* before the names of oceans, seas, rivers, canals, groups of islands, groups of lakes, and mountain ranges.

>   **the** Pacific Ocean
>
>   **the** Mediterranean Sea
>
>   **the** Mississippi River
>
>   **the** Suez Canal
>
>   **the** Hawaiian Islands
>
>   **the** Great Lakes
>
>   **the** Rocky Mountains

2. There is no article before singular islands, lakes and mountains:

>   Long Island
>
>   Lake Michigan
>
>   Mt. Everest

1. *The* is not used with names of countries unless the country's name includes the words *United* or *Union* (a group) or has a plural *-s* ending (also like a group).

Japan	**the** United States
Mexico	**the** United Arab Emirates
Canada	**the** Philippines
Russia	**the** former Soviet Union

2. *The* is not used with continents.

Africa	Europe
Antarctica	North America
Asia	South America
Australia	

3. Use *the* with world areas and regions.

the Far East	**the** South
the Middle East	**the** Midwest
the North	**the** East

4. Use *the* with place phrases containing *of.*

I come from Saudi Arabia.	I come from **the** kingdom **of** Saudi Arabia.
I live in New York state.	I live in **the** state **of** New York.
I go to McGill University.	I go to **the** University **of** Toronto.

Exercise 1

Correct the following sentences.

Where would you like to go on your next vacation?

1. My next trip is to Canada. I want to see ⌃the Great Lakes, ⌃the Rocky Mountains, and ⌃the Pacific Ocean.

2. I am from Mexico, but my friend is from ⌃the United Arab Emirates. I would like to visit him in his country after I leave ⌃the United States.

3. I hear ~~the~~ Seattle is really a beautiful place. I want to go hiking in ⌃the Olympic Mountains and climb Mt. Rainier.

4. This September I am going to visit ~~the~~ Harvard University. Then I will travel around ~~the~~ Boston and Vermont.

5. On my next vacation, I want to go to ~~the~~ Colorado. I really want to see Rocky Mountains.

6. I want to travel to ~~the~~ Greece and Egypt. It would be wonderful to swim in the Mediterranean Sea, travel down the Nile River, and see the Suez Canal.

Part 2 Singular Count Nouns

A count noun is a noun that can be counted:

| one apple | two apples |
| one chair | two chairs |

Singular count nouns must have an article (or other counting word):

a chair   one chair

A Singular Indefinite Nouns

1. Singular indefinite nouns must use *a* or *an*. (*Indefinite* means we don't know which one.)

   No: I ate apple for lunch.
   No: There is chair in the room.

   Yes: I ate **an** apple for lunch.
   Yes: There is **a** chair in the room.

Exercise 2

Write **C** for correct and **I** for incorrect.

Miscellaneous Sentences

1. __I__ I need to buy car.

2. __I__ I ate hamburger.

3. __C__ He has a child.

4. __I__ They bought new house.

5. __I__ She told me about trip she wanted to take.

2. Use *a* before a noun (or an adjective + a noun) that begins with a consonant sound. Use *an* before a noun (or an adjective + a noun) that begins with a vowel sound (a, e, i, o, u).

a book

a dog

a university (sounds like "yuniversity")

a unit (sounds like "yunit")

a d

an orange

an interesting thought

an hour (sounds like "our")

an uncle

an s (sounds like "es")

Exercise 3

Fill in the blanks with *a* or *an*.

What would you like to have that you don't have?

1. __a__ CD player

2. __an__ elevator in my apartment building

3. __an__ expensive car

4. __a__ scholarship

5. __a__ house

6. __a__ pet

7. __a__ racing bike

8. __an__ M.A. degree

B Singular Definite Nouns

1. Use *the* with singular definite count nouns. (*Definite* means we know which one.)

The apple in **the** bowl looks delicious.

He sat in **the** chair by the window.

2. A good test to see if the noun is definite or not is to ask the question "Which one?"

I ate an apple for lunch.
(Which apple? Any apple—it's not specific.)

The apple in the bowl looks delicious.
(Which apple? The apple in the bowl—it is specific.)

C First and Second Mention

1. Use *the* if you have mentioned the same noun earlier or if you are talking about a specific thing.

   I bought **a** hamburger and some fries. Unfortunately **the** hamburger wasn't cooked enough.

2. Phrases and adjective clauses after the noun often make the noun specific.

   The story **in the first chapter** was very entertaining. (specific story)
   The bread **that she made** was the best I've ever had.

   In some cases, the phrases and adjective clauses don't make the noun specific:

   I need to get a car that won't always need to be repaired. (any car)
   My neighbor saw an accident right in front of my house.

Exercise 4

Fill in the blanks with the correct article or Ø.

An Unfortunate Experience

My unfortunate experience occurred about two months ago. I was driving

downtown to buy _____a_____ dress for my best friend's wedding. Just before I

got downtown, my tire went flat. I looked at _____the_____ tire, and it had

_____a_____ nail in it. I didn't have _____a_____ phone in my car, and nobody

stopped to help me. I waited for _____an_____ hour and finally decided to walk.

_____the_____ policeman saw me. He was going to give me _____the_____ ticket for

jaywalking! But I told him about _____a_____ problem with my car, and he

called _____a_____ tow truck. _____The_____ truck arrived about ten minutes later,

and soon _____the_____ tire was fixed. I finally got downtown, but _____the_____ trip

took much longer than I had planned.

D Possessive and Demonstrative Adjectives

1. Possessive adjectives (*my, your, his, her, its, our, their*) and demonstrative adjectives (*this, that, these,* and *those*) do not take articles; they are already definite.

   No: I talked to my a sister.

   No: I talked to a my sister.

   Yes: I talked to my sister.

   No: We went to that a restaurant.

   No: We went to a that restaurant.

   Yes: We went to that restaurant.

E Adjectives

Adjectives alone do not take articles:

No: It is a nice.

Yes: It is nice.

Yes: It is a nice day.

No: She was a beautiful.

Yes: She was beautiful.

Yes: She was a beautiful dog.

Exercise 5

Correct the following sentences.

How did you experience culture shock?

1. Living in different country can be a difficult. I stayed home a lot and didn't

   see my friends so much.

2. I didn't enjoy my hobbies very much. But I tried to find new things to do.

   Now I am interested in new hobby: golf.

3. When I was student, I was so busy. I'm not sure I had culture shock.

4. I tried to find calm place to think.

5. I tried to have fun and go to party every weekend. I wanted to have a

enjoyable time.

6. The best thing for me was to find aᵃactivity I enjoyed and keep a busy.

7. I always felt tired, and I was afraid I had ᴳserious health problem.
   ∧

8. Little things made me ᵃ angry, so I would call friend a lot and talk.
   ✗

Exercise 6

Correct the following sentences.

What is your favorite junk food?

1. Potato chips are the best. I just ate bag of potato chips.

2. I love chocolate, and I eat candy bar every day.

3. Junk food is not healthy, so I eat fruit. I eat a orange every morning

   for breakfast.

4. Give me milkshake, and I am happy.

5. Every night before I go to bed, I eat bowl of vanilla ice cream.

Part 3 Plural Count Nouns and Noncount Nouns

So far, you have studied singular count nouns. Now we will look at plural count nouns and noncount nouns.

Plural Count Nouns	Noncount Nouns
apples	fruit
desks	furniture
people	food

1. If one of these nouns is indefinite, do not use an article. (Remember, *indefinite* means that if you ask *which,* the answer is general, not specific.)

   I like apples.   Furniture has become very expensive.

   People need to be loved.   Food is necessary.

2. An adjective in front of the noun usually does not make the noun specific, so you don't need an article:

   I really don't like green apples.

   All people need to be loved.

   Wood furniture has become very expensive.

   Ethiopian food is very hot.

3. If one of these nouns is definite, use *the*. (Remember, *definite* means that you are talking about a specific or known thing.)

   The apples we picked yesterday weren't really ripe.

   The chairs at that furniture store aren't expensive.

   The Ethiopian food we ate last night was delicious.

   Review:

	Count		Noncount
	Singular	*Plural*	
General (Indefinite)	a / an	Ø	Ø
Specific (Definite)	the	the	the

Exercise 7

Fill in the blanks with the correct article or *Ø*.

What do you like or dislike about the town you are living in now?

1. ____The____ food in this city is expensive.

2. ____The____ people here are very friendly.

3. I can have ____Ø____ fun at the beach.

4. There are ____Ø____ beautiful mountains to look at.

5. I can go to ____Ø____ interesting shops.

6. There is ____Ø____ fascinating scenery, very different from my hometown.

Exercise 8

Correct the following sentences.

Miscellaneous Sentences

1. ~~The~~ Music at the party last night was very nice.

2. I studied ~~the~~ history.

3. The teacher gave me ~~an~~ information.

4. I like to listen to ~~the~~ music.

5. My host family likes ~~the~~ Japanese food.

6. ~~The~~ gas is very expensive these days.

7. The Gas in my car had water in it.

8. It's very important to study European history if you want to understand more about ~~the~~ politics of these countries.

9. I don't really like ~~the~~ hamburgers they serve at that fast food place.

10. Little by little I could understand ~~the~~ English spoken in my college classes.

Part 4 Special Definite Nouns

Usually a noun is definite or specific when there is only one, or when both the speaker and the listener both know which noun the speaker is talking about.

1. Use *the* when there is only one:

   the moon   **the** sun   **the** earth

2. Use *the* in the following expressions:

the first	**the** last	**the** most wonderful	one of **the**
the second	**the** best	**the** same	some of **the**
the third	**the** oldest		most of **the**

   This is **the first** time I've studied English.

   My sister is in **the third** grade.

   When was **the last** time you ate watermelon?

   Tom is **the tallest** boy in his class.

   Our interests are **the same.**

   One of the students in our class writes nearly fluently.

3. Use *the* when both the speaker and the listener know what is being discussed:

> Please pass **the** salt.
>
> I'll pour **the** milk.
>
> (Everyone at the table knows which salt or milk.)

> How did you like **the** movie?
>
> How did you like **the** concert?
>
> (Both people know which movie or concert.)

> **The** weather is beautiful.
>
> I'm so tired of **the** rain.
>
> Could you please open **the** window?
>
> Tom is in **the** kitchen.
>
> **The** police stopped me.
>
> She's talking on **the** telephone.
>
> **The** mail hasn't come yet.

4. Use *the* with some special expressions. In American English, *the* is often used with places known to the community or family:

> I'm going to **the** store.
>
> Let's go to **the** beach.
>
> We went to **the** zoo.
>
> I need to return this book to **the** library.
>
> My sister is in **the** hospital. (American English only)
>
> She is going to **the** doctor tomorrow.

Exercise 9

Fill in the blanks with the correct article or *Ø*.

These People All Live in Watertown.

1. Jack lives near _____the_____ zoo.

2. Sam has a house near _____the_____ library.

3. Jack's apartment is next to _____the_____ hospital.

4. Kim's office is across from _____the_____ store.

5. Pat's condominium is across from _____the_____ beach.

Correct the sentences.

Miscellaneous Sentences

1. It's too loud here. I think I'll study in ^the^ library.

2. Yoshi felt sick, so he went to ^the^ doctor.

3. It's such a beautiful day. Let's go to ^the^ beach.

4. At home, I always listen to ^the^ radio.

5. We stopped at store to get some food.

6. ^The^ Last time I saw my grandmother was a year ago.

7. It was ^the^ first time I drove a car.

8. The food at that restaurant is almost ^the^ same as the food

    at other restaurants.

9. It was ^the^ second apartment I lived in.

10. One of problems with my writing is ^The^ articles.

Part 5   Special Count and Noncount Expressions

1. Some everyday expressions in English don't take an article, although the noun is usually count. This can happen when the noun refers to an activity.

No Article	Article
I go to bed at 9:00. (activity = sleep)	I bought a bed.
She's sick and in bed. (activity = rest or sleep)	My book is on the bed.
I always go to church. (activity = pray)	I live near a church.
I'm in college. (activity = study)	There is a college nearby.
She's at school right now. (activity = study)	She's waiting at the school to be picked up.

Note: Some expressions that refer to a habit can also be noncount. They are more like idiomatic expressions:

   I **eat breakfast** at 8:00 A.M.

   We had steak **for dinner.**

2. With adjectives, the noun becomes count again:

> We had **a big dinner.**
>
> I eat **a small breakfast** every morning.

Exercise 11

Fill in the blanks with the correct article or Ø. Then ask another student the questions and write the answers.

Student Interview: What is your daily routine?

Questions   *Answers*

1. What time do you eat _____ breakfast?   _____

2. Do you like to eat _____ big breakfast or

   _____ small breakfast?   _____

3. Do you like to lie in _____ bed after

   you wake up?   _____

4. Do you go to _____ school early or

   later in the morning?   _____

5. How many hours do you spend at

   _____ school?   _____

6. What is your favorite food

   for _____ dinner?   _____

7. What time do you go to _____ bed?   _____

Exercise 12

Correct the sentences.

Miscellaneous Sentences

1. My sister is in high school. She goes to private high school.

2. Lawrence is very sick. He's staying in the bed.

3. He's pretty religious. He goes to the church daily.

4. She's not hungry. She ate huge dinner.

5. My back hurts. I need new bed.

6. College I attend is having a dance Friday night.

7. I'm hungry. I need to eat a lunch. I usually eat lunch at this time.

Chapter Review

Exercise 13

Fill in the blanks with the correct article or *Ø*.

What do you think are some basic differences between men and women?

1. _____ women are more _____ gentle.

2. _____ men don't like to talk as much as _____ women.

3. _____ men make better _____ soldiers.

4. _____ woman can have _____ baby.

5. _____ man likes to solve _____ his problems quickly; _____

    woman likes to think about _____ her problems and then solve them.

6. It's difficult to compare because all men are not _____ same, and all

    women are not _____ same.

Exercise 14

Fill in the blanks with the correct article or *Ø*.

The Perfect Computer

If I buy _____ computer, here are _____ things I need. I want _____ large color screen that is _____ very clear. _____ computer needs to be _____ fast and have _____ lot of memory because I want to have _____ graphics programs and games. _____ cost is another factor. If it is _____ really expensive, I will see if I can find _____ used one. I also want to send _____ e-mail, so I need a modem (_____ connection from _____ computer to my phone). Finally, _____ most important factor is that it is _____ easy to learn and use. Is there _____ machine like this or is this _____ dream?

Exercise 15

Correct the mistakes in the following paragraph.

A Frightening Experience

Last year, I saw horror movie with my a friend. A movie was about vampire who wanted to eat people. After movie, we went to restaurant to have a dinner. I was still very frightened. As we were eating dinner, it started to rain. Then, I heard loud thunder and saw flashes of lightning. All of lights in restaurant went out, and it became very dark. Suddenly, I felt hand on my shoulder. I screamed because I imagined it was vampire. Then man said, "I'm sorry. I'm trying to find flashlight." It was restaurant manager.

Exercise 16

Correct the mistakes in the following paragraph.

A Wonderful Vacation

Last year, I had a wonderful vacation. My husband and I took trip to the Germany, Switzerland, and Austria. We rented car and drove all around. I loved taking boat ride down Rhine River and visiting beautiful castle. My husband enjoyed seeing the Lake Geneva and climbing in the Alps. We drank beer in the Munich and saw a opera in Vienna. I got to see house where Mozart lived in Salzburg. People we met on trip were very friendly. If I get chance to go back to Europe, I want to visit places we didn't have time to see.

Exercise 1

1. My next trip is to Canada. I want to see <u>the</u> Great Lakes, <u>the</u> Rocky Mountains, and <u>the</u> Pacific Ocean.

2. I am from Mexico, but my friend is from <u>the</u> United Arab Emirates. I would like to visit him in his country after I leave <u>the</u> United States.

3. I hear <u>Seattle</u> is really a beautiful place. I want to go hiking in <u>the</u> Olympic Mountains and climb Mt. Rainier.

4. This September I am going to visit <u>Harvard</u> University. Then I will travel around <u>Boston</u> and Vermont.

5. On my next vacation, I want to go to <u>Colorado</u>. I really want to see <u>the</u> Rocky Mountains.

6. I want to travel to <u>Greece</u> and Egypt. It would be wonderful to swim in <u>the</u> Mediterranean Sea, travel down <u>the</u> Nile River, and see the Suez Canal.

Exercise 2

1. __I__ I need to buy car.

2. __I__ I ate hamburger.

3. __C__ He has a child.

4. __I__ They bought new house.

5. __I__ She told me about trip she wanted to take.

Exercise 3

1. <u>a</u> CD player

2. <u>an</u> elevator in my apartment building

3. <u>an</u> expensive car

4. <u>a</u> scholarship

5. <u>a</u> house

6. <u>a</u> pet

7. <u>a</u> racing bike

8. <u>an</u> M.A. degree (the sound is "<u>em</u>")

Exercise 4

My unfortunate experience occurred about two months ago. I was driving downtown to buy <u>a</u> dress for my best friend's wedding. Just before I got downtown, my tire went flat. I looked at <u>the</u> tire, and it had <u>a</u> nail in it. I didn't have <u>a</u> phone in my car, and nobody stopped to help me. I waited for <u>an</u> hour and finally decided to walk. <u>A</u> policeman saw me. He was going to give me <u>a</u> ticket for jaywalking! But I told him about <u>the</u> problem with my car, and he called <u>a</u> tow truck. <u>The</u> truck arrived about ten minutes later, and soon <u>the</u> tire was fixed. I finally got downtown, but <u>the</u> trip took much longer than I had planned.

(Continued)

Exercise 5

1. Living in <u>a</u> different country can be <u>difficult</u>. I stayed home a lot, and didn't see my friends so much.

2. I didn't enjoy my hobbies very much. But I tried to find new things to do. Now I am interested in <u>a</u> new hobby: golf.

3. When I was <u>a</u> student, I was so busy. I'm not sure I had culture shock.

4. I tried to find <u>a</u> calm place to think.

5. I tried to have fun and go to <u>a</u> party every weekend. I wanted to have <u>an</u> enjoyable time.

6. The best thing for me was to find <u>an</u> activity I enjoyed and keep <u>busy</u>.

7. I always felt tired, and I was afraid I had <u>a</u> serious health problem.

8. Little things made me <u>angry</u>, so I would call <u>a</u> friend a lot and talk.

Exercise 6

1. Potato chips are the best. I just ate <u>a</u> bag of potato chips.

2. I love chocolate, and I eat <u>a</u> candy bar every day.

3. Junk food is not healthy, so I eat fruit. I eat <u>an</u> orange every morning for breakfast.

4. Give me <u>a</u> milkshake, and I am happy.

5. Every night before I go to bed, I eat <u>a</u> bowl of vanilla ice cream.

Exercise 7

1. <u>The</u> food in this city is expensive.

2. <u>The</u> people here are very friendly.

3. I can have <u>Ø</u> fun at the beach.

4. There are <u>Ø</u> beautiful mountains to look at.

5. I can go to <u>Ø</u> interesting shops.

6. There is <u>Ø</u> fascinating scenery, very different from my hometown.

Exercise 8

1. <u>The</u> music at the party last night was very nice.

2. I studied <u>history</u>.

3. The teacher gave me <u>information</u>.

4. I like to listen to <u>music</u>.

5. My host family likes <u>Japanese food</u>.

6. <u>Gas</u> is very expensive these days.

7. <u>The</u> gas in my car had water in it.

8. It's very important to study European history if you want to understand more about <u>the</u> politics of these countries.

9. I don't really like <u>the</u> hamburgers they serve at that fast food place.

10. Little by little I could understand <u>the</u> English spoken in my college classes.

(Continued)

Exercise 9

1. Jack lives near <u>the</u> zoo.
2. Sam has a house near <u>the</u> library.
3. Jack's apartment is next to <u>the</u> hospital.
4. Kim's office is across from <u>the</u> store.
5. Pat's condominium is across from <u>the</u> beach.

Exercise 10

1. It's too loud here. I think I'll study in <u>the</u> library.
2. Yoshi felt sick, so he went to <u>the</u> doctor.
3. It's such a beautiful day. Let's go to <u>the</u> beach.
4. At home, I always listen to <u>the</u> radio.
5. We stopped at <u>the</u> store to get some food.
6. <u>The</u> last time I saw my grandmother was a year ago.
7. It was <u>the</u> first time I drove a car.
8. The food at that restaurant is almost <u>the</u> same as the food at other restaurants.
9. It was <u>the</u> second apartment I lived in.
10. One of <u>the</u> problems with my writing is articles.

Exercise 11

1. What time do you eat <u>Ø</u> breakfast?
2. Do you like to eat <u>a</u> big breakfast or <u>a</u> small breakfast?
3. Do you like to lie in <u>Ø</u> bed after you wake up?
4. Do you go to <u>Ø</u> school early or later in the morning?
5. How many hours do you spend at <u>Ø</u> school?
6. What is your favorite food for <u>Ø</u> dinner?
7. What time do you go to <u>Ø</u> bed?

Exercise 12

1. My sister is in high school. She goes to <u>a</u> private high school.
2. Lawrence is very sick. He's staying in <u>bed</u>.
3. He's pretty religious. He goes to <u>church</u> daily.
4. She's not hungry. She ate <u>a</u> huge dinner.
5. My back hurts. I need <u>a</u> new bed.
6. <u>The</u> college I attend is having a dance Friday night.
7. I'm hungry. I need to eat <u>lunch</u>. I usually eat lunch at this time.

(Concluded)

Exercise 13

1. Ø Women are more Ø gentle.
2. Ø Men don't like to talk as much as Ø women.
3. Ø Men make better Ø soldiers.
4. A woman can have a baby.
5. A man likes to solve Ø his problems quickly; a woman likes to think about Ø her problems and then solve them.
6. It's difficult to compare because all men are not the same, and all women are not the same.

Exercise 14

If I buy a computer, here are the things I need. I want a large color screen that is Ø very clear. The computer needs to be Ø fast and have a lot of memory because I want to have Ø graphics programs and games. The cost is another factor. If it is Ø really expensive, I will see if I can find a used one. I also want to send Ø e-mail, so I need a modem (a connection from the computer to my phone). Finally, the most important factor is that it is Ø easy to learn and use. Is there a machine like this or is this a dream?

Exercise 15

Last year, I saw a horror movie with my friend. The movie was about a vampire who wanted to eat people. After the movie, we went to a restaurant to have dinner. I was still very frightened. As we were eating dinner, it started to rain. Then, I heard loud thunder and saw flashes of lightning. All of the lights in the restaurant went out, and it became very dark. Suddenly, I felt a hand on my shoulder. I screamed because I imagined it was a vampire. Then a man said, "I'm sorry. I'm trying to find a flashlight." It was the restaurant manager.

Exercise 16

Last year, I had a wonderful vacation. My husband and I took a trip to Germany, Switzerland, and Austria. We rented a car and drove all around. I loved taking a boat ride down the Rhine River and visiting a beautiful castle. My husband enjoyed seeing Lake Geneva and climbing in the Alps. We drank beer in Munich and saw an opera in Vienna. I got to see the house where Mozart lived in Salzburg. The people we met on the trip were very friendly. If I get a chance to go back to Europe, I want to visit the places we didn't have time to see.

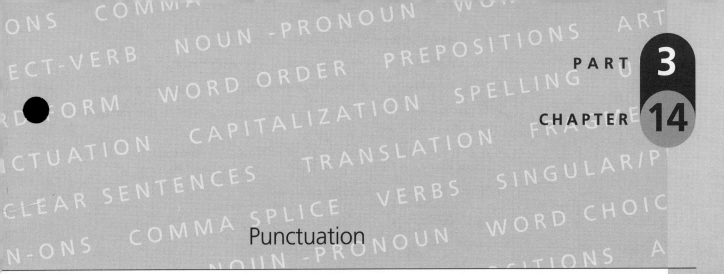

CHAPTER 14

Punctuation

Punctuation errors are mistakes using punctuation marks (. , ; : ". . ." '
! ?). Native speakers of English also learn the rules for using punctuation
correctly.

A Periods

1. Can you find the punctuation errors in these sentences?

   No: It rained yesterday

   Yes: It rained yesterday.

   No: He came here to study for a year, this was his dream.

   Yes: He came here to study for a year. This was his dream.

   - Use a period at the end of a sentence that is a statement.
     Note: In British English, a period is called a "full stop."

   - Be sure to use a period to separate two complete sentences. Do not
     use a comma.

     See Comma Splice on page 113 for more information.

2. Can you discover the problems in the following sentences?

   No: Mr Smith went to see Dr Jones.

   Yes: Mr. Smith went to see Dr. Jones.

   No: I told my prof. that I needed to see my dr.

   Yes: I told my professor that I needed to see my doctor.

   No: My friend lives on Underwood Ave..

   Yes: My friend lives on Underwood Ave.

   Note: In formal writing, write out words such as "Avenue."

   No: Now I'm studying E S. L. in the U. S A.

   Yes: Now I'm studying E. S. L. in the U.S.A.

   Yes: Now I'm studying ESL in the USA.

- Use a period at the end of an abbreviation.

- Use abbreviations for titles only before a person's name.

- If the abbreviation is at the end of the sentence, use only one period.

- In general, use a period after each letter in an abbreviation that stands for two or more words.

- A few common abbreviations (*USA, ESL*) do not need periods, but use periods for each letter or none at all. Do not mix the two.

- Here is a list of common abbreviations:

  Mr. Abelson

  Mrs. Cox

  Ms. Rice

  Dr. Stevens   (Doctor)

  Prof. Gonzales   (Professor)

  St. Anthony   (Saint)

  Stephen Jones, Sr.   (Senior)

  Stephen Jones, Jr.   (Junior)

  Fourth St.   (Street)

  Carnation Ave.   (Avenue)

  10:30 P.M. or 10:30 p.m.

  5000 B.C.

  800 A.D.

Exercise 1

Add periods where necessary.

Famous People and Places

1. Florence Nightingale lived from 1820 to 1920 she is known as the founder of modern nursing.

2. Dr Martin Luther King, Jr received the Nobel Peace Prize in 1964.

3. Two famous American streets are Pennsylvania Ave in Washington D C and Wall St in New York.

4. St Francis of Assissi is known partly for his love of animals and nature.

5. Cleopatra was a famous queen who lived from 69 B C to 39 B C in Egypt.

B Commas

1. The following No sentences have mistakes in the way the comma was written. Can you find the problems?

No: My children went to school, but I stayed home.

Yes: My children went to school, but I stayed home.

No: James wanted to study at a university

   , but he needed a scholarship.

Yes: James wanted to study at a university,

   but he needed a scholarship.

- Make sure your comma is larger than a period so that it is easy to read and people don't confuse it with a period.

- Do not use a comma to begin a new line. Put the comma after the word at the end of the previous line.

2. Commas show a small pause in the sentence when it is read aloud. Do you know the rules for using commas? Study the following sentences and each rule below them.

No: I used to live in Atlanta Georgia. Then I moved to Montreal Canada.

Yes: I used to live in Atlanta, Georgia. Then I moved to Montreal, Canada.

- Use commas to separate cities, provinces, states, and countries.

No: I plan to visit Australia, and New Zealand.

Yes: I plan to visit Australia and New Zealand.

Yes: I plan to visit Australia, New Zealand, and Hong Kong.

Note: The comma before *and* is optional.

- Use commas to separate three or more items in a series or list.

No: My grandparents would like to travel and their grandchildren would love to go with them.

Yes: My grandparents would like to travel, and their grandchildren would love to go with them.

- Use commas when you connect two sentences with these words: *and, but, so, yet, or, nor,* and *for* (meaning *because*). Do not use a comma before *and* if it does not connect two sentences.

See Less Formal Compound Sentences on page 35 for more information.

No: When the weather gets better we can do more outdoor sports.

Yes: When the weather gets better, we can do more outdoor sports.

No: My teacher spoke slowly, because it was the first day of class.

Yes: My teacher spoke slowly because it was the first day of class.

- Use a comma after an adverb clause (a dependent clause that begins with words like *before, when, if,* and *because*) at the beginning of a sentence. Do not use a comma or other punctuation if the adverb clause is the second clause.

See Adverb Clauses on page 279 for more information.

No: In the winter I love to feel the cold air on my face.

Yes: In the winter, I love to feel the cold air on my face.

No: My son loves riding a motorcycle. He knows however that they are dangerous.

Yes: My son loves riding a motorcycle. He knows, however, that they are dangerous.

- Use a comma after an introductory phrase.

- Use two commas to separate unnecessary information in the middle of a sentence.

No: There are three reasons, why I want to learn English.

Yes: There are three reasons why I want to learn English.

- Don't use commas to break up a sentence. One comma is never used between the subject and verb or between the verb and object.

Exercise 2

Write C for correct and I for incorrect. Then correct the mistakes.

Body Language

1. _____ Body language includes movement of the head face arms hands and body.

2. _____ Some people move their hands wildly when they tell a story.

3. _____ In some cultures looking a person straight in the eye means you are telling the truth but it is not polite in other cultures.

4. _____ If a person stands close to you, you may feel uncomfortable because the normal distance between people may be greater in your culture.

5. _____ When I visited Sofia Bulgaria I was confused because people nodded their heads up and down to mean "no" instead of "yes."

C Semicolons

A semicolon (;) looks like a combination of a colon (:) and a comma (,). It is used in formal writing to connect two closely related sentences.

1. Can you find the problems in these sentences?

No: The team had several players with injuries however, they felt confident about winning.

Yes: The team had several players with injuries; however, they felt confident about winning.

No: I have As on all my tests, consequently, I don't feel so much pressure for the final exam.

Yes: I have As on all my tests; consequently, I don't feel so much pressure for the final exam.

- Use a semicolon before a transition word when you connect two closely related sentences. Use a comma after the transition word.

  Note: A period could also be used to separate these sentences.

- Here are common transition words and the punctuation used to connect two sentences:

; in addition,	; however,	; therefore,	; for example,
; furthermore,	; on the other hand,	; consequently,	; for instance,
; moreover,	; nevertheless,	; as a result,	
	; nonetheless,		

See More Formal Compound Sentences on page 45 for more information.

2. How is a semicolon used here?

No: Life without my father was very difficult, I missed him terribly.

Yes: Life without my father was very difficult; I missed him terribly.

- It is possible, but not very common, to separate two closely related sentences with only a semicolon.

Exercise 3

Add commas and semicolons where necessary.

About Languages

1. There are about 5,000 languages spoken in the world however some of

   these languages are disappearing.

2. Some alphabets have more letters than others for instance the Cambodian alphabet has seventy-two letters compared to twenty-six in English.

3. Most children learn the language they hear in their family quite easily furthermore children who grow up hearing two languages may become bilingual.

4. Linguists believe that humans are biologically prepared to learn a language most children learn the language they hear in their family almost effortlessly.

5. Dr. Ludwig L. Zamenhof wanted a universal language to help people speak together easily therefore he invented *Esperanto* in the 1880s.

D Other Punctuation

Here are rules and examples for using other punctuation.

1. Use a colon (:) after a noun when you list information:

   No: They have three wishes for the next year, health, wealth, and happiness.

   Yes: They have three wishes for the next year: health, wealth, and happiness.

2. Use quotation marks (". . .") around the exact words that someone said.

   No: My friend said It's my birthday.

   Yes: My friend said, "It's my birthday."

   Note: There is a comma after *said* and the period comes inside the quotation mark.

   See Appendix 5 on page 341 for more information.

3. Use a question mark (?) at the end of a question.

   No: He asked, "Where should I go."

   Yes: He asked, "Where should I go?"

4. Use an exclamation point (!) to show surprise. Don't overuse it.

No: The plane began to gently roll! A few people screamed! I wasn't scared!

Yes: The plane began to gently roll. A few people screamed. I wasn't scared.

Yes: When I awoke, there was a snake in my sleeping bag!

5. An apostrophe (') has two uses:

a. Use an apostrophe (usually + *s*) to show possession (belonging to someone or something).

No: Yukiko parents are coming to visit.

Yes: **Yukiko's** parents are coming to visit.

No: My sisters house is being remodeled.

Yes: My **sister's** house is being remodeled.   (one sister)

Yes: My **sisters'** house is being remodeled.   (two sisters)

Note: If there are two or more sisters, the apostrophe goes after the *s*.

No: My car has a problem. It's engine is leaking oil.

Yes: My car has a problem. **Its** engine is leaking oil.

Note: Its with no apostrophe means *belongs to it.*

b. Use an apostrophe in contractions (two words put together).

No: I dont care about it.

Yes: I **don't** care about it.

No: Its hard to run a marathon.

Yes: **It's** hard to run a marathon.

Note: It's with an apostrophe means *it is.*

Exercise 4

Correct the mistakes.

What are the characteristics of a good language school?

1. The teachers say, "I will give you extra help.

2. These are the three most important characteristics, excellent teachers a computer lab and small classes.

3. Each teachers caring attitude for the students is very important to me.

4. The classes are small. Fifteen students is good!

5. The school has a lot of opportunities for: conversation practice with

   native speakers.

6. My friends tell me that "they think a school with many activities

   is also important."

Chapter Review

Exercise 5

Correct the mistakes.

What city have you never been to but would like to see?

1. I would like to visit Paris France, because it is so romantic.

2. I want to visit Kyoto, because it has so many temples and its so beautiful.

3. I think I'd like to visit Hong Kong because of it's shopping.

4. I have never been to New York but I would like to see it because of its

   excitement and energy.

5. There are three cities I would like to visit, Sydney, Bangkok,

   and Rio de Janeiro.

6. I want to go to Florence Italy because of the artwork

   , there.

7. My friends have told me that Salzburg Austria is like a city from a fairy

   tale and I would love to see it.

8. When I save enough money to buy a plane ticket I want to go to Nairobi

   Kenya so that I can see all the wildlife in the parks.

Exercise 6

There are six punctuation mistakes in the following paragraph. Can you find and correct them?

Acupuncture

Acupuncture uses needles to reduce pain or heal a person it began in China more than 2,000 years ago and is very different from Western medicine. Acupuncture treats the whole body! Acupuncturists believe, there is a life energy going through a persons body. Needles are put in different acupuncture points to balance this life energy. This helps with some of the following problems, back pain, high blood pressure, stress , addictions, and depression.

Exercise 1

1. Florence Nightingale lived from 1820 to <u>1920. She</u> is known as the founder of modern nursing.

2. <u>Dr.</u> Martin Luther King, <u>Jr.</u> received the Nobel Peace Prize in 1964.

3. Two famous American streets are Pennsylvania <u>Ave.</u> in Washington <u>D.C.</u> and Wall <u>St.</u> in New York.

4. <u>St.</u> Francis of Assissi is known partly for his love of animals and nature.

5. Cleopatra was a famous queen who lived from 69 <u>B.C.</u> to 39 <u>B.C.</u> in Egypt.

Exercise 2

1. __I__ Body language includes movement of the head, face, arms, hands, and body.

2. __C__ Some people move their hands wildly when they tell a story.

3. __I__ In some cultures(,)* looking a person straight in the eye means you are telling the truth, but it is not polite in other cultures.

4. __C__ If a person stands close to you, you may feel uncomfortable because the normal distance between people may be greater in your culture.

5. __I__ When I visited Sofia, Bulgaria, I was confused because people nodded their heads up and down to mean "no" instead of "yes."

* Note: After a short introductory phrase, a comma is optional.

Exercise 3

1. There are about 5,000 languages spoken in the world; however, some of these languages are disappearing.

2. Some alphabets have more letters than others; for instance, the Cambodian alphabet has seventy-two letters compared to twenty-six in English.

3. Most children learn the language they hear in their family quite easily; furthermore, children who grow up hearing two languages may become bilingual.

4. Linguists believe that humans are biologically prepared to learn a language; most children learn the language they hear in their family almost effortlessly.

5. Dr. Ludwig L. Zamenhof wanted a universal language to help people speak together easily; therefore, he invented *Esperanto* in the 1880s.

(Concluded)

Exercise 4

1. The teachers say, "I will give you extra help."

2. These are the three most important characteristics: excellent teachers, a computer lab, and small classes.

3. Each teacher's caring attitude for the students is very important to me.

4. The classes are small. Fifteen students is good.

5. The school has a lot of opportunities for conversation practice with native speakers.

6. My friends tell me that they think a school with many activities is also important.

Exercise 5

1. I would like to visit Paris, France because it is so romantic.

2. I want to visit Kyoto because it has so many temples and it's so beautiful.

3. I think I'd like to visit Hong Kong because of its shopping.

4. I have never been to New York, but I would like to see it because of its excitement and energy.

5. There are three cities I would like to visit: Sydney, Bangkok, and Rio de Janeiro.

6. I want to go to Florence, Italy because of the artwork there.

7. My friends have told me that Salzburg, Austria is like a city from a fairy tale, and I would love to see it.

8. When I save enough money to buy a plane ticket, I want to go to Nairobi, Kenya so that I can see all the wildlife in the parks.

Exercise 6

Acupuncture uses needles to reduce pain or heal a person. It began in China more than 2,000 years ago and is very different from Western medicine. Acupuncture treats the whole body. Acupuncturists believe there is a life energy going through a person's body. Needles are put in different acupuncture points to balance this life energy. This helps with some of the following problems: back pain, high blood pressure, stress, addictions, and depression.

CHAPTER 15

Capitalization

A capitalization error occurs when a small letter is written instead of a capital (big) letter, or a capital letter is written instead of a small letter. Native speakers of English also learn the rules for capitalization. See Appendix 6 on page 343 for a handwriting sample of small and capital letters.

A · Capitalization in a Sentence

Can you find the capitalization problems in these sentences?

No: I had a really bad headache. therefore, I stayed home.

Yes: I had a really bad headache. Therefore, I stayed home.

No: I asked my father, "did you ever feel confused?"

Yes: I asked my father, "Did you ever feel confused?"

No: He wanted to help his friends, but only if
        They wanted help.

Yes: He wanted to help his friends, but only if they wanted help.

No: For example, In my country, people take off their shoes inside
        a house.

Yes: For example, in my country, people take off their shoes inside
        a house.

No: I thought I understood what happened; However,
        I was wrong.

Yes: I thought I understood what happened; however,
        I was wrong.

- Capitalize the first word in a sentence.
- Capitalize the first word in a quotation if it is the first word of a sentence.
- Do not capitalize the first word in a new line unless it is the beginning of a sentence.

- Do not capitalize words after commas.
- Do not capitalize words after semicolons.

See Punctuation on page 277 for more information on commas and semicolons.

Exercise 1

The following story needs some capital letters. Change small letters to capital letters where necessary.

My First Plane Ride

i'll never forget my first airplane ride. I was about ten years old. I sat in the window seat and buckled my seatbelt. when the plane started racing down the runway, I could feel my heart pounding in my chest. as the plane lifted into the air, my stomach tickled and my ears popped. watching the buildings, cars, houses, and people on the ground grow tiny as we went higher and higher fascinated me. it was a wonderful experience.

Exercise 2

Change small letters to capital letters where necessary.

An Excerpt from a Conversation

my aunt asked my mother, "do you really want to leave your home to live in another country?"

"I think so," my mother answered. "my family needs a better place to live."

B People

Here are some rules and examples for using capital letters with people.

1. Capitalize the names of people and the pronoun *I*. Do not capitalize other pronouns (*you, he, she, it, we, they*) unless they begin a sentence.

   Steven, Sara, and I went downtown. I thought they would like it. We had a great time.

2. Capitalize a title (*Mr., Doctor, President, Professor, Captain*, etc.) with a name. Use a small letter for a title without a name.

Mrs. Alvarez has an appointment with Dr. Roberts.

I plan to go to medical school to become a doctor.

3. Capitalize the name of a family relationship (*Father, Mother, Aunt*) if it is used like a name. Use a small letter if you use *my father, her mother, Susan's aunt*.

All his life, Father has worked very hard, just like Aunt Margaret and Uncle Thomas.

My father and my mother live here, but my grandparents live with their youngest daughter in another city.

Exercise 3

Write C for correct and I for incorrect. Then correct the mistakes.

Family and Friends

1. _____ My father is related to the prime minister in my home country.

2. _____ Maria's Cousin Elizabeth is a Captain in the military.

3. _____ Last year I lived with Professor Adams. He and his wife were my

host parents.

4. _____ My Aunt and Uncle are both Doctors.

5. _____ Aziz and Khaled are cousins. Their mothers are sisters.

C Time Expressions and Names of Places

1. Use capital letters with the names of days, months, and holidays. Use small letters with the names of seasons.

This year Easter will be on Sunday, April 5.

I really like spring and fall, but I don't like winter.

2. Use capital letters with names of streets, cities, states, provinces, regions, countries, continents, mountains, lakes, rivers and islands. Do not capitalize these words when they are not part of a name.

Name (Proper Noun)	Not a Name (Common Noun)
1142 First Ave. S.	my street
Montreal	a city
Arkansas	a state
the South	walk south (a direction)
Ecuador	a country
Asia	a big continent
the Alps	the mountains
Mount Kilamanjaro	a mountain
Lake Geneva	a lake
the Mississippi River	a river
Long Island	an island

Examples:

There are many wonderful vacation spots in the Appalachian Mountains.
It's hot! Let's go to the mountains and swim in a cool lake.

Exercise 4

Write C for correct and I for incorrect. Then correct the mistakes.

Places I Want to Visit

1. _____ I like any Mountain because I love to hike.

2. _____ Skiing is my favorite Winter sport, and I would like to try the

    canadian rockies.

3. _____ I visited St. Petersburg last january and fell in love with its

    beauty. I want to see it again in the summer.

4. _____ New York is very exciting compared to the city I come from.

5. _____ Hawaii is wonderful because of the beaches and warm climate.

6. _____ I just got back from the Bahamas on Saturday. I'd love to go

    there again.

7. _____ I want to go on a tour of ancient cities in Mexico.

8. _____ I'd say Switzerland. It's such a beautiful Country.

D Other Uses

In general, use a capital letter for the specific name of anything. Here are some rules and examples.

1. Use a capital letter for the name of races, nationalities, and languages.

    The registration form asks students if they consider themselves African American, Asian American, Caucasian, Native American, or of Hispanic descent.

    Pataporn is Thai, and Kitty is Chinese.

    Yelena speaks Russian, English, French, and German.

2. Use a capital letter for the name of schools, companies, stores, clubs, and other organizations. Use a small letter if the specific name is not given.

    After I graduate from the University of British Columbia, I'll work at Anderson Construction Company.

    I went to high school before I attended the university and then got a job with a construction company.

3. Use a capital letter for the name of commercial products (the exact name of a company's product). Use a small letter for the type of product (no special name):

    At McDonald's I had a Big Mac and a Coca-Cola.

    I love hamburgers and pop.

    I had a headache, so I took an aspirin.

4. Use a capital letter for the name of a specific school class. Use a small letter for the name of a general subject (unless it is a language).

    Next quarter, I'll study Introduction to Business, Child Psychology, and Biology 103.

    The college offers many courses in business, psychology, and English.

5. Use a capital letter for the title of a book, newspaper, magazine, article, movie, television show, song, or story, including a story or essay that you write.

    Capitalize the first and main words, but use a small letter for prepositions, articles, connecting words (*and, but, or, so*) and *to* in infinitives when they are not the first word.

    Last night I read *Newsweek* and watched *Home Improvement* on TV.

    The title of my essay is "The Difference between Marketing and Sales."

Exercise 5

Correct the mistakes.

Studies and Careers in Business

1. I'm studying Marketing. I hope to get a job in a Company.

2. I'm taking Accounting 205. Luckily, I like Math, so it's not difficult.

3. When I was in High School, I really enjoyed my Business class.

4. The *Los Angeles times* listed over a hundred jobs in Sales.

5. I'm fluent in spanish and english, so I'm looking for a job as

   a bilingual secretary.

6. I love Computers, so I hope to get a job with IBM, Gateway, or another

   Computer Company.

Chapter Review

Exercise 6

Write C for correct and I for incorrect. Then correct the mistakes.

Geography Trivia: Did You Know?

1. _____ The Nile is the longest river in the world.

2. _____ The vatican is the smallest Country in the world.

3. _____ Death valley in california is the hottest place in the u.s.

4. _____ The biggest city in Canada is Toronto.

5. _____ The canary islands belong to Spain.

6. _____ Hawaii is the U.S. state that gets the most rain.

7. _____ If you put all of the Countries in alphabetical order, the first

   Country is afghanistan.

8. _____ The only country that has a map on its flag is Cyprus.

Correct the mistakes.

A Memorable Trip: My Flight to Cairo

1. I flew from Los Angeles to London on april 1, early on a saturday morning.

2. I knew it would be a long trip, and took a lot of reading, including books for my Psychology and Business classes.

3. I had an eighteen-hour layover in London. I got a room and slept for a while. I have found that if I take one Aspirin, I sleep better, so I did that.

4. Unfortunately, when I left London, my Trip became more interesting than I wanted.

5. The Woman next to me was airsick for several hours during the flight.

6. The couple in front of Me had a five-month-old Baby who cried most of the flight. The Mother could do nothing to comfort Him.

7. The man next to me was Japanese, and he didn't speak any english.

8. We had to land at another Airport and wait twenty-four more hours for another plane.

9. When I got to Cairo, I called my Uncle Bill to come pick me up.

10. He probably didn't expect me to burst into tears when I saw him, too exhausted from the Trip to do anything but cry.

Exercise 8

Correct the mistakes.

My Goals

I guess the most important thing for me to do is improve my english abilities. English is very difficult for me. I studied It a lot in my Country, and although I can read It pretty well, I can't speak well. I plan to spend a lot of time talking to Native Speakers. I also want to get good grades so that when I finish e.s.l. I can get into the college I want. My Major is engineering, and I want to go to a good University. If I get accepted to one, My parents will pay for me to attend, So I really need to get good grades. I also hope to enjoy myself while I am here, too. If I get out and do things, I will have more chances to speak english, and I will improve more quickly.

Exercise 1

<u>I'll</u> never forget my first airplane ride. I was about ten years old. I sat in the window seat and buckled my seatbelt. <u>When</u> the plane started racing down the runway, I could feel my heart pounding in my chest. <u>As</u> the plane lifted into the air, my stomach tickled and my ears popped. <u>Watching</u> the buildings, cars, houses, and people on the ground grow tiny as we went higher and higher fascinated me. <u>It</u> was a wonderful experience.

Exercise 2

<u>My</u> aunt asked my mother, "<u>Do</u> you really want to leave your home to live in another country?"

"I think so," my mother answered. "<u>My</u> family needs a better place to live."

Exercise 3

1. __C__ My father is related to the prime minister in my home country.

2. __I__ Maria's <u>cousin</u> Elizabeth is a <u>captain</u> in the military.

3. __C__ Last year I lived with Professor Adams. He and his wife were my host parents.

4. __I__ My <u>aunt</u> and <u>uncle</u> are both <u>doctors</u>.

5. __C__ Aziz and Khaled are cousins. Their mothers are sisters.

Exercise 4

1. __I__ I like any <u>mountain</u> because I love to hike.

2. __I__ Skiing is my favorite <u>winter</u> sport, and I would like to try the <u>Canadian Rockies.</u>

3. __I__ I visited St. Petersburg last <u>January</u> and fell in love with its beauty. I want to see it again in the summer.

4. __C__ New York is very exciting compared to the city I come from.

5. __C__ Hawaii is wonderful because of the beaches and warm climate.

6. __C__ I just got back from the Bahamas on Saturday. I'd love to go there again.

7. __C__ I want to go on a tour of ancient cities in Mexico.

8. __I__ I'd say Switzerland. It's such a beautiful <u>country</u>.

Exercise 5

1. I'm studying <u>marketing</u>. I hope to get a job in a <u>company</u>.

2. I'm taking Accounting 205. Luckily, I like <u>math</u>, so it's not difficult.

3. When I was in <u>high</u> <u>school</u>, I really enjoyed my <u>business</u> class.

4. The *Los Angeles Times* listed over a hundred jobs in <u>sales</u>.

5. I'm fluent in <u>Spanish</u> and <u>English</u>, so I'm looking for a job as a bilingual secretary.

6. I love <u>computers</u>, so I hope to get a job with IBM, Gateway, or another <u>computer</u> <u>company</u>.

(Concluded)

Exercise 6

1. __C__ The Nile is the longest river in the world.

2. __I__ The <u>Vatican</u> is the smallest <u>country</u> in the world.

3. __I__ Death <u>Valley</u> in <u>California</u> is the hottest place in the <u>U.S.</u>

4. __C__ The biggest city in Canada is Toronto.

5. __I__ The <u>Canary</u> <u>Islands</u> belong to Spain.

6. __C__ Hawaii is the U.S. state that gets the most rain.

7. __I__ If you put all of the <u>countries</u> in alphabetical order, the first <u>country</u> is <u>Afghanistan</u>.

8. __C__ The only country that has a map on its flag is Cyprus.

Exercise 7

1. I flew from Los Angeles to London on <u>April</u> 1, early on a <u>Saturday</u> morning.

2. I knew it would be a long trip, and took a lot of reading, including books for my <u>psychology</u> and <u>business</u> classes.

3. I had an eighteen-hour layover in London. I got a room and slept for a while. I have found that if I take one <u>aspirin</u>, I sleep better, so I did that.

4. Unfortunately, when I left London, my <u>trip</u> became more interesting than I wanted.

5. The <u>woman</u> next to me was airsick for several hours during the flight.

6. The couple in front of <u>me</u> had a five-month-old <u>baby</u> who cried most of the flight. The <u>mother</u> could do nothing to comfort <u>him</u>.

7. The man next to me was Japanese, and he didn't speak any <u>English</u>.

8. We had to land at another <u>airport</u> and wait twenty-four more hours for another plane.

9. When I got to Cairo, I called my <u>uncle</u> Bill to come pick me up.

10. He probably didn't expect me to burst into tears when I saw him, too exhausted from the <u>trip</u> to do anything but cry.

Exercise 8

I guess the most important thing for me to do is improve my <u>English</u> abilities. English is very difficult for me. I studied it a lot in my <u>country</u>, and although I can read it pretty well, I can't speak well. I plan to spend a lot of time talking to <u>native</u> <u>speakers</u>. I also want to get good grades so that when I finish <u>E.S.L.</u> I can get into the college I want. My <u>major</u> is engineering, and I want to go to a good <u>university</u>. If I get accepted to one, <u>my</u> parents will pay for me to attend, <u>so</u> I really need to get good grades. I also hope to enjoy myself while I am here, too. If I get out and do things, I will have more chances to speak <u>English</u>, and I will improve more quickly.

CHAPTER 16

Spelling

English spelling is difficult for both native and non-native speakers. As you know, English words are often not spelled the way they sound.

Many people appreciate the Spell Check that comes in word processing programs so that they can check their spelling when they write on a computer. However, even if the computer finds a misspelled word and gives you several choices for correct words, you need to have some spelling skills to know which is the correct choice. The same is true for the pocket spelling books or computer dictionaries you can buy.

If you improve your spelling, you can be more confident about your editing when you don't use a computer, and you can save time by not needing to look up so many words in a dictionary or spelling book.

A Suggestions for Improving Spelling

1. Review the spelling rules and common spelling errors in this chapter until you have a good understanding of them and can use the rules as you write in English.

2. Keep a spelling list of words you have misspelled in your writing. (See page 373 in the Student Notebook section.) Write the misspelled word, and then write it correctly five times. It helps for some students to say each letter as they write it, focusing on how the word looks and how the letters sound. Close your eyes until you "see" the word in your mind.

   Try to notice anything that helps you remember the spelling. Sometimes you can divide the word into smaller words. For example, *together* is spelled by writing *to get her* in one word.

Here is a sample of a student's spelling list with ways to remember the correct spelling.

Misspelled	Correct	Notes
1. langage	language language language language language	"guage — need "guage — u + age (= u age — get older) when you study a language
2. writting	writing writing writing writing writing	write + ing — follow the rule, just take away e, no double t
3. alot	a lot a lot a lot a lot a lot	a lot — needs to be two words or "a lot of idioms in English have two words"
4. collage	college college college college college	coll - ege — e on each side of g
5. diffecult	difficult difficult difficult difficult difficult	difficult — double f and i on each side of double f

3. If you find you continue to have problems with spelling, consider learning more about the sound / spelling system of English. There are many good books and some books with tapes that can help you.

B Basic Spelling Rules

1. Two words in this sentence are misspelled. Can you describe why they are wrong?

   No: My fathr has a lot of enrgy.

   Yes: My **father** has a lot of **energy.**

   - Every syllable (sound) in English needs a vowel (*a, e, i, o, u*) or semivowel (*w, y*). (The letters *w* and *y* sometimes have a vowel sound and sometimes a consonant sound.)

   - Here is one way to think about this rule:

     fa-ther   two syllables: each syllable needs a vowel
     1 2

     en-er-gy   three syllables: each syllable needs a vowel or
     1 2 3   semivowel (*y*). (Say the word slowly to hear each syllable.)

2. Can you see the basic spelling problem in this sentence?

   No: I hop I wrot him that letter.

   Yes: I **hope** I **wrote** him that letter.

   - Most words with long vowel sounds end in silent *e*.

   - Here are examples of short and long vowel sounds:

short vowel		long vowel	
hat	(ae)	hate	(ey)
hop	(a)	hope	(ow)
kit	(i)	kite	(ay)
cut	(u)	cute	(ew)

Exercise 1

There are two spelling mistakes in each sentence. Can you find and correct them?

New Year's Day

1. New Year's Day is a big holday in my famly.

2. Evry year we get together to celebrate and exchang gifts.

3. The childrn get a lot of toys and mney from the adults.

4. Everybdy stays up lat and watches the fireworks.

5. Last year, I tried to stay awak all night, but I fell asleep before my

   cousns did.

C Prefixes and Suffixes

Can you discover the spelling problems in these sentences?

No: The party officeres were dissappointed with the election results.

Yes: The party **officers** were **disappointed** with the election results.

No: I tryed to get my paper written on time, but I couldn't.

Yes: I **tried** to get my paper written on time, but I couldn't.

- Follow the rules for adding prefixes like *dis-* to the beginning of words, or suffixes like *-ed, -en,* and *-s* to the end of words.

See Appendix 7 on page 345 for spelling rules for adding prefixes and suffixes.

Exercise 2

Underline your preference for each situation. Then find and correct one mistake in each sentence.

Choices

1. For exercise, do you prefer jogging or rideing a bike?

2. On a hot day, do you prefer eatting an ice-cream cone or drinking

   a cold soda?

3. In general, do you prefer writting a letter or getting a letter?

4. In a small group, do you prefer mostly talking or mostly listening?

5. To help with a dinner, do you prefer preparing the meal or cleanning up?

Exercise 3

Write **C** for correct and **I** for incorrect. Then correct the mistakes.

What is an accomplishment you are proud of?

1. _____   I raised six children who are now happy and successful adults.

2. _____   I tryed out for the Olympic Swim Team and almost made it.

3. _____   My sister and I planned a family reunion. Everyone came and we

   all enjoied it a lot.

4. _____ When an accident occured in front of my house, I rescued the

driver. I discovered that I could stay calm in a stressful situation.

5. _____ After quitting college because of some problems, I went back and

finished my degree.

D Homonyms

Homonyms are words that have the same sound but different spellings. These are often difficult for native speakers of English, too. If you use the wrong word, your computer's Spell Check won't notice the mistake.

Check your knowledge of homonyms by writing the correct spelling in the blank.

buy or *by*   a preposition: music _____ Beethoven

                       pay money for something _____

hear or *here*   a place _____

                       similar to *listen* _____

hole or *whole*   space in the ground _____

                       all of something _____

its or *it's*   it is _____

                       belongs to it _____

meat or *meet*   to see someone _____

                       food from an animal _____

one or *won*   1 _____

                       opposite of *lost* _____

peace or *piece*   opposite of *war* _____

a part of something _____

right or *write*   opposite of *left*; not wrong _____

you do this with a pen _____

son or *sun*   hot star in the sky _____

a boy child _____

their, there or *they're*   belongs to them _____

they are _____

a place _____

threw or *through*   a preposition: *look _____ a window*

throw a ball (past tense) _____

to, too or *two*   2 _____

also _____

_____ go (or _____ *the store*)

which or *witch*   a scary woman in children's stories _____

tells _____ one

Check your answers: by, buy; here, hear; hole, whole, it's, its; meet, meat; one, won; peace, piece; right, write; sun, son; their, they're, there; through, threw; two, too, to; witch, which)

Exercise 4

Circle the correct word(s) for the meaning of the sentence.

A Science Fiction Story

1. My (son / sun) loves to (right / write) stories (which / witch) are

   sometimes rather unusual.

2. In one story, he (through / threw) a ball (through / threw) a window,

   and it turned into a spaceship heading towards the (son / sun) with him

   as the pilot.

3. When the spaceship got (their / they're / there), he could (here / hear)

   a strange noise.

4. (It's / Its) hard to believe, but he saw some wild aliens he wanted to

   (meat / meet).

5. The aliens and (their / they're / there) pets were friendly, and they got

   into the spaceship and returned (to / too / two) Earth (to / too / two).

E **Is It *ie* or *ei*?**

Can you find the spelling errors in this sentence?

No: I recieved a reciept from the casheir, but I lost it.

Yes: I **received** a **receipt** from the **cashier**, but I lost it.

- In general, follow this rule:
  Use *i* before *e* except after *c*, and in sounds of *a*, as in *neighbor* and *weigh*.

- Here are examples of this rule:
  i before *e:* believe, brief, cashier, niece
  After *c:* ceiling, deceive, receipt
  Sounds like *a* = eight, neighbor, sleigh, weigh

- Here are a few *ei* words that don't follow the rule:
  their, either, neither, weird, foreign, leisure, height

Exercise 5   Write C for correct and I for incorrect. Then correct the mistakes.

Keeping in Touch

1. _____ More and more people are calling their freinds instead of writing
   to them.

2. _____ It seems few people write letters, even to foreign countries.

3. _____ Many average citizens are getting fax machines and computers
   with e-mail, and they are sending and recieving short messages
   instead of letters.

4. _____ I seem to get niether letters nor postcards from my relatives now.

5. _____ Some people believe it's weird to write a letter. They think the
   post office won't be necessary in the future!

F American or British?

Can you find the problem in this sentence?

No: I heard a comedian at the theater, but I didn't enjoy her sense
     of humour.

Yes: I heard a comedian at the **theater,** but I didn't enjoy her sense
      of **humor.**

Yes: I heard a comedian at the **theatre,** but I didn't enjoy her sense
      of **humour.**

- In general, use American spelling in the U.S. and use British spelling in Great
  Britain, Canada, and other countries with British influence. In any case, use one
  style or the other. Don't mix the two.

  Note: Some theaters in the U.S. use the "theatre" spelling, and a few shopping centers use the
  "centre" spelling.

- Here are examples of the most common spelling differences:

American	British
cent**er**	cent**re**
real**ize**	real**ise**
col**or**	col**our**
defen**se**	defen**ce**
trave**led**	trave**lled**
che**ck**	che**que**

Exercise 6

Circle your preferences. Then correct the spelling so that all of the sentences are American or British, but not a mix of both.

Which do you prefer?

1. Seeing a movie in a movie theatre or at home on a VCR?

2. Food with a lot of strong flavors or food that is not so spicy?

3. Being the center of attention or not being noticed so much?

4. Bright, loud colours or soft, calm colors?

5. Using traveller's checks or using credit cards?

6. Getting to know your neighbors or not knowing your neighbours?

7. Apologizing immediately for bad behaviour or waiting until later

   to apologise?

G Other Common Spelling Errors

Many native and nonnative speakers of English have problems with the following words. Many of these words have spellings that you don't expect because the spelling doesn't follow the sound or the common spelling rules. If any of these words are difficult for you, notice the difficult part of the spelling. Practice the difficult words until you can spell them correctly.

Difficult word	Silent letter
ache (headache, backache)	**ch** + silent **e** for the final "k" sound
answer	looks like "an s**w**er," but there's a silent "w"
February	silent **r,** spelled like "Feb - **r**u - ary"
friend	silent **i,** fri + end
government	silent **n** (in fast speech)
guess	silent **u**
often	silent **t**
tomorrow	silent second **r**
tongue	silent **ue**
which	silent **h**

	Pronunciation difficulties
library	l/r - li**br**ary ("l" = 1, "r" = 2)
of course	of cou**r**se (not "cause")
something	always somethin**g**
think / thing	final sound - thin**k** (idea) or thin**g**
Thursday	**Thu**rsday (not "Tirsday")

	Other hints to remember
again	a + **gain** ("gen" spelled like "gain")
build / built	"i" sound is spelled **ui**
business	spelled like "**bus + i + ness**"
choose / chose	choose = present tense; chose = past tense
cough	sounds like "kawf"; spelled c + **ough**
country	remember **ou**
doctor	**o**r
early	spelled like "**ear**" plus "ly"
enough	sounds like "eenuf"; spelled e + n**ough**
forty	four, fourteen, but forty (**no u**)
grammar	**ar**
separate	se + p**a** + rate ("e" = 2, "a" = 2)
stomach	spelled like "st**o**m + "a**ch**," final k sound
truly	"true" + "ly" = **drop the silent e**
Tuesday	**ue**
Wednesday	spelled like "**Wed** + **nes** + day"
writing	remember, just one **t**, drop the **e**, add "-ing"

Study the list of difficult words. Then, without looking at the list, guess the word from the definition or clue. Write the word, thinking about the spelling.

Guess the Word

1. the second month of the year = _____

2. opposite of *late* = _____

3. opposite of *enemy* = _____

4. day after Monday = _____

5. day before Thursday = _____

6. place in your body where your food goes = _____

7. opposite of *join together* = _____

8. company = _____

9. the U.S. or Canada, for example = _____

10. one more time = _____

11. not seldom = _____

12. place you can borrow books = _____

13. day after today = _____

14. this book helps you edit your _____

15. honestly or sincerely = _____

16. you don't need more, you have _____

17. thirty-nine plus one = _____

18. opposite of *question* = _____

19. a pain in your head = _____

20. person who knows a lot about health = _____

Chapter Review

Exercise 8

Write **C** for correct and **I** for incorrect. Then correct the mistakes. (There may be two errors in one sentence.)

Facts about Canada

1. _____ Canada is the second largest country in the world.

2. _____ Canada has ten provinces and two territorys.

3. _____ Canada's population is approximatly 29 million, wich is relatively small.

4. _____ Ottawa is the capital city, and Toronto is the largest city, with almost four million people.

5. _____ Canada is a membr of the British Commonwealth, so it's official head-of-state is the Queen of England.

Exercise 9

There are eight mistakes in the following paragraph. Can you find and correct them?

Hummingbirds

The hummingbird is the world's smallest bird. It eates half its wieght in nectar, a sweet juice from flowers, evry day. Hummingbirds lick the nectar with thier tonges at the speed of 1.3 licks a secnd. A hummingbird flys very fast. It can reach speedes of 60 miles (100 km) per hour. However, hummingbirds can't walk. They can only perch or stand.

Exercise 1

1. New Year's Day is a big <u>holiday</u> in my <u>family</u>.

2. <u>Every</u> year we get together to celebrate and <u>exchange</u> gifts.

3. The <u>children</u> get a lot of toys and <u>money</u> from the adults.

4. <u>Everybody</u> stays up <u>late</u> and watches the fireworks.

5. Last year, I tried to stay <u>awake</u> all night, but I fell asleep before my <u>cousins</u> did.

Exercise 2

1. For exercise, do you prefer jogging or <u>riding</u> a bike?

2. On a hot day, do you prefer <u>eating</u> an ice-cream cone or drinking a cold soda?

3. In general, do you prefer <u>writing</u> a letter or getting a letter?

4. In a small group, do you prefer mostly talking or mostly <u>listening</u>?

5. To help with a dinner, do you prefer preparing the meal or <u>cleaning</u> up?

Exercise 3

1. ___C___ I raised six children who are now happy and successful adults.

2. ___I___ I <u>tried</u> out for the Olympic Swim Team and almost made it.

3. ___I___ My sister and I planned a family reunion. Everyone came and we all <u>enjoyed</u> it a lot.

4. ___I___ When an accident <u>occurred</u> in front of my house, I rescued the driver. I discovered that I could stay calm in a stressful situation.

5. ___C___ After quitting college because of some problems, I went back and finished my degree.

Exercise 4

1. My (<u>son</u> / sun) loves to (right / <u>write</u>) stories (<u>which</u> / witch) are sometimes rather unusual.

2. In one story, he (through / <u>threw</u>) a ball (<u>through</u> / threw) a window, and it turned into a spaceship heading towards the (son / <u>sun</u>) with him as the pilot.

3. When the spaceship got (their / they're / <u>there</u>), he could (here / <u>hear</u>) a strange noise.

4. (<u>It's</u> / Its) hard to believe, but he saw some wild aliens he wanted to (meat / <u>meet</u>).

5. The aliens and (<u>their</u> / they're / there) pets were friendly, and they got into the spaceship and returned (<u>to</u> / too / two) Earth (to / <u>too</u> / two).

(Continued)

Exercise 5

1. __I__ More and more people are calling their <u>friends</u> instead of writing to them.

2. __C__ It seems few people write letters, even to foreign countries.

3. __I__ Many average citizens are getting fax machines and computers with e-mail, and they are sending and <u>receiving</u> short messages instead of letters.

4. __I__ I seem to get <u>neither</u> letters nor postcards from my relatives now.

5. __C__ Some people believe it's weird to write a letter. They think the post office won't be necessary in the future!

Exercise 6

(Use either the British or American spelling, but be consistent. Don't mix the two.)

British	**American**
1. theatre	theater
2. flavours	flavors
3. centre	center
4. colours, colours	colors, colors
5. traveller's cheques	traveler's checks
6. neighbours, neighbours	neighbors, neighbors
7. apologising, behaviour	apologizing, behavior
apologise	apologize

Exercise 7

1. the second month of the year = February
2. opposite of *late* = early
3. opposite of *enemy* = friend
4. day after Monday = Tuesday
5. day before Thursday = Wednesday
6. place in your body where your food goes = stomach
7. opposite of *join together* = separate
8. company = business
9. the U.S. or Canada, for example = country
10. one more time = again
11. not seldom = often
12. place you can borrow books = library
13. day after today = tomorrow
14. this book helps you edit your <u>writing</u>
15. honestly or sincerely = truly
16. you don't need more, you have <u>enough</u>
17. thirty-nine plus one = forty
18. opposite of *question* = answer
19. a pain in your head = headache
20. person who knows a lot about health = doctor

(Concluded)

Exercise 8

1. __C__   Canada is the second largest country in the world.

2. __I__   Canada has ten provinces and two <u>territories</u>.

3. __I__   Canada's population is <u>approximately</u> 29 million, <u>which</u> is relatively small.

4. __C__   Ottawa is the capital city, and Toronto is the largest city, with almost four million people.

5. __I__   Canada is a <u>member</u> of the British Commonwealth, so <u>its</u> official head-of-state is the Queen of England.

Exercise 9

The hummingbird is the world's smallest bird. It <u>eats</u> half its <u>weight</u> in nectar, a sweet juice from flowers, <u>every</u> day. Hummingbirds lick the nectar with <u>their</u> <u>tongues</u> at the speed of 1.3 licks a <u>second</u>. A hummingbird <u>flies</u> very fast. It can reach <u>speeds</u> of 60 miles (100 km) per hour. However, hummingbirds can't walk. They can only perch or stand.

CHAPTER 17

Final Editing Assessment

After you have finished the chapters you chose to do in the Editing Focus section of this book, take this Final Editing Assessment. You will find out how much you have learned about editing carefully for correct English. The suggested time for this assessment is 45 minutes.

Read the sentence carefully. If there is no error, choose C for correct. If there is an error, choose I for incorrect. Use the answer sheet on the next page. For more detailed instructions, see page 3.

Answer Sheet

Tear this answer sheet out of your book and use it to take the Final Editing Assessment on pages 319 to 321. Circle C for *correct* if there is no error. Circle I for *incorrect* if there is an error.

1.	C	I	26.	C	I	51.	C	I
2.	C	I	27.	C	I	52.	C	I
3.	C	I	28.	C	I	53.	C	I
4.	C	I	29.	C	I	54.	C	I
5.	C	I	30.	C	I	55.	C	I
6.	C	I	31.	C	I	56.	C	I
7.	C	I	32.	C	I	57.	C	I
8.	C	I	33.	C	I	58.	C	I
9.	C	I	34.	C	I	59.	C	I
10.	C	I	35.	C	I	60.	C	I
11.	C	I	36.	C	I	61.	C	I
12.	C	I	37.	C	I	62.	C	I
13.	C	I	38.	C	I	63.	C	I
14.	C	I	39.	C	I	64.	C	I
15.	C	I	40.	C	I	65.	C	I
16.	C	I	41.	C	I	66.	C	I
17.	C	I	42.	C	I	67.	C	I
18.	C	I	43.	C	I	68.	C	I
19.	C	I	44.	C	I	69.	C	I
20.	C	I	45.	C	I	70.	C	I
21.	C	I	46.	C	I			
22.	C	I	47.	C	I			
23.	C	I	48.	C	I			
24.	C	I	49.	C	I			
25.	C	I	50.	C	I			

Fragment

(The sentence, or one of the sentences, is not a complete sentence.)

1. Arizona a state in the southwest part of the United States.

2. In Arizona, you can see beautiful deserts, dramatic mountain ranges, and fantastic rock formations.

3. Many tourists visit northern Arizona. Because they want to see the Grand Canyon.

4. Arizona has a multicultural and varied population. Such as Native Americans, Mexican Americans, and many older retired people.

5. If you travel to Arizona. You shouldn't go in the summer because it can be very hot.

Run-on or Comma Splice

(Two sentences are written incorrectly as one sentence.)

6. My uncle is an interesting man, he has unusual hobbies and a fun job.

7. He likes to ride a unicycle, and he knows how to juggle very well.

8. He loves to entertain children by juggling on his unicycle; however, he has never wanted to perform professionally.

9. My uncle works as an international reporter for a newspaper he has traveled all over the world.

10. Whenever my uncle is in town, I enjoy spending time with him and hearing all about his latest travels.

Verbs

(The problem can be the verb tense or verb form.)

11. A war has started in my country in 1995.

12. After the war got worse, my family and I came to Canada in 1996.

13. I have been studied English since January.

14. Now my husband and children are working hard to adjust to life in a new country.

15. After we will get good jobs, our life will be better.

Singular/Plural

(The noun form for *one* or *more than one* isn't correct.)

16. One of my friends and I went camping last weekend.

17. We brought a tent and other camping equipment last weekend.

18. While we were hiking near the campground, we saw some deer and a bear.

19. We needed to hang our foods from a tree so wild animal wouldn't come into our tent.

20. Many person at the campground were afraid.

Subject–Verb Agreement

(The subject and verb don't match.)

21. Each student in my class is very friendly.

22. The women who is in my conversation group help me practice English.

23. Our teacher give us a lot of chances to speak in class.

24. Listening to music are my favorite class activity.

25. There are some activities, such as dictations, that I don't like.

Noun–Pronoun Agreement

(Words such as *he, him, his, it* are not used correctly.)

26. My brother he works at a restaurant.

27. I ate there last week and enjoyed very much.

28. My friends ordered some pizza from the restaurant. Everyone liked it.

29. Some day, my brother wants to have own restaurant.

30. Owning a restaurant has been his dream all of his life.

Word Choice

(One or more words are wrong. A different word or expression should be used in English.)

31. I very enjoy rollerblading and skiing.

32. Every Saturday in the winter, I play skiing with my friends.

33. Most of my friends are students from other countries.

34. If they speak English very fast or use big words, I sometimes don't hear what they say.

35. Spending time with my friends is a good way for me to practice English.

Word Form

(The wrong form of a word is used.)

36. I just finished to fill out a job application.

37. This application was the most difficult one I've seen.

38. The directions on the application were very confusing.

39. Other problem was it asked for a short essay, and I hate writing essays.

40. I'm worried that I won't get this job.

Word Order

(The words are correct, but they are in the wrong place in the sentence.)

41. My neighbor is very helpful who lives in the next apartment.

42. Really, he is friendly and kind.

43. He often gives me fresh vegetables from his son's garden.

44. I can ask him for help when I don't know what should I do.

45. I've never had such a kind neighbor.

Prepositions

(Words such as *on, in, at,* or *to* are used incorrectly.)

46. I've been really busy in this week.

47. I'm going back my country next week, so I am getting ready to go.

48. I've been here since five years, so I have a lot of packing to do.

49. I've visited to several cities, and I have many souvenirs.

50. I'm looking forward to seeing my best friend when I arrive at the airport.

Articles

(The words *a, an,* or *the* are used incorrectly.)

51. August 31, 1997 was very sad day.

52. Princess Diana was killed in a car accident in a tunnel under the Seine River in Paris, France.

53. I remember when I heard news on radio.

54. Diana was a very popular.

55. She was possibly the most famous woman in the world.

Punctuation

(The marks , ; : ' ". . ." are used incorrectly.)

56. Omaha, Nebraska is the largest city in Nebraska.

57. Much of the state of Nebraska is very flat, however, Omaha has many hills.

58. When I visited Omaha, I enjoyed seeing the zoo, the art museum, and the train museum.

59. In Omaha, its usually very hot during the summer.

60. My friend who lives in Omaha told me "she enjoys living there."

Capitalization

(A big or small letter is used incorrectly.)

61. My Aunt and Uncle live in Montreal, Canada.

62. Their children speak English at home, but French at school.

63. They both teach Business Classes at McGill University.

64. Before they had children, they lived and worked in Europe and Africa.

65. I think they are my favorite Relatives.

Spelling

(A word is not spelled correctly.)

66. Some ESL students like speaking and listening, but others prefer grammar and writing.

67. It's always difficult to learn anther langage well.

68. My friend, who is forty, says it's harder to memorize new vocabulary when you are older.

69. I dissagree because my grandmother is studing Spanish and learning a lot.

70. All students need to find thier learning style and try hard to do thier best.

Final Editing Assessment Results

When you get your corrected answer sheet, follow these steps.

1. Put a slash (/) through the number of your incorrect answers. For example, if you answered items 1, 4, and 5 incorrectly, draw a slash through those numbers on the right side of the page.

Final Editing Assessment Results

Fragment	1	2	3	4	5
Run-on or Comma Splice	6	7	8	9	10
Verbs	11	12	13	14	15
Singular / Plural	16	17	18	19	20
Subject–Verb Agreement	21	22	23	24	25
Noun–Pronoun Agreement	26	27	28	29	30
Word Choice	31	32	33	34	35
Word Form	36	37	38	39	40
Word Order	41	42	43	44	45
Prepositions	46	47	48	49	50
Articles	51	52	53	54	55
Punctuation	56	57	58	59	60
Capitalization	61	62	63	64	65
Spelling	66	67	68	69	70

2. Count up your total score: number correct _____ (out of 70). This gives you a general idea of your overall score.

3. Compare your results with the Beginning Editing Assessment on page 10. We hope you will see improvement, especially in the areas that were your weaker areas.

Appendices

Irregular Verbs

This Appendix goes with Editing Focus Chapter 5, Verbs.

Here are the simple, simple past, and past participle forms for common irregular verbs:

Simple Form	Simple Past	Past Participle
be	was / were	been
beat	beat	beaten / beat
become	became	become
begin	began	begun
bend	bent	bent
bet	bet	bet
bite	bit	bitten / bit
bleed	bled	bled
blow	blew	blown
break	broke	broken
bring	brought	brought
build	built	built
buy	bought	bought
catch	caught	caught
choose	chose	chosen
come	came	come
cost	cost	cost
cut	cut	cut
dig	dug	dug
do	did	done
draw	drew	drawn
drink	drank	drunk
drive	drove	driven
eat	ate	eaten
fall	fell	fallen

Simple Form	Simple Past	Past Participle
feed	fed	fed
fight	fought	fought
find	found	found
fly	flew	flown
forget	forgot	forgotten
forgive	forgave	forgiven
freeze	froze	frozen
get	got	gotten
give	gave	given
go	went	gone
grow	grew	grown
have	had	had
hear	heard	heard
hide	hid	hidden
hit	hit	hit
hold	held	held
hurt	hurt	hurt
keep	kept	kept
know	knew	known
lead	led	led
leave	left	left
lend	lent	lent
let	let	let
lose	lost	lost
make	made	made
mean	meant	meant
meet	met	met
pay	paid	paid
put	put	put
quit	quit	quit
read	read (rhymes with *bed*)	read (rhymes with *bed*)
ride	rode	ridden
ring	rang	rung
run	ran	run
say	said (rhymes with *bed*)	said (rhymes with *bed*)
see	saw	seen

Simple Form	Simple Past	Past Participle
sell	sold	sold
send	sent	sent
shake	shook	shaken
shoot	shot	shot
shut	shut	shut
sing	sang	sung
sit	sat	sat
sleep	slept	slept
speak	spoke	spoken
spend	spent	spent
stand	stood	stood
steal	stole	stolen
swear	swore	sworn
swim	swam	swum
take	took	taken
tell	told	told
think	thought	thought
throw	threw	thrown
understand	understood	understood
wake	woke / waked	woken / waked
wear	wore	worn
win	won	won
write	wrote	written

Nouns

This Appendix goes with Editing Focus Chapter 6, Singular / Plural, and Chapter 7, Subject–Verb Agreement.

A Definition

Nouns are names of people, animals, places, things, and ideas. Here are some examples:

people: man, girl, banker, student, teacher, neighbor, uncle, James, Marilyn

animals: cat, dog, mouse, cow, horse, elephant, zebra

places: country, city, neighborhood, bank, grocery store, cafe, school, Texas

things: book, chair, lamp, sweater, shirt, grass, tree, street, car

ideas: peace, love, happiness, time

B Count Nouns

Count nouns are nouns that we can count. For example, we can say *one book, two books; one dog, several dogs; one flower, a few flowers;* or *There weren't many students in class.* Count nouns have both singular and plural forms. There are both regular and irregular plural count nouns.

1. Most count nouns form the plural by adding *-s* or *-es.*

   See Appendix 7 for spelling rules.

Singular	Plural
one chair	many chairs
one table	two tables
one brush	several brushes
one box	some boxes
one toy	several toys
one fly	a few flies
one radio	three radios
one potato	a lot of potatoes

2. Some count nouns have a special irregular plural form.

Singular	Plural
a woman	women
a man	men
one child	children
one person	many people
a mouse	some mice
one goose	many geese
one tooth	many teeth
a foot	two feet

3. Some irregular nouns have the same singular and plural forms.

Singular	Plural
one deer	three deer
a fish	many fish
one sheep	several sheep
a species	many species (= type of animal)

4. Some count nouns come in pairs. They use only the plural form.

Plural

jeans

pants

trousers

shorts

pajamas

glasses

scissors

pliers

5. Some irregular nouns are always plural.

Plural

clothes

groceries

police

congratulations

C Noncount Nouns

Noncount nouns cannot be counted. For example, we can say *some pollution, a little rain,* or *There wasn't much traffic.* We often use another word when we need to measure or count them, for example, *a piece of fruit, two inches of rain* and *a basketball game.*

Nature: rain, snow, ice, dew, grass, lightning, thunder, scenery

Liquids: water, milk, soda, beer, wine, gasoline, oil, shampoo, lotion

Solids: bread, cheese, butter, margarine, ice cream, wood, cotton, wool, soap, chalk

Gases: air, fog, smog, pollution, smoke, oxygen, hydrogen

Grains and powders: corn, wheat, flour, rice, cereal, salt, pepper, sugar, dust

Name of a group: furniture, luggage, food, fruit, meat, mail, postage, money, change, transportation, traffic, homework, vocabulary, slang, trash

Gerunds: walking, running, swimming, skating, skiing, shopping

Sports: baseball, basketball, football, soccer, tennis

School subjects: biology, chemistry, English, geography, math, psychology, science

Ideas: time, space, life, happiness, love, peace, knowledge, information, news

Word Form

This Appendix goes with Editing Focus Chapter 10, Word Form.

A Parts of Speech

Noun: name of a person, animal, place, thing, or idea

Examples: girl, cat, school, pencil, happiness

Adjective: word that describes a noun

Examples: big, small, intelligent, sad, expensive

Verb: word that shows action and *be, seem, appear*

Examples: walk, talk, think, speak, write; is, was, seem, appear

Adverb: word that describes a verb, an adjective, or another adverb

Examples: quickly, fast, softly, very, too

B Word Endings

Sometimes the ending of the word can help you know which word form it is, especially for nouns and adjectives. For example, look at the word *use* and its different forms:

Noun	Adjective	Verb	Adverb
user (person)	usable	use	
usefulness	useful	used	usefully
uselessness	useless		uselessly

Here are some common word endings for nouns, adjectives, verbs, and adverbs.

Nouns

-er	teacher, helper, user, worker (a person)
-or	ancestor, author, doctor, counselor (a person)
-ist	psychologist, scientist, geologist, Buddhist (a person)
-ism	Buddhism, capitalism, socialism, communism
-tion	creation, action, information, invention
-sion	confusion, invasion, persuasion
-ment	announcement, improvement, pavement, retirement
-ence	difference, independence, excellence
-ance	maintenance, insurance
-ness	kindness, happiness, sadness, usefulness
-ty	beauty, electricity, honesty, royalty
-ology	astrology, biology, geology, meteorology (usually name of an area of study)
-dom	freedom, kingdom, stardom

Adjectives

-able	adaptable, capable, usable
-ful	beautiful, careful, wonderful, useful
-less	careless, hopeless, mindless, useless
-ous	famous, humorous, gorgeous
-ible	incredible, terrible, horrible
-ive	expensive, expressive
-ic	electric, tragic, academic
-al	electrical, mental, musical, royal
-y	pretty, happy, healthy, funny

Verbs

-ate	hesitate, investigate
-ed	walked, talked, stayed (for regular, simple past tense or past participle)
-ize	computerize, criticize, organize

Adverbs

-ly	quickly, slowly, carefully, happily

Note: These word endings often help you know the word form. However, not all of the word forms end in these endings. For example, *fast* and *very* are adverbs, but they don't end in -*ly*. *Sad* and *tall* are adjectives that don't have the typical adjective word endings. In addition, some word endings can be confusing. *Ugly* and *friendly* are adjectives that end in -*ly*, which is often an adverb ending. To be sure of the word form, check a dictionary.

C Country / Nationality / Language

Here are some countries with the adjective form and the language, if it is a form of the same word. These countries are in groups according to the ending of the adjective form. (Note spelling exceptions for certain words.)

Country (noun)	Nationality (adjective)	Language (noun)
	-n, -an, -ian, -ean	
Argentina	Argentinean	
Australia	Australian	
Austria	Austrian	
Brazil	Brazilian	
Cambodia	Cambodian	Cambodian
Canada	Canadian	
Colombia	Colombian	
Egypt	Egyptian	
Ecuador	Ecuadorian	
India	Indian	
Indonesia	Indonesian	Indonesian
Iran	Iranian	
Italy	Italian	Italian
Kenya	Kenyan	
Korea	Korean	Korean
Malaysia	Malaysian	Malaysian
Mexico	Mexican	
Morocco	Moroccan	
Nicaragua	Nicaraguan	
Nigeria	Nigerian	
Norway	Norwegian	Norwegian
Panama	Panamanian	
Peru	Peruvian	
Russia	Russian	Russian
South Africa	South Africa	
Uganda	Ugandan	

Country (noun)	Nationality (adjective)	Language (noun)
-n, -an, -ian, -ean		
Ukraine	Ukrainian	Ukrainian
United States	American	
Venezuela	Venezuelan	
-ese		
China	Chinese	Chinese
Congo	Congolese	
Japan	Japanese	Japanese
Lebanon	Lebanese	
Portugal	Portuguese	Portuguese
Vietnam	Vietnamese	Vietnamese
-ish		
Denmark	Danish	Danish
England	English	English
Finland	Finnish	Finnish
Ireland	Irish	Irish
Poland	Polish	Polish
Spain	Spanish	Spanish
Sweden	Swedish	Swedish
Turkey	Turkish	Turkish
Other endings		
The Czech Republic	Czech	Czech
Croatia	Croat	Croatian
France	French	French
Germany	German	German
Greece	Greek	Greek
Iceland	Icelandic	Icelandic
Iraq	Iraqi	
Israel	Israeli	
Kuwait	Kuwaiti	
The Netherlands/Holland	Dutch	Dutch
New Zealand	New Zealander	
Pakistan	Pakistani	
Saudi Arabia	Saudi	
The Slovak Republic	Slovak	Slovak
Switzerland	Swiss	
Thailand	Thai	Thai

Gerunds and Infinitives

This Appendix goes with Editing Focus Chapter 5, Verbs, and Chapter 10, Word Form.

A Verb + Gerund or Infinitive

These verbs are followed by a gerund or an infinitive with the same meaning.

Example: **I love skiing.**   **I love to ski.**

love	prefer	can't stand	begin
like	hate	start	continue

Note: Forget, regret, remember, and *stop* take either a gerund or an infinitive. However, the meanings of the gerunds and infinitives can be very different.

Example: I **stopped smoking.** (I don't smoke anymore.)

I **stopped to smoke.** (First, I stopped what I was doing. Then I smoked.)

B Verb + Infinitive

These verbs are followed by an infinitive only.

Example: I **need to buy** the textbook.

afford	fail	promise
agree	hope	refuse
appear	intend	seem
ask (for yourself)	learn	volunteer
care	need	wait
decide	offer	want
demand	plan	wish
deserve	prepare	would like
expect	pretend	

C Verb + Object + Infinitive

These verbs are followed by an object (someone, person's name, *me, you, him, her, it, them*) and an infinitive.

Example: Teresa **invited Maria to go** to a party.

advise	encourage	let*	teach
allow	expect (someone)	order	tell
ask (someone)	hire	persuade	want (someone)
convince	invite	remind	warn
dare	need (someone)	require	

*See note on page 210.

D Verb + Gerund

These verbs are followed by a gerund only.

Example: She **finished writing** her essay.

admit	finish	practice
avoid	give up	quit
discuss	go	recommend
dislike	keep	suggest
enjoy	miss	understand

E Verb with Preposition + Gerund

These verbs are followed by a preposition and a gerund.

Example: We've **talked about moving** to Utah.

believe in	participate in
succeed in	
argue about	approve of
complain about	take advantage of
talk about	
worry about	insist on
	keep on
apologize for	
have a good reason for	look forward to
forgive (someone) for	object to
thank (someone) for	

F Be + Adjective + Preposition + Gerund

These words use a *be* verb with an adjective and a preposition followed by a gerund.

Example: Kerry **is interested in studying** sign language.

be excited about	be interested in
be worried about	
	be famous for
be afraid of	be responsible for
be in charge of	
be proud of	be accustomed to
	be used to

G Expression + Gerund

These expressions are followed by a gerund only.

Example: We **had a good time playing** basketball.

have a difficult time	have a good time
have difficulty	have fun
have a hard time	
have trouble	be busy

Quotations

This Appendix goes with Editing Focus Chapter 14, Punctuation.

1. Use quotation marks to show the exact words somebody said.

   The teacher said, "There is no homework for tomorrow."

   "There is no homework for tomorrow," the teacher said.

   "There is," the teacher said, "no homework for tomorrow."

   - The punctuation goes inside the quotation marks.
   - Use commas to separate the quotation from the rest of the sentence.
   - If you have two sentences, you don't need to use new quotation marks.

     The teacher said, "There is no homework for tomorrow. Your next assignment is due on Monday."

2. Indirect speech does not use quotation marks:

   No: He said "that he could come."

   Yes: He said, "I can come."

   Yes: He said that he could come.

3. If you are quoting a question or an exclamation, use the punctuation that goes with it. Do not use a comma.

   "When is the next assignment due?" she asked.

   "Go away!" he screamed.

Capitalization

This Appendix goes with Editing Focus Chapter 15, Capitalization.

Here are examples of capital (big) and lowercase (small) letters in English.

A **Printing**

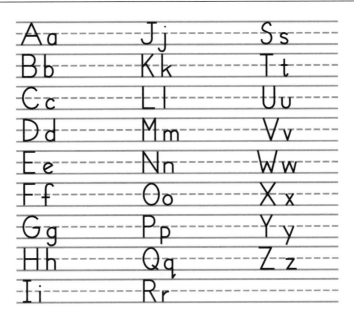

B **Cursive**

Spelling

This Appendix goes with Editing Focus Chapter 5, Verbs; Chapter 6, Singular/Plural; and Chapter 16, Spelling.

Words to Know

vowel   the letters *a, e, i, o, u*

consonant   the letters that are not vowels (*b, c, d, f, g, h, j, k, l, m, n, p,* etc.)

syllable   how many separate parts in a word

  Examples: see = one syllable, mo vie = two syllables, vid e o = three syllables

stress   the stronger and louder sound of a syllable

  Examples: **'mo** vie (The stress is on the first syllable.)

  re **'lax** (The stress is on the second syllable.)

prefix   a word part added to the beginning of a word

  Examples: **un** + sure = unsure, **dis** + agree = disagree

suffix   a word part added to the end of a word

  Examples: beauty + **ful** = beautiful, dog + **s** = dogs

A Adding -s or -es

1. For most words, add -s.

Nouns		Verbs (third person, singular)	
car	cars	speak	speaks
book	books	want	wants
cake	cakes	hope	hopes

2. For words that end with the letters *ss, ch, sh, x,* and *zz,* add *-es.*

   (The *-es* adds an extra syllable so that it is easier to say.)

Nouns		Verbs	
class	classes	miss	misses
inch	inches	push	pushes
box	boxes	buzz	buzzes

3. For words that end in *y:*

   If the letter before the *y* is a vowel, add *-s.*

Nouns		Verbs	
boy	boys	say	says
key	keys	pay	pays

   If the letter before the *y* is a consonant, change the *y* to *i* and add *-es.*

Nouns		Verbs	
baby	babies	try	tries
fly	flies	cry	cries

4. For words that end in *o:*

-s		-es		Both -s and -es are OK	
auto	autos	do	does	mosquito	mosquitos / mosquitoes
kilo	kilos	go	goes	tornado	tornados / tornadoes
memo	memos	echo	echoes	volcano	volcanos / volcanoes
photo	photos	hero	heroes	zero	zeros / zeroes
piano	pianos	potato	potatoes		
radio	radios	tomato	tomatoes		
solo	solos				
video	videos				
zoo	zoos				

5. For words that end in a single *f* or *fe:*

   Most words change *f* to *v* and add *-es*

calf	calves	shelf	shelves
half	halves	thief	thieves
knife	knives	wife	wives
leaf	leaves	wolf	wolves

   Exceptions (add only *-s*):

belief	beliefs
chief	chiefs
roof	roofs

B Adding a Prefix

Simply add the prefix (word beginnings such as *dis-, pre-, un-*) at the beginning of the word. You don't need to change the spelling of the main word.

dis + belief	=	disbelief
pre + register	=	preregister

un + able	=	unable
un + happy	=	unhappy

C Adding a Suffix

1. For words that end in *e*, drop the final *e* if the suffix (word endings such as *-ed, -ing, -able*) begins with a vowel. Keep the *e* if the word ending begins with a consonant. For *-ed*, just add *-d*.

   Drop e

hope + ed	=	hoped
come + ing	=	coming
believe + able	=	believable

   Keep e

safe + ty	=	safety
care + ful	=	careful
hope + less	=	hopeless

   Exceptions (words that don't follow this rule): noticeable, truly

2. For words that end in *y*, keep the *y* before *-ing*. Keep the *y* before *-ed* if the word ends in a vowel + *y*. If the word ends in a consonant + *y*, change the *y* to *i* and add *-ed* or other endings. (See Part A to review the rules for adding *-s* or *-es*.)

   Keep y

carry + ing	=	carrying
try + ing	=	trying
enjoy + ing	=	enjoying
play + ing	=	playing
enjoy + ed	=	enjoyed
play + ed	=	played

   Change y to i + word ending

carry + ed	=	carried
try + ed	=	tried
happy + ly	=	happily
happy + ness	=	happiness
funny + er	=	funnier
funny + est	=	funniest

3. For one-syllable words that end with a single vowel and a single consonant, double the consonant with word endings that begin with a vowel.

plan + ed	=	planned
plan + ing	=	planning
sad + er	=	sadder
sad + est	=	saddest

   (Note the difference with two vowels:
   rain–rained, feed–feeding, sleep–sleeping.)

4. For words that have the stress on the last syllable, double the consonant with word endings that begin with a vowel.

be 'gin + ing = beginning

for 'get + ing = forgetting   for 'get + able = forgettable

oc 'cur + ing = occurring   oc 'cur + ed   = occurred

(Note the difference with the stress on the first syllable: 'lis ten = listened, 'o pen = opened.)

5. For verbs that end in *ie,* change *ie* to *y* before adding *-ing.* For *-ed,* just add *d.*

-ing   **-ed**

lie + ing = lying   lie + ed = lied

tie + ing = tying   tie + ed = tied

Answer Keys— Beginning and Final Editing Assessments

Fragment

(The sentence, or one of the sentences, is not a complete sentence.)

1. __I__ British Columbia is a Canadian province with beautiful cities, <u>such</u> as Vancouver and Victoria.

2. __C__ Many tourists come to visit British Columbia from all over the world.

3. __C__ In Vancouver, visitors can walk around Stanley Park, go to several wonderful museums, or shop on Robson Street.

4. __I__ On a sunny day, the views around Vancouver are <u>beautiful because</u> you can see the mountains.

5. __I__ If you ever have the chance to go to Western Canada, <u>you</u> should try to visit British Columbia.

Run-on or Comma Splice

(Two sentences are written incorrectly as one sentence.)

6. __I__ At first, life was difficult for me in the United <u>States.</u> <u>I</u> didn't understand English.

7. __C__ I could speak only a few words of English, so it was very hard to communicate.

8. __I__ Luckily, I had some friends who spoke <u>English.</u> <u>They</u> could help me a lot.

9. __C__ When I needed to fill out applications or go to the doctor, my friends translated for me.

10. __C__ Now I can do everything by myself because I speak and understand English quite well, and I am getting along fine.

Verbs

(The problem can be the verb tense or verb form.)

11. __I__ The new city library near my house <u>was built</u> in 1990.

12. __I__ Every day I <u>go</u> to the library to study in a quiet place.

13. __C__ Yesterday I studied in the library for three hours.

14. __I__ Residents are <u>allowed</u> to check out books, CDs, and tapes from the library.

15. __I__ I <u>have had</u> my own library card since last August.

Singular / Plural

(The noun form for *one* or *more than one* isn't correct.)

16. __I__   Students usually have <u>homework</u> every day.
17. __I__   I always have to read <u>books</u> and write <u>summaries</u>.
18. __C__   I sometimes learn useful information in my reading assignments.
19. __I__   This week we are reading stories from several <u>countries</u>.
20. __I__   I'm learning about <u>traditions</u> and <u>customs</u> in Chile.

Subject–Verb Agreement

(The subject and verb don't match.)

21. __I__   Both the book and the tapes for our listening class <u>are</u> available in the college bookstore.
22. __I__   One of my favorite hobbies <u>is</u> looking at books in a big bookstore.
23. __C__   The people who work in the bookstore are very helpful.
24. __I__   Every student <u>needs</u> to know how to get to the bookstore.
25. __C__   The bookstore opens at 8:00 A.M. and closes at 8:00 P.M. on weekdays.

Noun–Pronoun Agreement

(Words such as *he, him, his, it* are not used correctly.)

26. __I__   My <u>friend works</u> at a CD store.
27. __C__   I bought a great new CD. I've listened to it many times.
28. __I__   If you need to get special CDs, you can order <u>them</u> at the store.
29. __I__   I hope to have <u>my</u> own music store someday.
30. __C__   It's a dream I've had all of my life.

Word Choice

(One or more words are wrong. A different word or expression should be used.)

31. __I__   I really enjoy meeting <u>people from other countries</u>.
32. __I__   Every Friday night I <u>go</u> bowling with my friends.
33. __C__   I was very tired last night, so I went to bed early.
34. __C__   When I am sick, I take some medicine.
35. __I__   I hope I will <u>have</u> a good life.

Word Form

(The wrong form of a word is used.)

36. __I__ My friend loves playing basketball and <u>swimming</u>. (or "to play basketball and to swim.")

37. __I__ He and <u>other</u> friends often have a basketball game after class.

38. __C__ My friend thinks basketball is the most exciting sport in the world.

39. __I__ However, when I watch basketball games, I'm very <u>bored</u>.

40. __C__ I'm unusual because almost all young men seem to like basketball.

Word Order

(The words are correct, but they are in the wrong place in the sentence.)

41. __I__ <u>I love my nieces and nephews</u> a lot.

42. __C__ I especially enjoy playing fun games with them.

43. __I__ My <u>nephew whom I babysit for often is</u> in the second grade.

44. __I__ Babysitting is good practice <u>for me to learn</u> how to be a parent.

45. __C__ However, I like it when I can give the kids back to their parents at the end of the day.

Prepositions

(Words such as *on, in, at,* or *to* are used incorrectly.)

46. __C__ I feel very sorry for my friend.

47. __I__ He has been <u>living here</u> for three years.

48. __I__ Now he has to go back <u>to</u> his country because his father died.

49. __I__ He has to quit school and get ready to leave <u>on</u> Friday.

50. __C__ I'll go to the airport with him to say good-bye.

Articles

(The words *a, an,* or *the* are used incorrectly.)

51. __C__ My aunt lives in a small apartment in a big city.

52. __I__ She moved to New York, which is <u>the</u> biggest city in the United States.

53. __C__ Unfortunately, the cost of living in New York City is very expensive.

54. __I__ My aunt is looking for <u>a</u> better job that pays more money.

55. __C__ She may take computer classes at a local college to improve her skills.

Punctuation

(The marks , ; : ' ". . ." are used incorrectly.)

56. __I__ Paul Newman, who is a good actor, is also an unusual businessman.

57. __C__ His company makes a variety of spaghetti sauces and salad dressings.

58. __C__ Unlike most companies, Newman's company gives all of its profits to help people who are poor, handicapped, or sick.

59. __C__ I really like to watch Newman's movies, and I feel good about buying his food products.

60. __I__ He's starred in some of my favorite films, such as *Butch Cassidy and the Sundance Kid* and *Nobody's Fool*.

Capitalization

(A big or small letter is used incorrectly.)

61. __C__ Many international students attend colleges and universities in North America.

62. __I__ At my <u>college</u>, they often study <u>business</u> classes.

63. __C__ I have several Vietnamese friends at school.

64. __I__ They speak <u>English</u> at school, but they use <u>Vietnamese</u> at home.

65. __C__ Next semester a friend and I will take Introduction to Psychology.

Spelling

(A word is not spelled correctly.)

66. __I__ I'm waiting to <u>receive</u> an important package in the mail.

67. __I__ I hope it will arrive <u>tomorrow</u>.

68. __C__ I ordered a new printer from a computer magazine.

69. __C__ Computers have become extremely important in modern society.

70. __I__ I'll be able to write essays for my <u>writing</u> class at home instead of using the computer lab.

Answer Key to Final Editing Assessment (Chapter 17)

Fragment

(The sentence, or one of the sentences, is not a complete sentence.)

1. ___I___   Arizona <u>is</u> a state in the southwest part of the United States.

2. ___C___   In Arizona, you can see beautiful deserts, dramatic mountain ranges, and fantastic rock formations.

3. ___I___   Many tourists visit northern Arizona <u>because</u> they want to see the Grand Canyon.

4. ___I___   Arizona has a multicultural and varied population**,** <u>such</u> as Native Americans, Mexican Americans, and many older retired people.

5. ___I___   If you travel to Arizona, <u>you</u> shouldn't go in the summer because it can be very hot.

Run-on or Comma Splice

(Two sentences are written incorrectly as one sentence.)

6. ___I___   My uncle is an interesting man**.** <u>He</u> has unusual hobbies and a fun job.

7. ___C___   He likes to ride a unicycle, and he knows how to juggle very well.

8. ___C___   He loves to entertain children by juggling on his unicycle; however, he has never wanted to perform professionally.

9. ___I___   My uncle works as an international reporter for a newspaper**.** <u>He</u> has traveled all over the world.

10. ___C___   Whenever my uncle is in town, I enjoy spending time with him and hearing all about his latest travels.

Verbs

(The problem can be with verb tense or verb form.)

11. ___I___   A war <u>started</u> in my country in 1995.

12. ___C___   After the war got worse, my family and I came to Canada in 1996.

13. ___I___   I <u>have studied</u> / <u>have been studying</u> English since January.

14. ___C___   Now my husband and children are working hard to adjust to life in a new country.

15. ___I___   After we <u>get</u> good jobs, our life will be better.

Singular / Plural

(The noun form for *one* or *many* isn't correct.)

16. __C__   One of my friends and I went camping last weekend.
17. __C__   We brought a tent and other camping equipment last weekend.
18. __C__   While we were hiking near the campground, we saw some deer and a bear.
19. __I__   We needed to hang our <u>food</u> from a tree so wild <u>animals</u> wouldn't come into our tent.
20. __I__   Many <u>people</u> at the campground were afraid.

Subject–Verb Agreement

(The subject and verb don't match.)

21. __C__   Each student in my class is very friendly.
22. __I__   The women who <u>are</u> in my conversation group help me practice English.
23. __I__   Our teacher <u>gives</u> us a lot of chances to speak in class.
24. __I__   Listening to music <u>is</u> my favorite class activity.
25. __C__   There are some activities, such as dictations, that I don't like.

Noun–Pronoun Agreement

(Words such as *he, him, his, it* are not used correctly.)

26. __I__   My <u>brother works</u> at a restaurant.
27. __I__   I ate there last week, and enjoyed <u>it</u> very much.
28. __C__   My friends ordered some pizza from the restaurant. Everyone liked it.
29. __I__   Some day, my brother wants to have <u>his</u> own restaurant.
30. __C__   Owning a restaurant has been his dream all of his life.

Word Choice

(One or more words are wrong. A different word or expression should be used in English.)

31. __I__   I <u>really</u> enjoy rollerblading and skiing.
32. __I__   Every Saturday in the winter, I <u>go</u> skiing with my friends.
33. __C__   Most of my friends are students from other countries.
34. __I__   If they speak English very fast or use big words, I sometimes don't <u>understand</u> what they say.
35. __C__   Spending time with my friends is a good way for me to practice English.

Word Form

(The wrong form of a word is used.)

36. __I__   I just finished <u>filling</u> out a job application.

37. __C__   This application was the most difficult one I've seen.

38. __C__   The directions on the application were very confusing.

39. __I__   <u>Another</u> problem was it asked for a short essay, and I hate writing essays.

40. __C__   I'm worried that I won't get this job.

Word Order

(The words are correct, but they are in the wrong place in the sentence.)

41. __I__   My <u>neighbor who lives in the next apartment</u> is very helpful.

42. __I__   He is <u>really</u> friendly and kind.

43. __C__   He often gives me fresh vegetables from his son's garden.

44. __I__   I can ask him for help when I don't know what <u>I should</u> do.

45. __C__   I've never had such a kind neighbor.

Prepositions

(Words such as *on, in, at,* or *to* are used incorrectly.)

46. __I__   I've been really <u>busy this</u> week.

47. __I__   I'm going back <u>to</u> my country next week, so I am getting ready to go.

48. __I__   I've been here <u>for</u> five years, so I have a lot of packing to do.

49. __I__   I've <u>visited several</u> cities, and I have many souvenirs.

50. __C__   I'm looking forward to seeing my best friend when I arrive at the airport.

Articles

(The words *a, an,* or *the* are used incorrectly.)

51. __I__   August 31, 1997 was <u>a</u> very sad day.

52. __C__   Princess Diana was killed in a car accident in a tunnel under the Seine River in Paris, France.

53. __I__   I remember when I heard <u>the</u> news on <u>the</u> radio.

54. __I__   Diana <u>was very</u> popular.

55. __C__   She was possibly the most famous woman in the world.

Punctuation

(The marks , ; : ' "..." are used incorrectly.)

56. __C__ Omaha, Nebraska is the largest city in Nebraska.

57. __I__ Much of the state of Nebraska is very flat; however, Omaha has many hills.

58. __C__ When I visited Omaha, I enjoyed seeing the zoo, the art museum, and the train museum.

59. __I__ In Omaha, it's usually very hot during the summer.

60. __I__ My friend who lives in Omaha told me she enjoys living there.

Capitalization

(A big or small letter is used incorrectly.)

61. __I__ My aunt and uncle live in Montreal, Canada.

62. __C__ Their children speak English at home, but French at school.

63. __I__ They both teach business classes at McGill University.

64. __C__ Before they had children, they lived and worked in Europe and Africa.

65. __I__ I think they are my favorite relatives.

Spelling

(One or more words are not spelled correctly.)

66. __C__ Some ESL students like speaking and listening, but others prefer grammar and writing.

67. __I__ It's always difficult to learn another language well.

68. __C__ My friend, who is forty, says it's harder to memorize new vocabulary when you are older.

69. __I__ I disagree because my grandmother is studying Spanish and learning a lot.

70. __I__ All students need to find their learning style and try hard to do their best.

Student Notebook

Error Chart

Name: _____ **Title:** _____ **Writing #** _____

After your teacher has marked your writing, use this chart to record which types of errors occurred.
Put a check (✓) in the correct row for each error. Then add up the totals and write them on your Progress Chart.

Editing Focus Chapter	Error Type	Symbol	Totals
1	Unclear Meaning / Translation	(Uncl)	
2	Fragment	(Frag)	
3	Run-on Sentence	(Run-on)	
4	Comma Splice	(CS)	
5	Verb Tense / Verb Form	(V)	
6	Singular / Plural	(S/Pl)	
7	Subject–Verb Agreement	(SV)	
8	Noun–Pronoun Agreement	(N-Pn)	
9	Word Choice	(WC)	
10	Word Form	(WF)	
11	Word Order	(WO)	
12	Preposition	(Prep)	
13	Article	(Art)	
14	Punctuation	(Punc)	
15	Capitalization	(Cap)	
16	Spelling	(Sp)	

Note: Your teacher will give you a new Error Chart for each writing assignment that you complete.

Progress Chart

Name: _____

This chart will help you see your progress. You'll see which areas are improving and which areas need more study. Record the totals from the Error Chart for each writing assignment.

Title

Editing Focus Chapter		Writing:	1	2	3	4	5	6	7	8	9	10
1	Unclear Meaning / Translation	(Uncl)										
2	Fragment	(Frag)										
3	Run-on Sentence	(Run-on)										
4	Comma Splice	(CS)										
5	Verb Tense / Verb Form	(V)										
6	Singular / Plural	(S/Pl)										
7	Subject–Verb Agreement	(SV)										
8	Noun–Pronoun Agreement	(N-Pn)										
9	Word Choice	(WC)										
10	Word Form	(WF)										
11	Word Order	(WO)										
12	Preposition	(Prep)										
13	Article	(Art)										
14	Punctuation	(Punc)										
15	Capitalization	(Cap)										
16	Spelling	(Sp)										
	Total Number of Errors:												
	Grade:												

Sentence Types Chart

Name _____ **Writing #** _____ **Title** _____

Use this chart to see the sentence variety in your writing. Look at each sentence in your writing. Decide which type of sentence it is and put a check (✔) in the row. Then add up the totals and mark them on your Sentence Types Progress Chart.

Sentence Type	Total
Question	
Simple Sentence	
Compound Sentence	
Complex—Adverb Clause	
Complex—Adjective Clause	
Combination	
Incorrect Sentence (Fragment, Run-on, CS)	

Sentence Types Progress Chart

Name _____

Record the totals from the Sentence Types Chart. You will see your sentence variety. If you use only a few types of sentences, you will see which types of sentences to try to include in future writing assignments.

Title

Sentence Type	Writing	1	2	3	4	5	6	7	8	9	10
Question											
Simple Sentence											
Compound Sentence											
Complex—Adverb Clause											
Complex—Adjective Clause											
Combination											
Incorrect Sentence (Fragment, Run-on, CS)											

Unclear Errors

Some part of your sentence is not clear or does not sound like English. It may be a direct translation from your language. Write your common incorrect sentences with their corrections here.

Incorrect: *I hope to see my family next vacation because I have been one year I have never seen them.*

Correct: *I hope to see my family next vacation because I haven't seen them for one year.*

Incorrect:

Correct:

Incorrect:

Correct:

Incorrect:

Correct:

Incorrect:

Correct:

Incorrect:

Correct:

Incorrect:

Correct:

Word Choice Errors

A different word or expression should be used. Write your common word choice errors here.

	Incorrect	Correct
1.	*find my goals*	*achieve / reach my goals*
2.		
3.		
4.		
5.		
6.		
7.		
8.		
9.		
10.		
11.		
12.		
13.		
14.		
15.		
16.		
17.		
18.		
19.		
20.		

Spelling Errors

Keep a list of your common spelling mistakes. Write the misspelled word correctly five times. Then write some notes that will help you remember the correct spelling.

Misspelled	Correct	Notes
1. *langage*	*language language language language language*	*guage—need guage*
2.		